# THE NUCLEAR NORTH

## C.D. HOWE SERIES IN CANADIAN POLITICAL HISTORY

*Series editors: Robert Bothwell and John English*

This series offers fresh perspectives on Canadian political history and public policy from over the past century. Its purpose is to encourage scholars to write and publish on all aspects of the nation's political history, including the origins, administration, and significance of economic policies; the social foundations of politics and political parties; transnational influences on Canadian public life; and the biographies of key public figures. In doing so, the series fills large gaps in our knowledge about recent Canadian history and makes accessible to a broader audience the background necessary to understand contemporary public-political issues.

*The Nuclear North* is the sixth volume in the series. The other volumes are:

*Grit: The Life and Politics of Paul Martin Sr.,* by Greg Donaghy
*The Call of the World: A Political Memoir,* by Bill Graham
*Prime Ministerial Power in Canada: Its Origins under Macdonald, Laurier, and Borden,* by Patrice Dutil
*The Good Fight: Marcel Cadieux and Canadian Diplomacy,* by Brendan Kelly
*Challenge the Strong Wind: Canada and East Timor, 1975–99,* by David Webster

The series originated with a grant from the C.D. Howe Memorial Foundation and is further supported by the Bill Graham Centre for Contemporary International History.

C.D. Howe Series In
**Canadian Political History**

# THE NUCLEAR NORTH

*Histories of Canada in the Atomic Age*

EDITED BY SUSAN COLBOURN
AND TIMOTHY ANDREWS SAYLE

**UBC**Press · Vancouver · Toronto

29 28 27 26 25 24 23 22 21 20    5 4 3 2 1

Printed in Canada on FSC-certified ancient-forest-free paper (100% post-consumer recycled) that is processed chlorine- and acid-free.

---

**Library and Archives Canada Cataloguing in Publication**

Title: The nuclear north : histories of Canada in the atomic age / edited by Susan Colbourn and Timothy Andrews Sayle.
Names: Colbourn, Susan, 1987– editor. | Sayle, Timothy A., editor.
Series: C.D. Howe series in Canadian political history.
Description: Series statement: C.D. Howe series in Canadian political history | Includes bibliographical references and index.
Identifiers: Canadiana (print) 20200246488 | Canadiana (ebook) 20200246666 | ISBN 9780774863971 (hardcover) | ISBN 9780774863988 (paperback) | ISBN 9780774863995 (PDF) | ISBN 9780774864008 (EPUB) | ISBN 9780774864015 (Kindle)
Subjects: LCSH: Nuclear weapons—Government policy—Canada. | LCSH: Nuclear energy—Government policy—Canada. | LCSH: Cold War. | LCSH: Canada—Foreign relations—1945–
Classification: LCC UA600 .N83 2020 | DDC 355.8/251190971—dc23

---

Canadä

UBC Press gratefully acknowledges the financial support for our publishing program of the Government of Canada (through the Canada Book Fund), the Canada Council for the Arts, and the British Columbia Arts Council.

This book has been published with the help of a grant from the Canadian Federation for the Humanities and Social Sciences, through the Awards to Scholarly Publications Program, using funds provided by the Social Sciences and Humanities Research Council of Canada.

Printed and bound in Canada by Friesens
Set in Perpetua and and Minion by Apex CoVantage, LLC
Copy editor: Frank Chow
Proofreader: Judith Earnshaw
Indexer: Cheryl Lemmens
Cover designer: Will Brown

UBC Press
The University of British Columbia
2029 West Mall
Vancouver, BC V6T 1Z2
www.ubcpress.ca

# CONTENTS

# FOREWORD

Canada's nuclear history begins with geology, but it does not begin with uranium. Canada was a storehouse of minerals, mostly embedded in the Canadian Shield, with mining companies to match. In the early twentieth century, these companies found a home in Toronto – a large home, centred on the Toronto Stock Exchange, where mining stocks were born, flourished, and, not infrequently, died. Mining was a speculative business, which is to say, risky. Prospectors, promoters, and speculators were thick on the ground, and their projects far outnumbered viable mining firms. But there were enough of these, and by the 1920s Canada had developed a human and technological infrastructure of miners, mining engineers, and even a very few geologists, who could point the way to ores and, it was hoped, wealth. The wealth was displayed in large houses in the new suburbs of Canada's biggest cities, Toronto and Montreal.

Eldorado Gold Mines Limited was a typical speculation of the 1920s. A prospector-speculator named Gilbert LaBine claimed that gold was to be found at a certain location in Manitoba, and raised money accordingly, in both Canada and the United States. His mine was not viable, and Eldorado Gold Mines might have joined the long parade of failed mines in Canada. But LaBine knew how to read geological reports, and he had read of a new element, derived from uranium in pitchblende – radium. Radium was the wonder drug of the 1920s – one of the few that could be used to treat cancer, although it was recognized that it could cause cancer as well. It was hard to produce, but at one point in the 1920s it sold for $120,000 a gram and returned stunning profits to its manufacturer, a Belgian company. The Belgians could draw on an incomparably rich mine in their colony in the Congo, and by the late 1920s had eliminated virtually all rivals in the radium market.

To make a long story short, this was Canada's ticket of entry to the nuclear age. The Eldorado "Gold Mine" became a miner and refiner of uranium and radium. The mine was on Great Bear Lake, in the Northwest Territories, and the refinery, in Port Hope, Ontario, was the only uranium/radium refinery outside Europe. Though far less wealthy than its Belgian rival, Eldorado formed a cartel with the Belgians in 1937, dividing up the world radium market between them. Uranium, from which radium was distilled, was, as far as Eldorado was concerned, virtually a waste product, useful only for colouring ceramics if you happened to fancy orange.

Eldorado's world, Gilbert LaBine's world, was unconnected to any larger developments, political, technological, or scientific. And even if LaBine had wanted to connect, he would have had difficulty. Canada was not the scientific centre of the world, and though its universities did produce physicists, they had to leave the country to complete their training, usually in the United States or Great Britain, and most of them did not come back.[1] While Canadian scientists participated in the development of nuclear physics, they did not do so in Canada or as Canadians.

Nuclear research in the 1930s took place at Cambridge, or Columbia, or Berkeley, or in Paris or Berlin. By 1938, it was well understood that a nuclear chain reaction could produce an incalculable amount of energy – or to put it in practical terms, an atomic bomb. There was even discussion in 1938–39 of a private enterprise bomb – French science plus Belgian uranium and money – but it was overtaken by events. It was a sign that the Belgians had a sophisticated understanding of what uranium could do, whereas LaBine and his colleagues saw uranium as merely a colour on a plate. LaBine, Eldorado, and Canadians in general were ignorant of these things, but the outbreak of the Second World War brought them to Canada's doorstep.

In the spring of 1940, the Germans defeated and occupied Belgium and France. German domination of continental Europe set in motion a flight of scientists and a transfer of knowledge and resources. Danger from mere proximity to Nazi-occupied Europe sent British scientists to the transatlantic part of the British Empire – to Canada, safe from German bombers.

Canada had space to offer, and money; it also had uranium and, most important, a uranium refinery. Or rather, Eldorado did.

Canadian prime minister Mackenzie King assigned his minister of munitions and supply, C.D. Howe, to establish a Canadian laboratory for a group of mainly British and French scientists and British engineers and technicians. They were to work in cooperation with the Americans to develop an atomic bomb. Initially, Canada's job was to feed them money and supplies, including uranium. At the same time, Eldorado had signed contracts to provide the American Manhattan Project with uranium, and, more importantly, the use of its refinery to produce refined uranium, an essential stage in converting raw ore into what is now called "weapons-grade" uranium: $U_3O_8$.

All this was conducted with as much secrecy as the Canadians, prodded by the British and Americans, could manage. Merging science and secrecy with Eldorado Gold Mines Limited was a challenge. The Canadian government decided that it would buy all the shares, or as many as it could find, from and through LaBine, at a set price. LaBine set off to find his shareholders and bought as many shares as he could, often at a lower price than the government paid him. In the meantime, officers of the company conducted their own business (or businesses) on the side, which eventually led to the arrest of Eldorado's secretary treasurer and its refinery manager, and to court cases in Toronto and New York City. The Canadian government finally and openly nationalized Eldorado in 1944, converting it to a Crown corporation. When the minister responsible, Howe, learned what had been going on in the company, he removed LaBine and placed Eldorado under his own executive assistant, W.J. Bennett. From 1946 onward, Eldorado would be in, but not of, the Canadian mining community.

That left the British atomic laboratory, located initially in Montreal and then transferred in 1945–46 to an isolated location in Chalk River, Ontario, on the Ottawa River. The "Montreal Laboratory" (referred to as the "Montreal Lab" by its occupants) worked on French ideas with British engineering, under the direction of one of the world's foremost atomic physicists, Sir John Cockcroft. The French had favoured heavy water to moderate an atomic reaction, and this heavy water direction became embedded in Canadian reactor technology. The Montreal Lab's particular assignment was to perfect the technology for a plutonium bomb, which eventually it did.

By then the war was over, and when the various imported scientists returned to France and Britain, they left behind one of the most successful reactor designs ever conceived, the National Research Experimental (NRX) reactor at Chalk River, which went critical in 1947 – the first outside the United States. They also left behind a cadre of scientists and technicians, many of them British in origin. Over the years, Chalk River became known for original and imaginative science, and was considered on a par, though smaller, with American and British atomic facilities. Only in the 1980s did government cheese-paring undermine its pure science orientation and convert it to "practical" science.

Wartime cooperation did not, however, leave a lasting political or international connection between the governments of Canada and Great Britain in the field of atomic research. The British were, after all, a great power, and in the final analysis they did not want their atomic projects cluttered up by reporting to another country, even one as friendly as Canada. This had obvious implications for defence and strategy, but it also meant that the British went their own way in producing a *British* reactor. It is worth noting that it was the British who broke the connection: had they not done so, Canada might have become involved in the British atomic bomb program. Instead, as a matter of cost and practicality, Canada refused to contemplate the expense and complications of its own atomic weaponry, relying instead on its American and British partners. Although this would later be taken as a great statement of moral principle and opposition to atomic weapons, it was nothing of the kind: the relevant minister, well aware of both the cost of a weapons program and Canada's shortage of scientists and engineers, did not bother discussing the idea with his colleagues. C.D. Howe simply announced the fact on the spur of the moment during a dull evening session of Parliament.

This takes us into the realm of civilian uses for atomic energy. It was clear that atomic reactors could be used to generate electricity, which could confer industrial advantage on the manufacturing nation at home as well as in sales abroad. (It can be seen as a component in *industrial strategy,* a popular and indeed inevitable form of technological and labour protectionism in virtually all countries.) National pride and national advantage conditioned atomic policies after the war, and in some respects they still do. The British were the first to see atomic research in those terms, but the

Canadians and Americans were not far behind. In industrial terms, the three countries drew apart, and by the mid-1950s each had produced a "national" reactor design. The British-designed and produced reactor, the Magnox, proved to be a flop. The simpler American light water design was practical and backed by the weight of American technology and manufacturing capacity. And there was the Canadian heavy water design, which eventually was called the CANDU (Canada Deuterium Uranium). The relative strengths of the Magnox and the CANDU may be illustrated by the desire of Britain's government-owned electricity grid to adopt the CANDU and not the Magnox in the early 1960s, which was quashed, however, by the British government of the day. Atomic research and atomic manufacturing have been so expensive and so greatly subsidized that they have remained instruments of national industrial policy to this day.

The backdrop to all of this was the Cold War. In the contest between liberal democracy and communist totalitarianism, Canada's place was never in doubt. Canada both absorbed and supplied technology. Its plutonium-producing reactor design was adopted by the United States for its production plants on the Savannah River. Canada provided the same efficient design to India, thereby inadvertently contributing to India's eventual nuclear bomb program. In the early 1950s, Chalk River tested fuel rods for the US nuclear submarine fleet. When Chalk River experienced the world's first serious reactor accident in 1952, American naval officers such as Lieutenant Jimmy Carter were on hand to help with the cleanup. At the same time, Canada supported non-proliferation, which meant there was a rather large hole in Canadian nuclear diplomacy. A program of nuclear exports was inevitably conducted in a fog of moral and strategic ambiguity – not just by Canada but also by any of its competitors.

Canada's most lucrative nuclear export was not technology but a mineral, uranium. Technological advances made the relatively low-grade ores found in Canada eminently useful. The Americans in the 1940s and 1950s did their best to corner the world supply of uranium, and the price rose proportionately, so that in the late 1950s uranium was by value one of Canada's major exports. Those exports fed the American nuclear weapons program, with which Canada was already technologically connected. Eventually, however, American enthusiasm for foreign uranium abated, and the bonanza years for Canadian uranium production ended. So did the strategic significance of uranium, which became more and more an ordinary commodity, consigned from the Port Hope refinery to exotic destinations such as Riga, in the Soviet Union.

This volume deals mainly with the place of nuclear fission in Canada's external relations. There is an alternate strain of history that deals with other aspects of Canadian atomic history, for from the heady days of radium at $120,000 a gram to the manufacture of CANDUs, it is obvious that atomic energy is a dangerous business for those handling nuclear materials. While nuclear energy has its idealistic side – the idea that it can be a safe and reliable universal tool to lift the world out of poverty – there is no getting around its perils or the dangerous residues it leaves behind.

The scientists and administrators of 1946 comforted themselves with the thought that these problems – of nuclear waste, for example, or reactor technology – would be solved, just as politicians and diplomats of subsequent years have argued that atomic weapons would never be used. The evidence in the first case, thirty-five years after Chernobyl and ten years after Fukushima, does not lead to abounding confidence in the second.

ROBERT BOTHWELL

## NOTE

1 Walter Zinn, born in Kitchener, Ontario, in 1904 and educated at Queen's University, had to leave Canada to obtain a PhD in what would later be called nuclear physics at Columbia University in New York City. Zinn went on to become one of the world's leading nuclear physicists, and director of the Argonne National Laboratory in 1946. Ironically, in the same year, the Canadian government tried to entice him back to Canada to head the new Chalk River atomic laboratory – without success.

# ACKNOWLEDGMENTS

This book would not have been possible without the support of others. Each chapter began as a paper for a conference held at the University of Toronto's Bill Graham Centre for Contemporary International History in September 2018. Sincere thanks go to John English and the Graham Centre for their support; without it, this collection would not have come to fruition.

At UBC Press, everyone involved made the process a seamless one. Randy Schmidt offered crucial advice and support, as he shepherded the project to completion. The entire production team was fantastic; thanks, in particular, to Katrina Petrik, Michelle van der Merwe, Frank Chow, and Cheryl Lemmens. We are also grateful to the two anonymous reviewers for their comments and suggestions. Thanks, too, go to the C.D. Howe Series in Political History.

More than anything, this project began as a reflection on Canadian nuclear history inspired by one person: Robert Bothwell. We dedicate this book to him.

# THE NUCLEAR NORTH

# INTRODUCTION

## *Nuclear If Necessary, but Not Necessarily Nuclear*

### Susan Colbourn

I n July 1945, the first nuclear weapon was detonated in the deserts of New Mexico. For those who knew of the Trinity test, the weapon's potential inspired awe – and fear. "I feel that we are approaching a moment of terror to mankind," William Lyon Mackenzie King, the long-serving Canadian prime minister, confided in his diary late that month, "for it means that, under the stress of war, men have at least not only found but created the Frankenstein which conceivably could destroy the human race."[1]

Canada had, of course, played a role in the creation of this Frankenstein's monster. Throughout the Second World War, Canada participated in the Manhattan Project as a junior partner to the United States and the United Kingdom in the development of the first atomic bomb. King's government paid for an atomic laboratory in Montreal during the war, in cooperation with the British. And the Manhattan Project relied on uranium mined and refined in Canada.[2] Canada's nuclear history, however, extends far beyond its wartime role as Igor to Dr. Frankenstein, predating the Trinity test.

## A NUCLEAR NATION

Canada's history as a nuclear nation began at home, with natural resources. In 1930, Manitoba-based prospector Gilbert LaBine found a deposit of silver and pitchblende at Great Bear Lake. Successive discoveries

3

in the 1940s and 1950s identified crucial deposits of uranium, such as those near Uranium City, Saskatchewan, and Elliot Lake, Ontario. In 2013, Canada churned out over 9,000 tonnes of uranium, extracted from mines dotting the landscape of northern Saskatchewan.[3] Demand ebbed and flowed over the decades, but these resources granted Canada a role in the development of nuclear weapons and the spread of nuclear power.

Canadians invested in their nuclear know-how, expanding on the foundations laid through the nation's ties to the Manhattan Project. At Chalk River, in Ontario's Laurentian Hills, the Zero Energy Experimental Pile (ZEEP) nuclear reactor went critical before the end of 1945. Two years later, the National Research Experimental (NRX) reactor did as well. Later breakthroughs, such as the Canada Deuterium Uranium (CANDU) heavy water reactor, powered Canadian homes and generated export sales.[4]

Wartime nuclear research also afforded Canada a seat at the first nuclear negotiating table, as the nascent United Nations established a dedicated committee to debate the international control of atomic energy. As with so many others, this was a seat Canada sought and kept; Canadians, one US official reported in the autumn of 1945, felt "that Canada should have a voice in the determination of policy concerning atomic power."[5] Canadian claims rest on access: Canada was part of an exclusive inner circle, one of the first three countries to hold the nuclear secret.

Nuclear issues have shaped Canadian life throughout the Cold War and beyond, both at home and abroad. Grappling with nuclear questions – and with Canada's own nuclear capabilities and resources – influenced the country's defence policy, diplomacy, trade relations, and global reputation. At home, the atomic age reshaped communities and landscapes, as the mining of nuclear materials became part and parcel of Canada's larger extraction economy. Elliot Lake emerged "literally overnight," as mining companies flooded in after the discovery of uranium ore in 1953.[6] Like it or not, Canadians were living in a nuclear nation.

## CANADIAN CONUNDRUMS

At first glance, the assertion that Canada is, in fact, a nuclear nation might still surprise some. Certainly, during the writing of this book, more than one colleague asked whether Canada had any nuclear history at all. Scholars of Canada will laugh, then rattle off a list of Canada's entanglements, starting with the discovery of pitchblende and the founding of the Montreal Laboratory. But the basic point remains, and it is a sharp reminder of how we define – or don't, as the case may be – being nuclear. Often, we associate the idea of being a nuclear nation with one particular technology and the ownership thereof: the atomic bomb.

The answer in the Canadian case, then, seems clear-cut: an obvious and resounding no. After participating in the Manhattan Project, Canada elected not to pursue a national atomic program of its own. The decision, as the oft-repeated tale goes, was a simple one: C.D. Howe made a spur-of-the-moment announcement, rejecting the prospect of a Canadian nuclear weapons program in response to a question in the House of Commons.[7] Thanks to Howe and his remark, Canada became the first nuclear non-proliferator. Subsequent generations harked back to this choice, holding it up as prime evidence of the country's longstanding commitment to arms control and disarmament starting at home.

But geography virtually ensured that Canada would be protected from the Soviet Union by the US nuclear arsenal, an outcome made all the more likely given that Canada lay directly between the two Cold War superpowers. Against the backdrop of the Cold War confrontation, successive Canadian governments committed and reaffirmed the country's participation in bilateral and multilateral nuclear alliances. Prime Minister Louis St. Laurent's government helped to forge the North Atlantic Treaty Organization (NATO), a defence arrangement underwritten by the military power of the United States and, in particular, Washington's nuclear forces. The North American Air Defense Command (NORAD), too, carved out another role for Canada in US nuclear strategy and the defence of the continent.[8] The foundation of Canadian defence policy was the coverage and security afforded by its place under the US nuclear umbrella.

Countless Canadian policies aimed at strengthening Washington's nuclear deterrent, and Ottawa offered Canadian territory and forces to support and defend the US nuclear force. Radar lines stretched out across the Canadian Arctic, designed to sound the alarm on a Soviet nuclear strike and allow enough time to launch a Western response. At NATO, Canadian forces prepared for a nuclear strike role should a conflict break out with the Soviet Union. Canadians trained to conduct nuclear strikes in Europe, and at home the government agreed to station US nuclear weapons on Canadian soil, realities that complicated the common refrain that Canada was not a nuclear power.[9]

To attempt to make sense of Canadian policies during this period is to engage in a battle of semantics. Canada did not own the nuclear weapons stationed on Canadian territory, nor did it own the warheads that its forces trained to fire. But what made the country a nuclear one? Was it simply a question of Canadian ownership of a national atomic program?

This awkward position was hardly secret at the time; in fact, it was the stuff of politics and public protest throughout the Cold War. Canadians repeatedly debated what kind of nuclear role the country should take on as part of its membership in NATO or in NORAD. Be it the political and public debates over the Bomarc missiles in the early 1960s or the testing of US air-launched cruise missiles some two decades later, Canadians argued about their obligations as an ally. Some went so far as to question whether Canada's alliance, with its nuclear connection, actually endangered Canadians rather than protecting them.

Prime Minister Pierre Elliott Trudeau transformed Canada's nuclear weapons policy. Part of a broader reassessment of Canada's international commitments and, in particular, the country's participation in the North Atlantic Alliance, Trudeau abandoned the country's existing nuclear operational roles. Canadian forces stationed in Europe would no longer have a nuclear strike role. At home, the government prepared to remove all nuclear weapons from Canadian soil. It took over a decade to complete that task, a testament to just how enmeshed Canada had become in the nuclear weapons enterprise. By the early 1980s, Canadian officials could finally guarantee that Canada did not have any nuclear weapons, but this did not change the fact that Canada adhered to and upheld nuclear alliances.[10] Even as Trudeau pursued initiatives to "suffocate" the arms race, his government freely affirmed and underscored the crucial role that nuclear weapons played in the "deterrent and defence policies of [the] West" to which Canada belonged.[11]

Canada's international reputation – both real and perceived – has been the subject of much debate. To some, Canada has an obvious and consistent track record as a champion of arms control and disarmament. Other, more critical voices identify a long history of Canadians aiding and abetting damaging nuclear policies. One 1980s pamphlet summed up this history succinctly with the slogan "Atomic Bombs: Canada's Gift to the World."[12]

Even after the removal of nuclear weapons from Canadian soil and the end of Canada's nuclear strike role at NATO, no small number of Canadians remained concerned about the country's relationship with nuclear weapons. Central to these worries was the role of the United States and Canada's ties to its more powerful neighbour to the south. "Despite its non-nuclear halo," the prominent peace activist Simon Rosenblum wrote in 1985, "Canada has been a willing auxiliary to American nuclear weapons policy since the development of the Hiroshima and Nagasaki bombs."[13]

For critics like Rosenblum, Canadian corporations' production of components used in nuclear weapons, such as missile guidance systems, were obvious examples of Canadian complicity in the nuclear arms race and with Washington's nuclear policies. Nor were nuclear weapons their only concern. A growing number of Canadians turned their attention to the dangers of nuclear energy in the 1970s, like those in Nova Scotia determined to stop the construction of a nuclear power plant on Stoddart Island.[14]

One 1980 flyer distributed by the Canadian Coalition for Nuclear Responsibility, for instance, highlighted the country's role in the Manhattan Project and the use of a Canadian reactor in India's May 1974 "peaceful nuclear explosion," along with the export of Canadian nuclear reactors to potential proliferators such as Argentina.[15] In doing so, it underscored the links between nuclear power and nuclear weapons as two sides of the same atomic coin.

Canadians have always recognized the Janus-faced nature of the harnessed atom and of their own relationship to all things nuclear. From the onset of the atomic age, Canadians have debated the role of nuclear power in Canada, the peril of nuclear weapons, and Canada's role in a nuclear world. Should Canada remain a member of an alliance dependent on nuclear deterrence? Should Canadian nuclear technologies be sold to potential nuclear proliferators across the globe and built in Canadians' own backyards? What of the costs of these nuclear technologies, and their impact on local communities and on the environment?

## TELLING NUCLEAR HISTORIES OF CANADA

Canadians' efforts to navigate the atomic age have been diverse, complicated, and at times contradictory, a fact showcased in the chapters that follow. Some of the themes that emerge will be familiar to students of Canadian history, such as functionalism's role in shaping postwar diplomacy, the perceived value of having a seat at the negotiating table, and chronic anxieties about Canada's relationship with the United States. These bedrocks of Canadian foreign policy, seen through a nuclear lens, help to break down an artificial divide between nuclear history and Canadian history – they are one and the same in the postwar world.

We already know a great deal about Canada's nuclear past. We know how a wide array of Canadians tried to make sense of the dangers of nuclear weapons, whether by developing civil defence plans or organizing campaigns to abolish these destructive devices.[16] Increasingly, with the growth of environmental history, we are learning more about how the nuclear industry transformed communities and landscapes across Canada.[17] High-profile nuclear episodes punctuate the country's political history after 1945; the Gouzenko affair, the Bomarc missile debates, and Pierre Trudeau's Peace Mission, to name but a few, remain popular subjects of study.[18]

Rarely, however, do we consider these histories in any holistic sense. If we reflect on these issues together, as part of one whole, what do these seemingly discrete episodes tell us about Canada's history? This collection takes a step in that direction, illustrating how Canada's nuclear history links the domestic to the global. Understanding Canada's nuclear past and, for that matter, the foundations of its still-nuclear present, brings together politics, trade, science, medicine, the environment, the military, and many more lines of historical inquiry. This collection of essays underscores the sheer number of issues with nuclear dimensions, of which the topics included here are only a small sampling. To highlight the degree to which nuclear history is woven into the very fabric of Canadian history in the atomic age, this book is divided into four sections, arranged thematically.

Setting the stage, Katie Davis sketches out in Chapter 1 the intersections between the postwar tradition of functionalism and the early wrangling over the atomic bomb. Having gained a seat on the United Nations Atomic

Energy Commission (UNAEC), Canadian diplomats attempted to navigate the politics of the early atomic age and of the burgeoning Cold War. The Canadian delegation supported the commission's efforts to develop a program of international control, but these efforts were hamstrung by the geopolitical realities of souring relations between the United States and the Soviet Union. General A.G.L. McNaughton, the head of the Canadian delegation at the UNAEC, attempted to bridge the growing divide. His efforts achieved few, if any, real successes. McNaughton was essential in the commission's first report, ensuring it was adopted and sent to the Security Council. The fact that the Soviet Union and Poland abstained during the vote illustrated the obvious limits of any Canadian diplomacy. Yet, as Davis demonstrates, Canada's presence on the UNAEC could be seen as significant in its own right: it was an example of functionalism in action.

In Chapter 2, Timothy Andrews Sayle picks up on a similar theme, telling a sometimes bizarre tale about how Canada leveraged nuclear weapons – and Canada's own nuclear strike role – to secure a place on another international committee, NATO's Nuclear Planning Group (NPG). Created in hopes of resolving the Western allies' chronic debates about who would decide to drop the bomb and with what degree of allied consultation, the NPG's membership was the source of much consternation. To win a seat at that table, Canada's permanent representatives in Brussels skillfully maneuvered to keep the country's diplomatic options open and ultimately leveraged Canada's nuclear capabilities to demand a place.

In Chapter 3, Michael Stevenson revisits one of the most crucial episodes in Canadian nuclear history as he considers the nuclear policies of John Diefenbaker's government and Canada's defence relations with the United States. Focusing in particular on Howard Green's tenure as Diefenbaker's secretary of state for external affairs, Stevenson challenges the prevailing interpretation of Green as naive. Green's handling of the disarmament and defence portfolios showed consistency and clarity, identifying a desired role for Canada to play on the global stage and the considerations that should shape the country's relations with the United States.

Jack Cunningham examines these same debates in Chapter 5, but from the view of the opposition benches. He traces Lester B. Pearson's thinking on nuclear weapons and on Canada's obligations as a member of nuclear alliances throughout the 1950s and into the 1960s. Pearson's approach to the nuclear issues of the day, including the acquisition of US nuclear weapons, reflected a striking consistency. As leader of the Opposition, Pearson repeatedly returned to the question of command and control of the West's nuclear weapons and how a decision would be made regarding their use. Even as he continued to highlight these themes, his policies and those of the Liberal Party responded to the changing political climate. The Liberals, as Cunningham highlights, argued over how best to calibrate a nuclear policy that ticked all the necessary boxes: addressing public anxieties about the dangers of nuclear weapons and assuaging concerns about the Canada-US relationship while also remaining a reliable ally in Western circles.

Offering another fresh perspective on the contentious debates of the early 1960s, Asa McKercher explores James Minifie's *Peacemaker or Powder-Monkey* in Chapter 4. Minifie's bestseller reflected a much larger debate taking place within Canadian society, as Canadians questioned the value of their close relationship with the United States and mused about the potential benefits of a neutralist path in the Cold War. However, even as some Canadians questioned the assumptions at the heart of the country's foreign and defence policies, neutralism did not mean isolationism but rather independence. McKercher links the circulation of ideas about neutralism to support for peacekeeping. Using Canadian military power in peacekeeping roles afforded neutralism's champions a way for Canada to remain engaged in the world without being in direct service of the United States.

Nor were Canadian anxieties about the country's place in the global order confined to the debates of the early 1960s. When Brian Mulroney's government contemplated the purchase of nuclear-propelled submarines in the late 1980s, the ensuing debates reflected much of the same jockeying over Canada's past and future. In Chapter 6, Susan Colbourn sketches out the broad contours of popular debate over the nuclear submarines, illustrating the diverse ways in which Canadians interpreted and marshalled their country's nuclear history to make their case, both for and against the submarines. Critics wondered about the submarines' value to the defence of Canada and to NATO as an alliance, the potential damage that might be done to Canada's global reputation as a champion of arms control and disarmament, and the shocking price tag of acquiring nuclear submarines.

To others more supportive of the submarines, however, the acquisition was a logical extension of Canada's existing experience with civilian nuclear reactors befitting an already-nuclear nation.

In Chapter 7, Matthew Wiseman picks up on related questions of expertise, as he delves into the history of No. 1 Radiation Detection Unit (1 RDU). Soldiers in this specialized unit of the Canadian Army observed nuclear weapons tests at the Nevada Test Site and at Australia's Maralinga Range. They also conducted decontamination work at Chalk River. The unit's creation was a direct response to the dangers of the nascent atomic age; its creators envisioned that the experimental group would enable the Canadian military to prepare itself to deal with radiological problems should a nuclear attack take place. Wiseman considers the circumstances surrounding the exposure of 1 RDU members to high levels of radiation, along with the broader impact of the unit's work on the health and safety of its personnel.

In Chapter 8, Ryan Dean and P. Whitney Lackenbauer examine Operation Morning Light, an eighty-four-day mission to recover the radioactive debris strewn across the Northwest Territories after a satellite crashed in early 1978. The nuclear-powered Soviet reconnaissance satellite Cosmos 954 malfunctioned and fell out of orbit, scattering radioactive wreckage as it crashed to earth. Canada and the United States coordinated an emergency response, bringing together military and civilian specialists to assess the problem and conduct an extensive cleanup and recovery mission. Operation Morning Light reflected the myriad and diverse issues touched by the atomic age, for the crash and cleanup encompassed environmental issues, health and safety concerns, the politics of the Cold War, and Indigenous-Crown relations, among others.

In Chapter 9, Se Young Jang turns our attention to another crucial aspect of Canada's nuclear policy: the export of Canadian nuclear reactors. Canadian policy shifted considerably in the wake of India's May 1974 nuclear test, which had used plutonium from a Canadian-provided civilian reactor. Hoping to improve Ottawa's reputation both at home and abroad, the Trudeau government doubled down on its non-proliferation policy, even if this emphasis threatened potential export deals to sell Canadian nuclear reactors overseas. And yet Canada's export policy remained inconsistent, applied on a case-by-case basis. After the Indian test, Canada stopped its negotiations to sell heavy water reactors to South Korea. Prior to any sale, Ottawa insisted that Seoul must accept far more rigorous nuclear safeguards and become party to the Nuclear Non-Proliferation Treaty (NPT). Strikingly, none of those same conditions were applied in the ongoing negotiations with Argentina.

Placing these histories in conversation with one another, this collection speaks to the diverse ways in which Canada and Canadians were enmeshed in the global nuclear order during the Cold War. Canadians developed and sold nuclear technologies, extracted resources that helped to fuel the nuclear arms race, and tried to reduce the risk of their own nuclear annihilation. Canada's natural resources, geographic position, alliance commitments, and national self-image all shaped the country's place in the international nuclear landscape.

Taken together, these chapters hint at just how many aspects of Canadian life have been shaped by Canada's presence in the atomic age. Canada's Cold War engagement with nuclear technologies brings together histories of science and technology, of domestic politics and international diplomacy, of economics and trade, and of social movements, to name but a few of the historical approaches employed by the contributors to this volume.

Revisiting old debates and introducing new lines of inquiry, this collection suggests the vast possibilities for scholars going forward to tell more entangled histories of Canada as a nuclear nation, how Canadians participated in the global nuclear order, and how the atomic age shaped the country. This is merely the tip of the iceberg, and we hope it will encourage more scholars to explore the complex connections between the history of Canada and that of the atomic age.

## NOTES

1 King diary entry no. 28630, July 27, 1945, Diaries of Prime Minister William Lyon Mackenzie King, Library and Archives Canada (LAC).
2 Robert Bothwell, *Nucleus: The History of Atomic Energy of Canada Limited* (Toronto: University of Toronto Press, 1988), 3–82; Donald H. Avery, *The Science of War: Canadian Scientists and Allied Military Technology during the Second World War* (Toronto: University of Toronto Press, 1988), 176–202.
3 Natural Resources Canada, "About Uranium," October 6, 2014, https://www.nrcan. gc.ca/energy/energy-sources-distribution/uranium-nuclear-energy/uranium-canada/ about-uranium/7695.

4   For an overview of Canada's CANDU policies, see Duane Bratt, *The Politics of CANDU Exports* (Toronto: University of Toronto Press, 2006).

5   Matthews note, November 10, 1945, RG 59, Office of the Secretary, Special Asst. to Sec. of State for Atomic Energy & Outer Space, General Records Relating to Atomic Energy Matters, 1948–1962, box 46, folder "Canada e. General, 1945–1952 [1 of 3]," US National Archives and Records Administration (NARA).

6   City of Elliot Lake, "Local History," https://www.elliotlake.ca/en/recreation-and -culture/local-history.aspx?hdnContent=.

7   Robert Bothwell, *The Big Chill: Canada and the Cold War* (Toronto: Irwin Publishing, 1998), 19.

8   NORAD was renamed North American Aerospace Defense Command in 1981.

9   For detailed treatments of Canada's defence relations with the United States in the early Cold War, see Richard Evan Goette, *Sovereignty and Command in Canada-US Continental Air Defence, 1940–57* (Vancouver: UBC Press, 2018); Joseph T. Jockel, *No Boundaries Upstairs: Canada, the United States, and the Origins of North American Air Defence, 1945–1958* (Vancouver: UBC Press, 1987); Andrew Richter, *Avoiding Armageddon: Canadian Military Strategy and Nuclear Weapons, 1950–63* (Vancouver: UBC Press, 2001).

10  Lysyshyn to Maté, June 5, 1989, box 140019, folder "Canadian Association of Municipal Nuclear Weapons Free Zones," City of Toronto Archives (CTA).

11  External Affairs to London, "Cdn Policy on Nuclear Wpns," October 18, 1982, RG 25, vol. 12587, file 27-11-1, pt. 4, LAC. On the "strategy of suffocation," see Paul Meyer, "Pierre Trudeau and the 'Suffocation' of the Nuclear Arms Race," *International Journal* 71, 3 (September 2016): 393–408.

12  Canadian Coalition for Nuclear Responsibility flyer, n.d. [1980], MG 28 I 218, vol. 43, folder "Canadian Coalition for Nuclear Responsibility – Articles – Reports 1980–1981," LAC.

13  Simon Rosenblum, *Misguided Missiles: Canada, Cruise and Star Wars* (Toronto: James Lorimer, 1985), 143–44.

14  Mark Leeming, "The Creation of Radicalism: Anti-Nuclear Activism in Nova Scotia, c. 1972–1979," *Canadian Historical Review* 95, 2 (June 2014): 217–41.

15  Canadian Coalition for Nuclear Responsibility flyer, n.d. [1980], MG 28 I 218, vol. 43, folder "Canadian Coalition for Nuclear Responsibility – Articles – Reports 1980–1981," LAC. On Canada's nuclear cooperation with India, see Mark Andrew Eaton, "Securitizing Development Assistance: India's Nuclear Program and Canadian Societal Views on Nuclear Reactor Exports, 1974–1978," *American Review of Canadian Studies* 47, 4 (2017): 408–26; Yogesh Joshi, "Between Principles and Pragmatism: India and the Nuclear Non-Proliferation Regime in the Post-PNE Era, 1974–1980," *International History Review* 40, 5 (2018): 1073–93.

16  On Canada's civil defence structures, see Andrew Burtch, *Give Me Shelter: The Failure of Canada's Cold War Civil Defence* (Vancouver: UBC Press, 2012). For discussions of anti-nuclear activism in Canada, see, for example, Tarah Brookfield, *Cold War Comforts: Canadian Women, Child Safety, and Global Insecurity* (Waterloo, ON: Wilfrid Laurier University Press, 2012), esp. 51–100; Mark Andrew Eaton, "Canadians, Nuclear Weapons, and the Cold War Security Dilemma" (PhD diss., University of Western Ontario, 2007).

17  See, for example, David Elijah Bell and Marissa Zappora Bell, "Port Hope Burning: The Trail of Eldorado, the Uranium Medical Research Centre, and Community Tension over Scientific Uncertainty," in *Nuclear Portraits: Communities, the Environment, and Public Policy,* ed. Laurel Sefton Macdowell (Toronto: University of Toronto Press, 2017), 238–74; Robynne Mellor, "Wildly Nuclear: Elliot Lake and Canada's Nuclear Legacy," Network in Canadian History and Environment (NiCHE), June 15, 2016, http://niche-canada.org/2016/06/15/wildly-nuclear-elliot-lake-and-canadas-nuclear-legacy/. For a comparative history of Canada's uranium extraction throughout the Cold War, see Robynne Mellor, "The Cold War Underground: An Environmental History of Uranium Mining in the United States, Canada, and the Soviet Union, 1945–1991" (PhD diss., Georgetown University, 2018).

18  Each has been the subject of recent scholarship. On the Gouzenko affair, see Dennis Molinaro, "How the Cold War Began . . . with British Help: The Gouzenko Affair Revisited," *Labour/Le Travail* 79 (2017): 143–55. Canadian nuclear policy and the debates of the early 1960s are the subject of Chapters 3, 4, and 5 in this volume. See also Isabel Campbell, "Pearson's Promises and the NATO Nuclear Dilemma," in *Mike's World: Lester B. Pearson and Canadian External Affairs,* ed. Asa McKercher and Galen Roger Perras (Vancouver: UBC Press, 2017), 275–96; Isabel Campbell, "The Defence Dilemma, 1957–1963: Reconsidering the Strategic, Technological, and Operational Contexts," in *Reassessing the Rogue Tory: Canadian Foreign Relations in the Diefenbaker Era,* ed. Janice Cavell and Ryan M. Touhey (Vancouver: UBC Press, 2018), 123–42; Nicole Marion, "'I Would Rather Be Right': Diefenbaker and Canadian Disarmament Movements," in *Reassessing the Rogue Tory,* 143–66; Asa McKercher, *Camelot and Canada: Canadian-American Relations in the Kennedy Era* (New York: Oxford University Press, 2016); Patricia I. McMahon, *Essence of Indecision: Diefenbaker's Nuclear Policy, 1957–1963* (Montreal and Kingston: McGill-Queen's University Press, 2009). On the Trudeau Peace Mission, see Luc-André Brunet, "Unhelpful Fixer? Canada, the Euromissile Crisis, and Pierre Trudeau's Peace Initiative, 1983–1984," *International History Review* 41, 6 (2018): 1145–67, doi: 10.1080/07075332.2018.1472623; Susan Colbourn, "'Cruising Toward Nuclear Danger': Canadian Anti-Nuclear Activism, Pierre Trudeau's Peace Mission, and the Transatlantic Partnership," *Cold War History* 18, 1 (2018): 19–36; Susan Colbourn, "The Elephant in the Room: Rethinking Cruise Missile Testing and Pierre Trudeau's Peace Mission," in *Undiplomatic History: The New Study of Canada and the World,* ed. Asa McKercher and Philip Van Huizen (Montreal and Kingston: McGill-Queen's University Press, 2019), 253–76.

*Part 1*

# A SEAT AT THE TABLE

# CHAPTER 1

# VERY CLOSE TOGETHER

*Balancing Canadian Interests on*
*Atomic Energy Control, 1945–46*

*Katie Davis*

T he early days of the atomic age were filled with great hope for a future fuelled by atomic energy, coupled with intense anxiety about postwar peace. The October 1945 edition of *Maclean's* described the contributions atomic energy would make to Canadian society in areas like medicine, agriculture, and power. Indeed, the lead story predicted, "the coming of atomic power ... may prove to be the most important single event in the whole history of mankind." But the significance of atomic energy was underscored by its duality: "Its possibilities for evil are tremendous, and its possibilities for good are equally great."[1] Harnessing the benefits of atomic energy required controlling its destructive potential. Failure to do so would be catastrophic.

There was a way out of this dilemma: international control of atomic energy. In this context, the United Nations Atomic Energy Commission (UNAEC), formed in 1946, sought to halt nuclear proliferation before it could begin. Fears of nuclear war were at the heart of its mission to bring atomic energy under the control of the nascent United Nations. Pundits and policy-makers frequently framed the UNAEC's work in life-or-death terms. International control, as one 1946 publication by the Federation of American Scientists put it, was the choice between "one world or none."[2] Either the world united to control the atomic bomb or it would perish in nuclear war.

But the developing Cold War challenged this goal from the outset. The Canadian representative to the UNAEC, General A.G.L. McNaughton, advised Ottawa in late 1946 that "the work of the Atomic Energy Commission must be considered in terms of general relations between the Soviet Union and the Western World." He advised that "a breakdown in these negotiations might well precipitate a crisis in the entire structure of the United Nations."[3] McNaughton saw atomic energy in an international context shaped by tense superpower relations and concerns about UN viability.

Canada's UNAEC delegation took the dangers of nuclear war seriously. As they tried to navigate the growing divide between the superpowers, Canadian diplomats prized unanimity. The complicated efforts to secure such unanimity demonstrated the challenges Canadian diplomacy faced during its postwar "golden age." Canadian diplomatic influence hinged on professionalism and expertise, augmented in the UNAEC by Canada's wartime participation in the Manhattan Project. But to navigate these earliest days of the Cold War, the Canadian delegation struggled to balance multilateral cooperation and Canada's bilateral relations with the United States. General McNaughton's leadership considerably advanced this dual policy, but superpower tensions, as they became increasingly insurmountable by the end of 1946, ultimately pushed Canada firmly into the US-led Western bloc.

While Canada's Western orientation might seem inevitable in retrospect, the Canadian delegation initially pursued cohesion and universal agreement in the UNAEC. The logic of "one world or none" demanded it. During the fluid period of 1945–46, Canadians had the leeway to maneuver between the superpowers to advance international control negotiations. The overriding importance of the issue combined with the Canadian preference for multilateralism made the UNAEC a key arena for maximizing Canada's postwar diplomatic influence.

By the end of 1946, however, the Canadians faced rapidly dissolving UNAEC negotiations. With the superpowers in polar opposition, the delegations were unable to agree on the content of the first report to the Security Council. Canada ultimately sided firmly with the United States. The loss of Canada as an important consensus builder in the UNAEC fundamentally changed the dynamics of the commission. By siding with the majority – those who supported the US position on international control – the Canadian delegation helped to strengthen the commission's impasse along Cold War lines. This deadlock, enshrined in the UNAEC's first report to the Security Council, ultimately ensured the failure of international control of atomic energy.

## ATOMIC FUNCTIONALISM IN THE EARLY COLD WAR

For most of its first year, however, the seemingly existential nature of international control negotiations combined with Canada's expertise on atomic issues gave Canadian diplomats an elevated purpose in the UNAEC. Canada occupied a uniquely influential position. The only permanent member without great power status, Canada gained this position due to its wartime cooperation with the United States and United Kingdom on the production of atomic bombs. As a member of an elite atomic club, Canada had influence with the US delegation, a crucial relationship given the US monopoly on atomic weapons.[4] Canada's renunciation of its own military nuclear program gave the delegation further diplomatic goodwill.[5] The country's atomic expertise and peaceful intentions augmented Canada's image as a reliable partner with which to negotiate international control. The Canadian delegation capitalized on this position, and encouraged the Americans to cooperate with the Soviets despite persistent disagreements between the superpowers – a divide that crystallized in the commission's first meetings and defined negotiations. At the same time, Canadian interests limited this influence. Canada could not afford to upset relations with the United States. Should international control negotiations break down, Canada needed strong relations with its southern neighbour. Because Canada had forgone a military atomic program of its own, it might need shelter under a US nuclear umbrella in the future. As Cold War divisions deepened in the late 1940s, this security requirement limited the extent to which Canada could push a middle ground between the superpowers.

Canada's inclusion in early atomic negotiations was a victory for functionalism.[6] Functionalism dictated that a country's expertise and contribution should determine representation and influence in international affairs. As Timothy Andrews Sayle demonstrates in Chapter 2, functionalism remained a part of Canada's approach to nuclear issues well into the 1970s. Canadians leveraged their professionalism and atomic expertise to make an impact in the new United Nations. Canadian diplomats in these early years, John English notes, "eschewed idealism and opted for the sensible rather than the sensational."[7] This sensibility guided the delegation through often-conflicting priorities, as Canada balanced multilateral and bilateral relations. When Canadian interests conflicted with US goals in the UNAEC, McNaughton trod carefully. He developed creative solutions to keep negotiations from stalling. In this context, functionalism was intimately linked to the life-or-death nature of international control. The importance of the UNAEC's mission made it essential that negotiations continue.

Throughout the commission's first year, McNaughton strove to overcome deadlock and create a conciliatory working atmosphere. Indeed, his adviser, George Ignatieff, said that McNaughton "set the hallmark of patience, pragmatism and mediation."[8] McNaughton seemed the "obvious choice" to represent Canada in the UNAEC.[9] An engineer by training and former head of the National Research Council, the scientific organization that later oversaw Canadian atomic research, McNaughton had strong connections to the scientific establishment and a solid understanding of atomic science. He was a wartime military leader and former minister of national defence with a keen understanding of what was at stake in the postwar peace. He aptly combined political, military, and scientific experience to perform his diplomatic role. He was, however, inexperienced as a diplomat. In one early instance, McNaughton chided a member of his own delegation in a commission meeting – a sign of both growing pains as a new diplomat and his confident determination.[10] This confidence proved essential for standing up to Bernard Baruch, the American delegate to the UNAEC, a hard-headed businessman unamenable to compromise. At the same time, McNaughton's cordial attitude in public meetings both assuaged Baruch's pride and made a good impression on the Soviets. He had a good working relationship with the Soviet representative, Andrei Gromyko, who found it "so easy to work with the General" because "*he* is never rude" – a tacit dig at the notoriously difficult Baruch.[11]

McNaughton offered crucial remedies to advance stalled negotiations, and his personality smoothed this tricky process. Although he accepted US leadership on the commission, he proposed resolutions to make US actions more palatable to the Soviets. He worked to quietly assuage US concerns and urge moderation, and his efforts to restrain the US delegation foreshadowed a similar Canadian strategy during the Korean War.[12] With

McNaughton's frequent urging of cooperation, the UNAEC's work progressed throughout 1946. Notably, he proposed a structure of private committee meetings that ensured frank discussion of the technical aspects of international control. At the same time, he was willing to take risks when the US delegation became belligerent, proposing a crucial amendment that made it possible for the commission to adopt its first report in December 1946.

This strategy proved untenable in a difficult international climate. Uniquely positioned to influence negotiations through atomic expertise and good relations with the United States, Canada saw its impact restricted by the growing divide between the superpowers. Despite McNaughton's skilled maneuvering, compromise had reached its limits by the end of the year. The Canadians ultimately deprioritized multilateral cooperation in the UNAEC to preserve good relations with the United States. This shift was considered necessary given Soviet intransigence. If universal agreement was impossible, a majority plan for international control would demonstrate the extent of the Soviets' unwillingness to cooperate – while obscuring the reality that the US position was also deeply intractable.

## CANADIAN POLICY FORMATION AND THE BARUCH PLAN

The United States, Canada, and the United Kingdom were among the first to advocate for international control of atomic energy. Atomic cooperation began during the Second World War, when they developed an atomic bomb as the absolute weapon against the Axis powers.[13] Canadians hosted British and French atomic researchers beginning in late 1942, mined uranium in the Northwest Territories, and established a small research reactor in Chalk River, Ontario. These contributions to the wartime atomic project earned Canada a seat at the table for postwar negotiations on atomic energy. In Washington in November 1945, Canadian prime minister W.L. Mackenzie King, US president Harry Truman, and British prime minister Clement Attlee issued a joint declaration on atomic energy, acknowledging their duty to "consider the possibility of international action" to control atomic energy. The three leaders emphasized that the responsibility "rests not on our nations alone, but upon the whole civilized world," laying the foundation for international control.[14] The United States and United Kingdom then gained Soviet support at a Moscow foreign ministers' conference in December 1945. They presented their resolution, embodying the Washington declaration, to the UN General Assembly in January 1946. The resolution passed unanimously and charged the UNAEC with "enquir[ing] into all phases of the problem" of atomic energy control.[15]

Preparing for the UNAEC's first meeting in June 1946, Canada developed its international control policy in the Advisory Panel on Atomic Energy.[16] The Advisory Panel lauded the Acheson-Lilienthal Report, the comprehensive study released by the US State Department in April 1946. The report recommended an international authority with ample safeguards to protect against the diversion of atomic materials for weaponized use.[17] The panel advised that Canada should support the US delegation if it adhered to the Acheson-Lilienthal Report in the UNAEC. Not only was the report a sound plan but the panel recognized that "Canada has a very important interest on general political grounds" in preserving cooperation with the United States.[18] The Department of External Affairs clarified these goals in instructions to McNaughton, cautioning that he should not "slavishly follow United States policies" because the Canadian delegation had "constructive suggestions to make of [its] own." However, McNaughton was advised not to push the US delegation beyond what it was willing to accept.[19] Canada could best contribute to the UNAEC by promoting cooperation while working behind the scenes with the US delegation. Keeping this tenuous balance characterized the Canadian delegation's approach throughout 1946.

Bernard Baruch's proposals made this strategy difficult, if not impossible, from the UNAEC's first meeting, which he opened by tabling a comprehensive plan for international control of atomic energy. While based on the Acheson-Lilienthal Report, Baruch's plan greatly strengthened enforcement and punishment measures. He also staunchly opposed using the Security Council's veto power when deciding punishments.[20] Baruch's far-reaching proposal was part of a larger strategy to protect the US atomic monopoly until a strong system of international control could be put in place. Only with harsh punishments would it be safe for the United States to give up its strategic advantage.[21] Though the first to speak in support of the Baruch plan, McNaughton recognized the difficulties inherent in this augmented version of the Acheson-Lilienthal plan. He correctly anticipated Soviet objections to the plan's enhanced enforcement measures, and reminded his colleagues of the difficult work ahead, noting that "mutual confidence [was] vital." He suggested that they first work on exchanging scientific information, rather than focusing on complex political questions like the Security Council veto.[22]

Underscoring Soviet objections to the Baruch plan, Andrei Gromyko tabled an alternate proposal at the next meeting that contradicted the Baruch plan in nearly every way. Gromyko proposed an international convention outlawing nuclear weapons that would precede all other international control measures. He opposed Baruch's proposal for comprehensive international inspection, instead suggesting that states pass their own domestic legislation for enforcement and punishment – a recommendation that gutted much of the Baruch plan. Finally, Gromyko opposed altering the Security Council's veto power. The Baruch plan hinged on removing this power to ensure equitable enforcement of an international control treaty.[23] Concerns about infringement of national sovereignty pervaded the Soviet approach. The Soviets were also unwilling to take the United States at its word. By pushing for a complete disarmament convention as the first step in negotiations, the Soviet delegation sought assurances that the United States was not merely leveraging its nuclear monopoly to secure its own agenda. The US monopoly amplified disagreement, exacerbated by the Gouzenko affair – the revelation of Soviet atomic espionage in Canada in September 1945 – which confirmed Soviet nuclear aspirations.[24] Public awareness of the Gouzenko affair by early 1946 hardened the US position, and raised skepticism about Soviet sincerity in international control negotiations.[25]

## FROM CONCILIATION TO ANTAGONISM

With deadlock firmly in place from the UNAEC's initial meetings in June 1946, McNaughton offered unconventional ways to push negotiations forward. He spoke frankly about the drawbacks of both the US and Soviet control plans. While Canada's atomic expertise permitted this role, Ottawa cautioned McNaughton to take care that his actions not be perceived by the superpowers as "an irresponsible piece of meddling."[26] McNaughton thus supported the Baruch plan as a sound start but recognized the legitimacy of Soviet critiques. He searched for middle ground when possible, and sought to moderate some of Baruch's more challenging demands.

The delegates met in plenary sessions throughout June and July, and formed committees to tackle points of disagreement such as the Security Council veto. The Working Committee sought common ground between US and Soviet proposals to determine the necessary powers of an international control agency. Committee 2 developed recommendations for safeguards, studying the technical requirements for atomic materials to be safely held by an international authority. Both committees' discussions involved complex debates over national sovereignty, and they worked with little success in the initial months.

With this slow progress in mind, the UNAEC took up a suggestion made by McNaughton in his first address to the commission months earlier. It resolved to postpone its discussion of political matters in both committees, and instead struck a committee to study the scientific feasibility of international control.[27] This Scientific and Technical Committee opted to hold closed-door, informal meetings in the hope of facilitating cooperation between participants. Further, in an international climate hardening into bipolarity, the committee's private meetings enabled frank discussions between atomic scientists and diplomats. Outside the commission, the superpowers clashed over territorial arrangements throughout 1945–46 – over the Soviet refusal to withdraw from Iran and the use of waters between the Soviet Union and Turkey. The Greek Civil War exacerbated tension as the United States feared a potential victory for communist forces there.[28] These international disagreements led to stalemates in the Security Council and raised doubts about the United Nations' efficacy. The Scientific and Technical Committee's unanimous report in September 1946 was a notable achievement given the impasse both in and out of the UNAEC.[29]

This report concluded that effective international control was possible from a scientific standpoint, and laid solid groundwork for the commission to refocus its attention on the far more difficult political tasks still ahead. McNaughton served as chairman when the commission finalized the report. The chairmanship rotated monthly, promoting fresh leadership perspectives during tense negotiations. Both the commission's plenary meetings and committee work were postponed until the scientific report was completed. At this crucial juncture, responsibility fell to McNaughton to restart negotiations and prevent another stalemate.[30] In this spirit, he sought to advance the commission's scientific work without getting bogged down again in political matters. He proposed that Committee 2, the safeguards committee, develop safeguards consistent with the report's conclusions.

McNaughton's plan was unanimously adopted with minor amendments.[31] At his urging, Committee 2 used informal sessions similar to those of the Scientific and Technical Committee. This method yielded another technical report by the end of the year.[32] Crucially, these new meetings fell outside of the standard record-keeping structure of the commission. Meeting transcripts were classified. McNaughton's insistence on informality meant that Committee 2 could proceed with greater frankness than previously possible. His problem solving at this juncture productively advanced commission negotiations, building on a successful phase of work by underscoring the importance of candid cooperation. McNaughton capitalized on a skill that the Canadian delegation was quickly mastering, showing that professionalism and consensus building both maximized Canadian influence and yielded results.

McNaughton's strategy worked well in committee meetings, but plenary sessions were a complicated arena where Baruch presided over the US delegation and sought to reassert his plan for international control. Despite this challenge, McNaughton did not want the spirit of cooperation developed in Committee 2's informal meetings to be lost in tense plenary sessions. He hoped their cordiality would provide a strong foundation for more difficult political discussions to come.[33] At the next plenary session in November, the delegates resolved to submit a progress report to the Security Council by December 31. This task would require substantial cooperation to develop a statement that encompassed the commission's technical and political positions.

Capitalizing on this conciliatory atmosphere, Baruch aimed to secure a report to the Security Council that endorsed his plan for international control. McNaughton counselled caution, concerned that a dramatic move might upset recent progress. Determined to reassert his plan, however, Baruch presented a resolution at a plenary session on December 5.[34] Although the resolution largely reiterated Baruch's original plan, McNaughton feared that forcing a vote on it might prompt a breakdown in negotiations. He thought it premature to ask delegates to formally align themselves with any plan in its entirety as many aspects of international control still required discussion. He worried that requiring the Soviets to take a stand on the issue might cause them to walk out of the negotiations. The Soviet delegation had already objected to Baruch's resolution and sought to prevent a vote altogether. Although McNaughton advised caution, Baruch was adamant "that now was the time for a decision . . . 'for all men to stand up and be counted.'"[35] He hoped that this roll call of support would underscore the split between the Soviets and the rest of the commission.

This placed McNaughton in a difficult position. From the beginning, Ottawa's strategy included two goals: to advance the work of the commission and to support the US delegation. At this point, these goals came into serious conflict. McNaughton's first instinct was to counsel caution and restraint, but during this particularly tense moment Baruch was obstinate. Given Baruch's personality, McNaughton altered course, taking on an active role in altering the US position. Supporting Baruch's resolution outright might precipitate a breakdown in negotiations if the commission members could not agree on the Security Council report. To resolve these differences, McNaughton wrote to Ottawa advising a new tactic – support the Baruch plan "in principle" but assert the right of commission members to amend it.[36] McNaughton thus sought to constrain US actions by tabling alternatives to Baruch's resolution. This recommendation was well received in Ottawa, prompting McNaughton to propose a Canadian amendment to the Baruch resolution.

At the next plenary session on December 17, McNaughton acted cautiously, reserving the amendment as a bold counter-maneuver should Baruch become intransigent. As he anticipated, Baruch immediately moved to vote on his resolution, declaring that "the time has come to match our words with action." Baruch argued that their work must be hastened by the unanimous disarmament resolution passed by the General Assembly three days earlier.[37] Introduced in the General Assembly by Soviet representative Vyacheslav Molotov, the idea of general disarmament, including nuclear disarmament, was part of a Soviet strategy to deprive the United States of its nuclear arsenal and ensure an equal footing for international control negotiations. As the General Assembly's work on disarmament advanced in favour of the Soviet approach, Baruch sought to undercut this progress by formally adopting the US approach in the UNAEC. He hoped that this move would make it impossible to implement the disarmament resolution.

In response to Baruch's demand for a vote, McNaughton again urged caution, this time in a plenary session – trading his private counsel for public rebuke. McNaughton suggested further discussion of Baruch's proposals in the Working Committee, rather than a formal vote in the plenary session. He recognized that the commission's report must "take full account" of the General Assembly resolution, and that elements of the Baruch plan – especially on the veto – conflicted with it.[38] Despite these reservations, McNaughton made clear that his government still agreed with "the principles on which [the Baruch] proposals are based." He also sought to moderate the significance of a forced vote. He argued that a vote for Baruch's resolution would not bind delegates to its every word, but rather indicated that they supported its principles in spirit. While other members joined McNaughton in supporting the Baruch resolution with this reservation in mind, Gromyko moved to delay voting. He asked for more time to study it in relation to the new General Assembly resolution. Baruch reluctantly supported Gromyko's request, but only for three more days.[39]

News of McNaughton's stand against Baruch broke in the *Globe and Mail* on December 20, described alongside Canada's contributions to the General Assembly resolution. Although the article emphasized McNaughton's caution in pushing back against Baruch, the subheading "Canadians Fight Hard" drew attention to the Canadian effort.[40] In Ottawa, however, some grew concerned about public perceptions of growing divisions between Canada and the United States. Indeed, Canadian adviser Escott Reid believed the commission was "on the eve of a very important crisis." In this context, Under-Secretary of State for External Affairs Lester Pearson reiterated McNaughton's intent to support the Baruch plan in principle rather than with a material vote. "If the Americans act stupidly in this matter and force a vote," Pearson argued, "we might well abstain."[41] But an abstention was not altogether desirable as it mimicked the Soviet tactic of non-participation. For the Canadian delegation, a critical issue such as international control required active participation, consensus building, and ultimately universal agreement. Concerns about what this split might mean for both Canada-US relations and international control rallied support at External Affairs behind the amendment.

At the same time, the US delegation courted the votes of commission members to pre-empt Canadian action. They called a meeting of several delegations thought to be amenable to the US position, excluding the Canadians. US representatives urged their counterparts to support Baruch's resolution and to ensure that a vote took place with no amendments and – of course – that it passed. The Canadian delegation learned of this meeting when a member of the British delegation approached them, angry that the Americans would try to strong-arm other delegates to get their way. This tactic emboldened the Canadian delegation to move forward with its amendment.[42] Escott Reid recognized that it seemed the US delegation was "beginning to realize that they [had] put themselves in a very embarrassing position."[43] Baruch's insistence on forcing a vote could precipitate a breakdown in the commission's negotiations. His actions threatened to make Canadian fears come true.

## THE CANADIAN AMENDMENT AND THE MAJORITY SHIFT

Fears of a breakdown in UNAEC negotiations were rooted in the commission's vital mission to preserve postwar peace through international control. Although the Canadians knew that the superpowers held opposing views on international control, they resolved to keep negotiations moving for as long as possible. This was no easy task given Baruch's insistence on his views and Gromyko's growing unwillingness to negotiate. To defuse this tense situation, McNaughton tabled an amendment to the Baruch resolution when the commission met again on December 20. He assured Gromyko that his amendment sought to reconcile the views of the United States and Soviet Union, and that there would be opportunities for discussion in the Working Committee. He reiterated that his government supported the underlying intent of the Baruch plan – the inexorable belief that international control of atomic energy was both possible and necessary. He stressed that the entire commission, including the Soviet delegation, agreed with this point. Thus he did not seek to subvert the Baruch resolution, only to make it palatable to everyone. The concise amendment stated that "the Commission approves and accepts the principles on which these findings and recommendations [of the Baruch resolution] are based." This wording recognized that the Soviets retained serious doubts about some of Baruch's proposals, but it also sought to enable them to express agreement with the underlying principle that atomic energy must be controlled through an international framework. The amendment also specified that the final report must reconcile the wording of the Baruch plan with the General Assembly's disarmament resolution.[44] This last piece was crucial, as it mandated that the report to the Security Council must essentially combine the US and Soviet positions.

Baruch immediately supported the Canadian amendment, which Reid described as "face-saving" for the US delegation.[45] A forced vote on Baruch's resolution would have prompted a complicated plenary debate that some members of the US delegation were now anxious to avoid. The Canadian move moderated Baruch's impetuousness in a way that was not possible from within his own delegation, which was stacked with Baruch's close business associates. Franklin Lindsay of the US delegation later admitted to the Canadians that their amendment had "helped the Commission out of a most difficult situation."[46]

The Canadian amendment was designed to enable the Soviet delegation to express support for Baruch's resolution without agreeing to every aspect of his plan for international control. This would enable the Soviets to vote, as Baruch insisted, while moderating the significance of that vote. It failed to secure Moscow's support, however. The Soviet delegation continued to insist that a vote on the Baruch resolution would be premature, even with the amendment. Gromyko objected to a final vote, but not to the consideration of Baruch's proposals in the Working Committee. The Polish delegation, in support of Soviet concerns, sought to moderate the language of the Canadian amendment. The Polish representative, Oskar Lange, proposed, changing "the Commission *approves and accepts* the principles" to "the Commission *draws attention to* the principles."[47] As a gesture of goodwill, McNaughton offered to abstain from voting on the Polish amendment and encouraged Lange to do the same for the Canadian one.[48] A majority rejected the Polish reframing of the amendment, supporting instead a vote on the original Canadian motion. Gromyko, in line with his earlier requests for more time, refused to vote. As a result, the vote on the Canadian amendment was 10–0 with Poland abstaining. No vote for the Soviet delegation was recorded, which functioned as an informal abstention.[49]

Although the Canadian amendment failed to secure Moscow's support, it preserved cordial relations within the commission – a hallmark of the Canadian approach. McNaughton recalled that Gromyko spoke "in a most conciliatory manner" during the meeting. Rather than objecting to any of the proceedings, he simply asked for more time. Similarly, McNaughton observed that the Polish delegation sought to preserve the commission's cooperation. According to him, Lange "begged that we should not now . . . create an atmosphere of disagreement." Though the Polish amendment was not accepted, McNaughton's suggestion that Lange abstain from voting enabled the Canadian amendment to pass with no votes against it. Otherwise, the Polish delegation might have cast a vote against the amendment to show its support for the Soviet position. McNaughton observed that Lange abstained due to the "spirit of conciliation shown by the Canadian delegation."[50] McNaughton's painstaking concentration on preserving UNAEC cooperation at this crucial juncture prevented a breakdown in negotiations without upsetting relations with the United States.

The danger of a complete breakdown was not over, however. The delegates still needed to adopt a report to be referred to the Security Council. The Working Committee met a week later to draft the report. The meeting was arduous, and became more intense when delegates turned to a discussion of the veto. Although the Canadians were never fond of the Security Council veto, McNaughton recognized the contentious nature of Baruch's desire to remove this power when deciding punishments for nuclear violations. As such, he sought to omit references to the veto in the report, both to bring it in line with the General Assembly resolution on disarmament and to placate the Soviets. By this point, however, Baruch had grown tired of these attempts to moderate his position, and he laid down his final view on the issue. Throughout the meeting, Ferdinand Eberstadt represented the US delegation, but when the subject turned to the veto, Baruch burst into the room. He proceeded to pontificate about the veto, ending with an ultimatum:

> Gentlemen, it is either – or. Either you agree that a criminal should have this right [to the veto] by voting against our [the US] position (or you fail to take a stand on the question by refraining from voting), or you vote for this sound and basic principle of enduring justice and plain common sense.[51]

Once again, Baruch demanded a vote, and in so doing he finally made clear his approach to UNAEC negotiations – either the commission's members would support the US position or the negotiations must end.

Even with the Canadian amendment, McNaughton never strayed from his careful strategy to promote progress through cordiality and respect. But when Baruch laid down this ultimatum, McNaughton shifted course. Rather than affirming the importance of cooperation, he stated that his chief aim at this juncture was to achieve a report, unanimous or otherwise. Canada would "conform to the views of the majority" on the text related to the veto, hoping to finalize a report by the deadline. Although he claimed that "the Canadian delegation takes an objective view," this emphasis on majority, rather than unanimous, decision making was a stark reversal of earlier tactics aimed at conciliation.[52]

Why did McNaughton alter his position at this crucial juncture? The failure to secure Soviet approval of the Canadian amendment signalled the difficulty of ever achieving unanimous agreement. The Canadian amendment sought to mediate between the superpowers' positions, but the Soviet abstention suggested that this might be impossible. During the Working Committee debates over the veto, Gromyko maintained his silence, refusing to discuss the issue. McNaughton noted Gromyko's continued abstention and recognized doubts raised by other delegations. In the same breath, however, he tacitly observed that the United States had enough support to win a majority regardless of some delegates' reservations.[53] At the same time, Baruch's ultimatum risked the dissolution of the UNAEC. If the Canadian delegation continued to press for unanimous agreement, it seemed unlikely that negotiations could ever progress beyond this point.

McNaughton's altered approach reflected a shift in Mackenzie King's thinking about the Soviets. After the failure of the Canadian amendment and Gromyko's persistent refusal to clearly state his views, King became convinced of Soviet insincerity. In his typical style, he reflected on this decision by recounting a dream: "It was President Roosevelt standing at full length but needing someone to support him. He beckoned me to give him my arms . . . and seemed anxious that others should see that we were very close together." King mused that this dream reinforced his confidence in his decision.[54] With growing doubts about the Soviet commitment to international control, the prime minister halted the Canadian delegation's attempts to omit the veto issue in the final report. "The fact that Russia is unwilling to include mention of the veto," he said, "specifically is the strongest reason why" it must be included.[55] McNaughton's shift in the Working Committee to conform with the majority instead of seeking unanimity illustrated this new approach.

The Canadian shift pushed the commission toward a report to the Security Council with majority, rather than unanimous, support. This shift toward majority rule shaped the tenor of all future negotiations, as the commission's majority grew increasingly hostile to the Soviet position. The Canadian delegation's role in precipitating this change was significant, beginning in the tenth plenary session on December 30. At this meeting, Gromyko once again asked for more time to consider the Baruch proposals. This time, McNaughton challenged the Soviet request, moving from painstaking conciliation to a firm stand alongside the United States. He pointed out that the Working Committee "had full opportunity to discuss, consider and revise the [Baruch] proposals." He noted that the committee had made revisions, and that if anyone failed to take advantage of this opportunity, "that is their misfortune, and ours too. This should not, however, prevent us from coming to a decision now."[56] Although the Canadian delegation retained some reservations about the report's content, McNaughton noted that "the present text is the one which will command the greatest measure of agreement" – an implicit reference to majority rule.

As McNaughton came down on the side of the majority, the Polish representative interjected with an appeal for cooperation reminiscent of his earlier attempt to alter the Canadian amendment. "We have obtained agreement basically on eighty-nine pages of the report," Lange noted, "with points of disagreement, maybe, running into a rather small number of sentences." He recommended that they refer the report to the Security Council without a vote attached to it.[57] Baruch, still bent on ensuring that every delegate "stand up and be counted," ignored Lange's recommendation and called for a vote. No one challenged him on this move. Lange stated that if that was the will of the commission, he would abstain. Gromyko maintained his earlier non-participation strategy and also abstained. The first report to the Security Council was thus adopted in a 10–0 vote with the Soviet Union and Poland abstaining. Unlike the vote on the Canadian amendment, these abstentions were not a mark of successful conciliation but rather underscored the divide between the superpowers. As the Polish delegate noted, disagreement on a few sentences stymied unanimity. But those disagreements, centred on the veto, were rooted in a jockeying for international influence that extended far beyond UNAEC negotiations.

## REFLECTIONS ON CANADIAN ATOMIC DIPLOMACY

Canada and the UNAEC's majority delegations honed their approach in negotiations as the divide with the Soviet Union deepened. The Soviet Union, Poland, and later Ukraine were publicly contrasted with "the majority," and blamed for lack of agreement. Canada's ability in 1946 to push for a strong, unanimous international control plan was due to its own nuclear capacity and continuing cooperation with the United States on atomic issues. This elevated atomic position gave Ottawa greater freedom to moderate the US approach, but it also demonstrated the limits of functionalism. While McNaughton persisted for months in balancing Ottawa's dual policies of commission cohesion and relations with the United States, this position was ultimately unsustainable. As the Cold War divide between the superpowers deepened, Canada had to fall in line – ultimately dashing hopes for UN unity on the dangerous problem of the atomic bomb.

Twelve years later, McNaughton reflected positively on his work in the UNAEC. The majority plan took shape beginning in January 1947 as the commission refined Baruch's proposals. "I was satisfied," McNaughton recalled, "that [the majority's] proposals . . . [were] an effective plan and I still think that this is true." But the impasse that developed in June 1946 never dissipated, and the UNAEC never fulfilled its central mission. In hindsight, McNaughton questioned the sincerity of the United States. He believed the US delegation was willing to "concede nothing which might compromise the [US atomic] technological advantage."[58] And he later derided the Baruch plan as "insincerity from beginning to end."[59] Canada's difficulties during the UNAEC's first year did not stem chiefly from Soviet opposition, but rather from US intransigence under Baruch's leadership. In Baruch's mind, his plan represented the only possible path to international control. He was unwilling to consider alternatives, seeing concessions on key issues like the veto as dangerous, even criminal.

In this context, McNaughton balanced a conflicting strategy based on advancing negotiations through consensus while supporting the US position in principle. On the ground, he saw the difficulty of balancing these two goals in a tense international climate. He offered policy recommendations to Ottawa while using his personal diplomatic skill to assuage US concerns. The prime minister supported this position to its breaking point, giving McNaughton considerable leeway to shape the Canadian approach for much of the year. But when the UNAEC conflict reached its height in late December, Ottawa chose the cautious path to preserve relations with its closest neighbour. Harbouring no illusions about Baruch's sincerity, the Canadian delegation saw Gromyko's persistent refusal in late December to take a stance as evidence that the Soviets had also dug in their heels. The Soviet refusal to give up the veto was the best evidence to suggest that their intentions were insincere. Indeed, the Soviets were well on their way to developing an atomic bomb of their own.

This episode in early Canadian nuclear diplomacy demonstrated the limits of functionalism. Expertise, professionalism, and personal relationships elevated Canada's role on the UNAEC, but these qualities could not overcome a hardening divide between the superpowers. Baruch's unwillingness to consider Soviet critiques exacerbated this conflict. Escott Reid bitterly remembered this limitation, recalling Baruch "doing his best to sabotage whatever slight possibility there might be of agreement."[60] Despite Reid's regrets, the shift to majority rule in the UNAEC was warmly received by the US delegation. Baruch reflected "that they owed more to Canada than to any of the other countries for having brought everything into line."[61]

As Reid rightly noted, however, the first report to the Security Council was a bittersweet success. The UNAEC's first year was the only period when cooperation with the Soviet Union on atomic energy might have been feasible. By the end of 1946, positions on both sides of the Iron Curtain hardened into an impasse that made agreement on a delicate issue like international control impossible. While the Canadian delegation worked to facilitate this agreement to a point, they re-evaluated their goals in this tense international climate and prioritized relations with the United States. Although there is no evidence to suggest that General McNaughton regretted this decision, his adviser, George Ignatieff, longingly reflected in hindsight on what the Canadians lost with it. "I've always regretted that we did not take Escott Reid's advice [to push Bernard Baruch to compromise] more seriously," he noted forty years later, "because in fact we never really recovered the ground that could have been made before proliferation of weapons began."[62]

## NOTES

1 Bruce Bliven, "Atomic Dawn: What's It Mean?" *Maclean's*, October 1, 1945, 5, 60, 62.

2 Dexter Masters and Katharine Way, eds., *One World or None* (New York: Whittlesey House, McGraw-Hill, 1946).

3 "Report by Delegation to the Atomic Energy Commission," November 29, 1946, *Documents on Canadian External Relations (DCER)*, vol. 12, *1946*, ch. 5, "Atomic Energy," Document 303, http://epe.lac-bac.gc.ca/100/206/301/faitc-aecic/history/2013-05-03/ www.international.gc.ca/department/history-histoire/dcer/details-en.asp@ intRefid=11522.

4 Although the United Kingdom and Canada worked on the Manhattan Project, the ability to produce and use atomic bombs remained solely with the United States. For the British position on international control, see Margaret Gowing, *Independence and Deterrence: Britain and Atomic Energy, 1945–1952*, vol. 1, *Policy Making* (London: Macmillan, 1974), 87–123.

5 The Canadian decision against developing nuclear weapons was announced on December 3, 1945. During Question Period in the House of Commons, C.D. Howe remarked: "Canada has not been working on the development of the atomic bomb. It has been working on the development of atomic energy for peace-time purposes." See *House of Commons Debates*, 20th Parliament, 1st Session, vol. 3, 2824. See also Robert Bothwell, *Nucleus: The History of Atomic Energy of Canada Limited* (Toronto: University of Toronto Press, 1988), 73–74; Brian Buckley, *Canada's Early Nuclear Policy: Fate, Chance, and Character* (Montreal and Kingston: McGill-Queen's University Press, 2000); and Michael Crawford Urban, "The Curious Tale of the Dog That Did Not Bark: Explaining Canada's Non–Acquisition of an Independent Nuclear Arsenal, 1945–1957," *International Journal* 69, 3 (September 2014): 308–33.

6 See Joseph Levitt, *Pearson and Canada's Role in Nuclear Disarmament and Arms Control Negotiations, 1945–1957* (Montreal and Kingston: McGill-Queen's University Press, 1993), 85, and John W. Holmes, *The Shaping of Peace: Canada and the Search for World Order, 1943–1957*, vol. 2 (Toronto: University of Toronto Press, 1982), 46.

7 John English, "'A Fine Romance': Canada and the United Nations, 1943–1957," in *Canada and the Early Cold War, 1943–1957*, ed. Greg Donaghy (Ottawa: Government of Canada, 1998), 80–81. Albert Legault and Michel Fortmann also highlight the professionalism of Canadian diplomats in *A Diplomacy of Hope: Canada and Disarmament, 1945–1988* (Montreal and Kingston: McGill-Queen's University Press, 1992), 64.

8 George Ignatieff, "General A.G.L. McNaughton: A Soldier in Diplomacy," *International Journal* 22, 3 (1967): 407.

9 Ibid., 404.

10  George Ignatieff, *The Making of a Peacemonger: The Memoirs of George Ignatieff* (Toronto: University of Toronto Press, 1985), 95.

11  Conversation with Mrs. McNaughton, undated, quoted in John Swettenham, *McNaughton*, vol. 3, *1944–1966* (Toronto: Ryerson Press, 1969), 119.

12  Denis Stairs terms this strategy "the diplomacy of constraint." See Greg Donaghy, "Diplomacy of Constraint Revisited: Canada and the UN Korean Reconstruction Agency, 1950–55," *Journal of the Canadian Historical Association* 25, 2 (2014): 159–85; Timothy Andrews Sayle, "A Pattern of Constraint: Canadian-American Relations in the Early Cold War," *International Journal* 62, 3 (Summer 2007): 689–705; Denis Stairs, *The Diplomacy of Constraint: Canada, the Korean War, and the United States* (Toronto: University of Toronto Press, 1974).

13  On wartime tripartite atomic cooperation, see Robert Bothwell, *Eldorado: Canada's National Uranium Company* (Toronto: University of Toronto Press, 1984); Bothwell, *Nucleus*; Margaret Gowing, *Britain and Atomic Energy, 1939–1945* (London: Macmillan, 1965); and Richard G. Hewlett and Oscar E. Anderson, *A History of the United States Atomic Energy Commission*, vol. 1, *The New World, 1939/1946* (University Park: Pennsylvania State University Press, 1962).

14  See Harry S. Truman, "The President's News Conference Following the Signing of a Joint Declaration on Atomic Energy," November 15, 1945, The American Presidency Project, https://www.presidency.ucsb.edu/node/231085.

15  United Nations General Assembly, "General Assembly Resolution 1 (I): Establishment of a Commission to Deal with the Problems Raised by the Discovery of Atomic Energy," January 24, 1946, https://undocs.org/en/A/RES/1(I).

16  Cabinet Conclusions, March 27, 1946, RG 2, Privy Council Office, Series A-5-a, vol. 2637, microfilm reel T-2364, item 6701, Library and Archives Canada (LAC); "Minutes of a Meeting of the Advisory Panel on Atomic Energy," April 15, 1946, *DCER*, vol. 12, ch. 5, Document 273, http://epe.lac-bac.gc.ca/100/206/301/faitc-aecic/history/2013-05-03/www.international.gc.ca/department/history-histoire/dcer/details-en.asp@intRefid=11485.

17  US Department of State, *A Report on the International Control of Atomic Energy* (Washington, DC: US Government Printing Office, 1946).

18  "Memorandum from Advisory Panel on Atomic Energy to Cabinet," May 7, 1946, *DCER*, vol. 12, ch. 5, Document 279, http://epe.lac-bac.gc.ca/100/206/301/faitc-aecic/history/2013-05-03/www.international.gc.ca/department/history-histoire/dcer/details-en.asp@intRefid=11491; Cabinet Conclusions, May 16, 1946, RG 2, Privy Council Office, Series A-5-a, vol. 2638, microfilm reel T-2364, item 6878, LAC.

19  Ignatieff to Associate Under-SSEA [Under-Secretary of State for External Affairs], June 8, 1946, *DCER*, vol. 12, ch. 5, Document 282, http://epe.lac-bac.gc.ca/100/206/301/faitc-aecic/history/2013-05-03/www.international.gc.ca/department/history-histoire/dcer/details-en.asp@intRefid=11494; Cabinet Conclusions, June 12, 1946, RG 2, Privy Council Office, Series A-5-a, vol. 2638, microfilm reel T-2364, item 6997, LAC.

20  Bernard Baruch, "Official Record of the First Meeting," June 14, 1946, in *United Nations Atomic Energy Commission, Official Records* (Lake Success, NY: United Nations, 1946), 4–14.

21  See Campbell Craig and Sergey Radchenko, *The Atomic Bomb and the Origins of the Cold War* (New Haven, CT: Yale University Press, 2008).

22 McNaughton, "Official Record of the Second Meeting," June 19, 1946, in *United Nations Atomic Energy Commission, Official Records* (Lake Success, NY: United Nations, 1946), 19–21.

23 Andrei Gromyko, "Official Record of the Second Meeting," 23–30.

24 On the Soviet atomic project, see David Holloway, *Stalin and the Bomb: The Soviet Union and Atomic Energy, 1939–1956* (New Haven, CT: Yale University Press, 1994).

25 The Gouzenko affair also increased the Canadian desire to demonstrate trustworthiness to the United States. For the intersection between Canadian policy, the Gouzenko affair, and the Cold War, see Robert Bothwell, "The Cold War and the Curate's Egg: When Did Canada's Cold War Really Begin? Later Than You Might Think," *International Journal* 53, 3 (Summer 1998): 407–18; and Dennis Molinaro, "How the Cold War Began . . . with British Help: The Gouzenko Affair Revisited," *Labour/Le Travail* 79 (Spring 2017): 143–55.

26 Ignatieff to Associate Under-SSEA, June 8, 1946, *DCER*, vol. 12, ch. 5, Document 282, http://epe.lac-bac.gc.ca/100/206/301/faitc-aecic/history/2013-05-03/www.international.gc.ca/department/history-histoire/dcer/details-en.asp@intRefid=11494.

27 United Nations Atomic Energy Commission (UNAEC), Committee 2, "Summary Record of the Fifth Meeting," August 6, 1946, AEC/C.2/SR/5, S-0936-0008-06, United Nations Archives (UNA).

28 A good primer on the early Cold War is Melvyn P. Leffler and David S. Painter, eds., *Origins of the Cold War: An International History*, 2nd ed. (New York: Routledge, 2005).

29 United Nations Department of Public Information, *Scientific and Technical Aspects of the Control of Atomic Energy* (Lake Success, NY: United Nations Department of Public Information, 1946).

30 McNaughton to Under-SSEA, September 21, 1946, *DCER*, vol. 12, ch. 5, Document 295, http://epe.lac-bac.gc.ca/100/206/301/faitc-aecic/history/2013-05-03/www.international.gc.ca/department/history-histoire/dcer/details-en.asp@intRefid=11509.

31 UNAEC, Committee 2, "Summary Record of the Seventh Meeting," October 8, 1946, AEC/C.2/SR/7, S-0936-0008-06, UNA.

32 UNAEC, "Notes on the Informal Discussion of Committee 2," AEC/C.2/W.1ff, S-0936-00010-07 and S-0936-00021-12, UNA.

33 McNaughton, "Official Record of the Sixth Meeting," November 13, 1946, in *United Nations Atomic Energy Commission, Official Records* (Lake Success, NY: United Nations, 1946), 75–82.

34 "Official Record of the Seventh Meeting," December 5, 1946, in *United Nations Atomic Energy Commission, Official Records* (Lake Success, NY: United Nations, 1946), 89–95.

35 McNaughton to SSEA [Secretary of State for External Affairs], December 12, 1946, *DCER*, vol. 12, ch. 5, Document 307, http://epe.lac-bac.gc.ca/100/206/301/faitc-aecic/history/2013-05-03/www.international.gc.ca/department/history-histoire/dcer/details-en.asp@intRefid=11528.

36 McNaughton to SSEA, December 15, 1946, *DCER*, vol. 12, ch. 5, Document 308, http://epe.lac-bac.gc.ca/100/206/301/faitc-aecic/history/2013-05-03/www.international.gc.ca/department/history-histoire/dcer/details-en.asp@intRefid=11530; SSEA to McNaughton, December 16, 1946, *DCER*, vol. 12, ch. 5, Document 309, http://epe.lac-bac.gc.ca/100/206/301/faitc-aecic/history/2013-05-03/www.international.gc.ca/department/history-histoire/dcer/details-en.asp@intRefid=11531.

37  United Nations General Assembly, "General Assembly Resolution 41 (I): Principles Governing the General Regulation and Reduction of Armaments," December 14, 1946, https://undocs.org/en/A/RES/41(I).

38  "Official Record of the Eighth Meeting," December 17, 1946, in *United Nations Atomic Energy Commission, Official Records* (Lake Success, NY: United Nations, 1946), 97–120.

39  Ibid.

40  *Globe and Mail*, December 20, 1946.

41  Pearson to SSEA, December 18, 1946, *DCER*, vol. 12, ch. 5, Document 311, http://epe.lac-bac.gc.ca/100/206/301/faitc-aecic/history/2013-05-03/www.international.gc.ca/department/history-histoire/dcer/details-en.asp@intRefid=11534.

42  Reid to SSEA, December 19, 1946, *DCER*, vol. 12, ch. 5, Document 315, http://epe.lac-bac.gc.ca/100/206/301/faitc-aecic/history/2013-05-03/www.international.gc.ca/department/history-histoire/dcer/details-en.asp@intRefid=11540.

43  Pearson to SSEA, December 18, 1946, *DCER*, vol. 12, ch. 5, Document 311.

44  McNaughton, "Official Record of the Ninth Meeting," December 20, 1946, in *United Nations Atomic Energy Commission, Official Records* (Lake Success, NY: United Nations, 1946), 123–26.

45  Reid to SSEA, December 19, 1946, *DCER*, vol. 12, ch. 5, Document 314, http://epe.lac-bac.gc.ca/100/206/301/faitc-aecic/history/2013-05-03/www.international.gc.ca/department/history-histoire/dcer/details-en.asp@intRefid=11539.

46  Ignatieff to SSEA, December 23, 1946, *DCER*, vol. 12, ch. 5, Document 317, http://epe.lac-bac.gc.ca/100/206/301/faitc-aecic/history/2013-05-03/www.international.gc.ca/department/history-histoire/dcer/details-en.asp@intRefid=11543.

47  Emphasis added.

48  Oskar Lange's background facilitated his rapport with the Anglo delegations. He was an economist whose theories merged Marxism with market economics. He worked extensively in the United Kingdom and United States, eventually becoming an American citizen. He later renounced his US citizenship to serve as the first ambassador of the Polish People's Republic to the United States. See "Dr. Lange Again Becoming a Pole to Be Envoy Here," *New York Times*, October 1, 1945.

49  "Official Record of the Ninth Meeting," 121–42.

50  McNaughton to SSEA, December 21, 1946, *DCER*, vol. 12, ch. 5, Document 316, http://epe.lac-bac.gc.ca/100/206/301/faitc-aecic/history/2013-05-03/www.international.gc.ca/department/history-histoire/dcer/details-en.asp@intRefid=11542.

51  UNAEC, "Verbatim Record of the Fifth Meeting of the Working Committee," December 27, 1946, AEC/C.1/PV/5, S-0936-0007-04, UNA.

52  Ibid.

53  Ibid.

54  Diaries of Mackenzie King, December 30, 1946, MG 26-J13, item 30363–30364, LAC.

55  Ibid. See also December 28, 1946, item 30359.

56  McNaughton, "Official Record of the Tenth Meeting," December 30, 1946, in *United Nations Atomic Energy Commission, Official Records* (Lake Success, NY: United Nations, 1946), 150–51.

57  Oskar Lange, "Official Record of the Tenth Meeting," 158–61.

58  McNaughton to Omond Solandt, September 22, 1958, A.G.L. McNaughton Fonds, MG 30-E133, vol. 320, LAC.
59  Interview with A.G.L. McNaughton, July 14, 1965, quoted in Swettenham, *McNaughton*, vol. 3, 119.
60  Escott Reid, *Radical Mandarin: The Memoirs of Escott Reid* (Toronto: University of Toronto Press, 1989), 221.
61  Diaries of Mackenzie King, January 1, 1947, MG 26-J13, item 30371–30372, LAC.
62  Roger Hill interview with George Ignatieff, "Oral History of Canadian Policy in NATO," March 1991, 91, RG 154, vol. 13, file 2100-17, LAC.

# CHAPTER 2

# "WE DO NOT WISH TO BE OBSTRUCTIONIST"

## How Canada Took and Kept a Seat on NATO's Nuclear Planning Group

*Timothy Andrews Sayle*

T he history of international relations since 1945 is a history of committees. Consigned to the dustbin of history is "great man" history, if there ever was such a thing. In its place is the history of greater and lesser mortals sitting in meetings, councils, and summits. This is especially true of any history related to international organizations, and truer again of Canadian international affairs since 1945, which have been purposely wrapped up in the history of such international organizations.[1]

Canada's efforts to shape the world in which Canadians live and prosper read like alphabet soup: a 2019 listing from Global Affairs Canada lists the following organizations and partners of the Government of Canada: APEC, EU, G7, G20, IAO, ICC, MOPAN, NATO, OAS, OSCE, ASEAN, OECD, UN, UNESCO, WTO, AfDB, ADB, CDB, EBRD, GEF, IDB, IFAD, IMF, RCM, UNICEF, UDP, UNHCR, UNFPA, WBG, WFP, and WHO.[2] This world of international organizations is not only one in which Canada operates but also one that Canada helped build; it is one that suits Canadian needs and helps achieve its goals. This is grand strategy by committee.

Grand strategies are traditionally thought to be supported by forces under arms, financial power, and diplomatic clout. But one of Canada's most important instruments of grand strategy is more nuanced: gaining and keeping committee membership. The short diplomatic account that follows might, in many ways, mirror countless other (and often minor) efforts in the history of Canada's postwar external affairs: first, negotiating for a seat at the table in a multilateral organization and, second, negotiating to keep that seat, from which influence can be exercised.

Committee membership is so central to Canadian international relations that it received direct mention in early formulations of the much-touted "functional principle." In 1942, Hume Wrong voiced a rather robust version of the principle: "Each member of the grand alliance should have a voice in the conduct of the war proportionate to its contribution to the general war effort." Lester Pearson, who served as ambassador to the United States, secretary of state for external affairs, and ultimately prime minister during part of the period under consideration here, offered a less lofty but no less fitting description: "Membership on bodies and committees would include those, but only those, who had a very real and direct interest in the work and could make an important contribution to it."[3] Rarely have there been statesmen who have so accurately identified the limits and possibilities of their state's power; none, perhaps, have identified a national grand strategy so limited in scope.

What makes the application of the functional principle to this particular episode so striking is that it may be the first and only time Canada used nuclear weapons – that is, its status as a nuclear weapons–capable state – to push itself onto a committee. To take the functional principle one step further, it is an intriguing case of Canada using claims of functionality – in this case, the country's nuclear abilities – to press for membership on a committee, and, even after giving up precisely the abilities that had entitled it to a seat in the first place, fighting to stay on that same committee.

Functionalism is only one lens to investigate Canada's efforts to get on – and stay on – NATO's Nuclear Planning Group (NPG). Canadian wrangling over the country's membership in the NPG, too, reveals the important role of Canadian diplomats in keeping options open for Ottawa, even when the prime minister and cabinet are fundamentally undecided about an issue. Finally, the diplomatic event reveals that Canadians, while working alongside like-minded states on cooperative organizations, cannot rely on friendships in other foreign offices, or on the shape of institutional organizations themselves, to look out for Canadian interests: that is the job of Canada alone.

Just as important is the light this episode sheds on a brief period of Canadian history in which Canadians were charged with unleashing nuclear hell on an enemy. Canadian historiography to this point has only scratched the surface of this issue, partially because the Government of Canada has, until recently, been unwilling to open its vault of nuclear secrets. We know in the broadest sense how Canada came to take on this role, but little about how the Government of Canada and responsible departments chose to take on the particular nuclear roles they did, and both the short-term and long-term impact that Canada's nuclear-capable role had on the management of Canadian external affairs.[4]

## NUCLEAR BACKSTORY

Canada played a significant role in supporting the nuclear sword of the United States, which, in turn, served as the nuclear sword of the North Atlantic Alliance during the Cold War. Since the frostiest beginnings of the Cold War, the Canadian government has delicately balanced the need to enable US nuclear forces with seeking to impose restraints on Washington's ability to launch nuclear war. Canadian geography, in the most direct flight path between the two Cold War superpowers, made Canadian air bases an essential transit area and refuelling zone for the bombers of the Strategic Air Command in the late 1940s and early 1950s. This need enabled the Canadians to develop a system of rules requiring consultation and approval in Ottawa of various types of Strategic Air Command missions.[5] Initially, these negotiations and Canadian concerns focused on the US decision to use nuclear weapons – essentially the decision of the president of the United States.

The authority to use nuclear weapons became more complicated in the 1950s. The Canadians, like the British and other allies, knew of nuclear weapons deployments off the Chinese coast, and heard rumours – one officer to another – that some US officers had received pre-delegated instructions to employ nuclear weapons in particular instances. Any understanding over who could use nuclear weapons and when became even more convoluted in 1954 when NATO adopted a new strategic concept (MC 48) that insisted NATO would immediately resort to the use of atomic weapons in case of war with the Soviet Union. Both the British and the Canadians worried that NATO's new specific reliance on early – and likely first – use of nuclear weapons could take decision making out of London and Ottawa and put it in the hands of American military commanders alone.[6] Secretary of State John Foster Dulles insisted that the allies not confront the question of just how NATO would go to war.

Dulles "worried" in particular about "subsequent discussion in the Council as to how the governments would exercise their right of decision in regard to the use of atomic weapons if an emergency developed." Such a discussion, he said, "would likely not be helpful and might be dangerous."[7] British foreign minister Anthony Eden had a conniption over the implementation of this policy but his Canadian counterpart, Lester Pearson, was more sanguine. Pearson himself recognized that "it was practically impossible to reconcile constitutional positions with practical necessities in a case of this kind." Instead, he urged, among the allies (particularly the Americans, British, and Canadians) "continuous consultation [to] keep our policies in alignment."[8]

The issue of how and when NATO would use nuclear weapons lay dormant in the North Atlantic Council (NAC) for several years after the adoption of MC 48. It crept back into alliance discussions after the Soviet launch of Sputnik in 1957. After the outgoing Eisenhower administration suggested the possibility of aiding in the creation of a NATO nuclear force, the question of control was raised again. The issue exploded in the early 1960s for two reasons. The first was an effort on the part of the John F. Kennedy administration to push for a "multilateral force" (MLF). While there were several ideas for just how the MLF would work in practice, it was most often conceived as a fleet of ships armed with nuclear-tipped ballistic missiles and manned by mixed crews from NATO states. Just who would pay for such a force, who would participate, and how it would fit into the NATO command structure – let alone how a multilateral force could and would receive authority to launch nuclear weapons – resulted in reams of papers and multitudes of fuzzy ideas about nuclear launch authority. One of the major announcements regarding the MLF had been made by Kennedy in a speech to the Canadian Parliament in 1961, and so for a brief period the MLF was referred to as the "Ottawa Force," until the Canadians made it clear that they were uncomfortable with this phrase. Not only did the Canadians want no part of the name of this force, they wanted no part of the force itself and did not participate in the formal NATO working groups that evolved to consider the idea.[9]

Second, at the same time as the endless discussions over the MLF were taking place, the United States strong-armed its NATO allies into adopting plans for the "demonstrative use" of nuclear weapons in case the Soviets closed access to West Berlin. In early 1962, NATO secretary general Dirk Stikker took the initiative to pull together the loose ends floating around from years earlier. He prepared a paper for the North Atlantic Council, NDP/62/2, in which he outlined the four most prominent new ideas for control and use of nuclear weapons. None of these ideas contained the notion that Canadians had clung to since 1954: that the North Atlantic Council would, as a whole, be responsible for deciding on the use of nuclear weapons. The Canadian government compelled Stikker to issue an amendment to his paper including the NAC option, but this episode reveals the total lack of agreement in the alliance about the procedures for the release of nuclear weapons. The "demonstrative use" provision seemed to indicate that their use had in fact become more likely, even short of war.[10]

Trying to understand the rules under which the United States might launch nuclear weapons, both inside and outside of NATO's integrated military command, was a complicated exercise. It grew even more complicated when the Canadian government accepted a nuclear role for Canadian forces assigned to NATO. Beginning in 1957, the United States had mooted the possibility of allowing non-nuclear states to purchase nuclear-capable weapons systems that could, in times of emergency, be fitted with US nuclear warheads.[11] After much debate and heartburn, Canada accepted such a role for its NATO-assigned forces. The Canadian brigade fielded ground-to-ground missile launchers designed and intended to fire nuclear warheads in case of contact with the enemy. Even more significant, the First Air Division was equipped with CF-104 fighters and assigned a "strike" role by NATO's Supreme Allied Commander. In case of war, Canadian pilots would fly over Warsaw Pact states and destroy targets by dropping nuclear bombs. The politics of the Canadian decision to take on a nuclear-capable role have been covered elsewhere.[12] The politics and strategy of how Canada managed its nuclear capability, and indeed used this capability as a bargaining chip in high politics, have remained secret until recently.

## FINDING A SEAT

On May 31, 1965, US secretary of defence Robert McNamara surprised his colleagues (and some of his own staff) at a meeting of NATO defence ministers by suggesting an "ad hoc select committee of defence ministers be set up to examine ways of improving participation in nuclear planning and consultation." McNamara explained that such a committee would continue the "progress on nuclear consultation" he had begun by sharing information on NATO's nuclear capabilities at the Athens and Ottawa meetings of allied foreign and defence ministers, in 1962 and 1963, respectively.[13] Little else was resolved at the meeting, and McNamara returned to Washington expecting that the Permanent Representatives would pick up the matter.

A few weeks after McNamara raised the idea of a committee, Thomas Finletter, the US Permanent Representative, brought up the matter in council. The idea, he said, was "a simple one – that getting together a group of defence ministers, few enough in number to facilitate discussion, might result in a valuable new impulse to nuclear consultation and improve its machinery." From Finletter's remarks it was evident to the other allies that the process by which this committee would work, and what precisely it would do, was hardly clear in American minds. Any committee, however, was certain to be "advisory" rather than designed to make a decision, and its primary goals were to "increase allied participation in nuclear planning" and to improve machinery and methods of consultation, including technical issues related to communications.[14]

Despite the limited detail Finletter offered, Canadian Permanent Representative George Ignatieff "immediately reacted favourably." The idea fit neatly with Canada's preferred resolution to the MLF goose chase: to adapt and use the NATO system rather than build new forces or structures. Ignatieff suggested that the group be made up of the alliance's three nuclear powers (France, the United Kingdom, and the United States) and three non-nuclear powers. The secretary general liked the formula and suggested that the Federal Republic of Germany (FRG), Italy, and Canada make up the other three. Immediately, the difficulties of membership became obvious. The French made clear that they would not participate, though they would not stop others from sitting on such a committee, and the

Dutch representative indicated that he had "no instructions that would permit him to accept Canada rather than the Netherlands" as a member. Even the formula itself was cast into doubt.[15] Finletter, on instructions from Washington, said there could be "no more than four or five" members. Only a group as small as this could meet McNamara's stated desire for the committee to be small and the Americans' unstated desire for the committee to serve as a means of meeting German demands for greater proximity to nuclear power after President Lyndon Johnson finally killed the MLF idea.[16]

Thus began the Canadian campaign for a seat on the "McNamara Committee," or what would first be called the "Select Committee," and then the "Special Committee." External Affairs sent Ignatieff a memorandum detailing the reasons Canada could and should have a seat at the table. First, because the Canadian Air Division was "one of the large nuclear capable forces in Western Europe," Canada had a "very real interest" in improving alliance control and communications. Second, in preparing to accept a nuclear role for Canadian forces in Europe, the Canadians had recently and extensively studied matters related to consultation and authorization for the use of nuclear weapons. External Affairs believed that Canada had "done more than most members to analyze the nuclear problems of the Alliance" and could contribute this expertise to the committee. Finally, the Canadians disagreed with some of their Western European allies who viewed the purpose of the committee as one to "improve nuclear relations between USA and Europe." Such a formulation left Canada on the sidelines. Ottawa's view was that the nuclear question was "an alliance-wide problem, hence [its] support of alliance-wide discussions."[17]

Ignatieff sensed that some NATO members were eager to exclude Canada from committee membership in favour of other European allies. With External Affairs' list of Canadian interests as his script, he called upon his American colleague to plead the Canadian case. Finletter reported to Washington that the Canadian was in a "very depressed state" because it seemed as if the Americans and the Europeans did not think Canada should be a member of the Special Committee. He made the case that the Canadians in Europe had the "next greatest nuclear delivery capability" after the Americans, British, and Germans, and also explained the contributions Canada could make based on Ottawa's nuclear studies. Finletter explained that Canadian membership would be a problem, but Ignatieff insisted that Canada would be "adamant in demanding participation."[18]

As Ignatieff approached Finletter in Paris, members of the Canadian Embassy in Washington began a simultaneous campaign to convince the State Department of Canada's worthiness of a seat on the committee. Finletter in Paris and George Vest of the Office of Atlantic Political and Military Affairs in Washington held the same line: they explained that the problem with Canadian membership would be the resulting size of the committee. If the Canadians insisted on membership, so would the Dutch. And if the Canadians and Dutch were on the committee, Turkey would request membership. Greece would follow suit, leading, as Vest said, to a "snow balling effect."[19]

By the end of July 1965, there was no agreement on membership, but there was obvious interest in the North Atlantic Council for "discussion of alliance nuclear arrangements on an alliance-wide basis." Manlio Brosio, the Italian diplomat and politician serving as NATO's secretary general, announced that these discussions would begin in September. Up to that point, the Canadians had both wished and assumed that the secretary general or his senior staff would be represented on the committee. The French, however, made clear to Brosio their view that he should not participate, and essentially vetoed the International Secretariat's representation in any discussion. The absence of the secretary general from the committee table only increased the stakes of membership for the smaller powers, who could now not rely on the good offices of the secretary general to ensure the interests of the whole alliance were taken into account.[20]

The US delegation had continuing instructions to hold the membership at five, plus an empty chair for France. West Germany, Italy, and either Canada or the Netherlands were to make up the three non-nuclear seats. The face-off was not a good one for Canada: the Dutch had previously participated in MLF discussions and Ignatieff assumed this would favour them; British officials told him as much.[21] If the Dutch held a seat and Canada did not, then the membership would essentially mirror the earlier working group on the MLF, and the Canadians feared the Special Committee would stray from its mission to consider consultation and communication, and start searching for new multilateral force solutions.[22]

In an effort to convince the Canadians to back down, Brosio privately suggested to Ignatieff that if both the Canadians and the Dutch could not sit on the committee, neither should. This would have the obvious benefit of meeting the strict American insistence that the committee could have no more than five members. In a clever parry, Ignatieff suggested that if the committee was to have fewer than six members, then it should have four, not five: the United States, United Kingdom, France, and Germany. Such a move would keep Italy out. If a proposal went forward for five members, Ignatieff warned, he "may then raise the question of whether Italy should be on considering that we [Canada] had the largest nuclear capable forces in Western Europe" after the nuclear powers and Germany. Brosio took the hint and said he "hoped this question would not arise." Ignatieff, to "ensure this point was not lost," made the same point to his Italian colleagues. Brosio promised to speak to the Americans on the Canadians' behalf, and urged the Canadians to make their own case in Washington.[23]

By the end of July, the British and Americans had come around to accepting six members for the committee (including the French phantom seat), but this did not resolve the Dutch-Canadian impasse. Both continued to insist on a seat. It seemed unlikely, however, that a membership of six could really, in the end, be limited to six. The Turkish delegation was willing to accept Canada as the sixth seat, but they could not accept the Dutch as members without insisting on their own membership, which would come with a Greek insistence on equality. Now there was the added fear that Turkish and Greek membership would lead to Belgian claims to a seat.[24]

The Americans had not relented in their efforts to convince the Canadians to abandon their hope for a place on the committee. In Paris, the acting US Permanent Representative offered bilateral consultations on nuclear issues if Canada "stepped down." In these bilateral discussions, the Americans promised, the Canadians would learn as much from the United States as they would if they sat on the Select Committee.[25] At the end of August, the Americans raised the ante: Secretary of Defense McNamara wrote directly to Minister of National Defence Paul Hellyer, asking him to abandon the Canadian bid.[26] Hellyer, along with Chief of the Defence Staff Frank Miller and the undersecretary of state for external affairs, were all willing to give in to McNamara. The direct request from McNamara was, in itself, extremely difficult for Hellyer to refuse. Some in Ottawa hoped that McNamara's request represented an opportunity to gain more bilateral consultation with Washington, though what this would mean in practice, and how much further it could go beyond the already close Ottawa-Washington bilateral relationship, was unclear.[27]

The Canadian ambassadors concerned did not see an attractive bargain. Charles Ritchie, the ambassador in Washington, and Ignatieff, writing from Paris, were both against dropping the Canadian bid for membership. Ritchie warned that the committee, unless it was carefully defined and limited, "could have long term implications for the political structure of NATO."[28] Ignatieff was wary of the Americans' insistence that the Special Committee would be limited to consultations and advice. The relationship of the committee to NATO's future was critical: this might be the forum in which the Americans satisfied the West German government's "interest in participation in nuclear control and strategy by offering [a] place on [the] directorate." Canada, he urged, should remain unwilling to give up its insistence on a seat as "leverage in order to clarify US intentions" on a host of issues: the future of the alliance, the future of non-proliferation policy, and the control of nuclear weapons.[29]

Hellyer did not immediately accede to McNamara's request. Instead, the Canadian Embassy in Washington approached the State Department in a bid to gain clarity on what the Americans expected the Special Committee to achieve. Canadian diplomats met with Assistant Secretary of State for European Affairs John Leddy and several officials concerned with NATO and Canadian affairs. The Canadians stressed that they "did not wish to be obstructive" – even though their obstruction was the source of their power – but warned they could not stand down on their bid for a seat without a better idea of how "such action might affect Canadian interests." They presented, orally, a series of questions sent from External Affairs about the nature of the new NATO committee and Washington's intentions. They made clear to Leddy that answers to these questions would not "ipso facto result in favourable Canadian reply to USA request."

Put on the spot, Leddy tried to turn the questions around on the Canadians. He took their first and main question, about the purpose of the committee, and described it as "puzzling." The purpose of the committee, he said, was to "move ahead on the Athens guidelines" and beyond that, he expected the Canadians to appreciate how hard it was "to tie down a high level body of this type to specifics." This uncertainty, of course, was precisely what concerned the Canadians. It was also obvious that the Special Committee was very much a product of McNamara's imagination, and that the State Department knew little more than the Canadians. In conversation, the Americans did acknowledge the public affairs problem facing the Canadians. Pearson's Liberals would be hard-pressed to explain why Canada had to forgo membership on the Special Committee while other non-nuclear countries, say, Italy or the Netherlands, were included. The Americans promised to provide full answers to the Canadian questions.[30]

Two weeks later, Leddy provided unofficial written answers – a "piece of paper" – to the Canadian questions, along with an "oral supplementary."[31] All the Canadians heard, however, was that the Americans could not guarantee that the Special Committee would remain as an ad hoc, limited group; because it was so "high powered" – made up of defence ministers – Washington could not predict its scope. Similarly, because of the ministerial membership, it was obvious that Special Committee meetings would be "accompanied by a good deal of publicity." No matter how much NATO members insisted that the Special Committee was simply an advisory group, a "public impression may well be created that [a] new NATO body has been or is in process of formation." Already in other allied states, especially Germany, the Special Committee was being presented this way in newspaper reporting.[32]

A few days after the meeting with Leddy, Ritchie spoke with Secretary of State Dean Rusk and delivered what was by now the standard Canadian opening line: "It was not our wish to be obstructionist." Still, he noted, Canada was "somewhat concerned" that the Special Committee might become "an important NATO body for discussion of nuclear problems." He also reiterated the domestic political problem for the Canadian government if it were not on the committee but "countries such as Netherlands and Italy with smaller forces with nuclear capability were members."[33] He took the same position with McNamara at a dinner in September, and reported that McNamara did not seem "resentful" of the Canadian effort to secure membership, and indeed "showed understanding for our position."[34] This, at least conceivably, limited the pressure on Hellyer to reply quickly to McNamara's earlier letter. The Canadians, despite their insistence to the contrary, remained obstructionist.

The obstruction served its purpose. Ignatieff's earlier threat to raise the appropriateness of Italian membership had made Brosio a champion of the Canadian position. While Brosio was NATO secretary general, he of course remained Italian; he was not about to allow his home country's seat to be jeopardized. In early October, he visited Washington and carried the Canadian brief.

On the evening of October 6, George Ball telephoned Secretary of State for External Affairs Paul Martin and told him that Brosio's visit had led to American agreement to expand the Special Committee's membership to eight or nine. Would Canada take a seat? Martin told Ball that he would respond the next day. In the interim, Martin, along with Hellyer and Miller, decided that Canada would take its seat. But the timing mattered. One of the reasons the Canadians had sought membership was to protect themselves from the domestic political charge of being left out. Now, with a Canadian federal election approaching, the Liberals wanted to avoid giving too much attention to their participation in matters related to nuclear weapons.[35] On October 7, the Canadian Embassy informed Ball that Canada would participate, but sought and gained American assurance that there would be no meeting of the new committee before November 8, 1965, Election Day in Canada.[36]

The Canadians immediately began preparing for the first meeting of the Special Committee. They wished to use their membership to press two goals: first, to put forward ideas that would "underline our legitimate interest in these discussions," and second, to steer discussion away from "highly controversial issues affecting the very future of the alliance." Canada did not want the Special Committee to discuss the relationship between the allies' non-proliferation policy and the alliance's nuclear arrangement; nor should it discuss the floundering MLF or a related British proposal for an Atlantic Nuclear Force; nor should any attention be given to the idea of a nuclear "directoire" in the alliance. Instead, the Canadians wanted to focus on "urgent and practical questions," especially the longstanding Canadian concern with "coordination of procedures for authorizations and use of nuclear weapons."[37]

These points, especially the matter of authorization, formed the basis of Hellyer's remarks at the first meeting of the Special Committee on November 28. He fired off a list of what the American delegate reported as "perceptive and difficult questions" regarding use of nuclear weapons, asking "whether a unanimity rule would apply in the Council on this subject. Could one country veto employment of weapons by a NATO commander? What if one or two countries failed to decide or unduly delayed their decision? What are the military implications of SACEUR having permission from some but not all of the NATO countries?" "Nobody," the US delegation reported, "answered these questions directly." It was a "prevailing assumption," however, that "governments would make their own decisions in their own capitals," and the North Atlantic Council was but a "useful facility to pool information on the nature of crises and to consult rapidly with other allies on their own reactions to and intentions in a crisis."[38] As long as Canada deployed nuclear-capable forces to the alliance, Hellyer and the Canadian delegation were on strong ground to continue raising concerns about how they would be deployed – and the Special Committee was the place to raise such questions.

The Canadian hunch that the Special Committee would be neither ad hoc nor temporary was quickly proven correct. One year after the first meeting, in December 1966, NATO officially created the Nuclear Defence Affairs Committee – an umbrella committee open to all NATO members – with a subordinate, but far more important, Nuclear Planning Group of limited membership. The NPG was to have a limited membership to ensure the goals McNamara had sought in the creation of the Special Committee. It was further subdivided into working groups on specific subjects. Membership in the NPG was not formally divided between rotating and non-rotating members, even though this was the de facto arrangement. For eighteen months beginning on January 1, the membership was to be composed of the United States, United Kingdom, West Germany, and Italy, essentially the permanent members, joined by Canada, the Netherlands, and Turkey. (Turkey would cede its seat to Greece after half the term.) After the first term, and beginning July 1, 1968, the Belgians and Danes would replace the Canadians and the Dutch, and the Greeks and Turks would switch again.[39] The system served NATO for the first two terms (three years), from the beginning of 1967 until the end of 1969, mainly because there was an even number of rotating members. In 1969, however, the Norwegians made clear that they would ask for a seat, and Canada, it seemed, would be the odd one out.

## KEEPING A SEAT

The fact that the Norwegians had not yet had a turn on the NPG strengthened their claim to a seat beginning January 1, 1970. To Ross Campbell, Ignatieff's successor as Canadian Permanent Representative, it was obvious that either the original "gentleman's agreement" would have to be revised or it would once again come to a showdown between the Dutch and the Canadians.[40] For the rest of the year, Campbell faced down opposition from the Americans, supported by the British and Germans, to revising the gentleman's agreement and enlarging the NPG. Having received no instructions on the issue until very late, he acted on his own to create the impression in Brussels that Canada would wish to resume full membership.[41]

In 1966, Ignatieff had been able to insist, time and again, that Canada deployed one of the largest nuclear-capable forces in the alliance. Campbell was on less sure ground. Pierre Trudeau was now prime minister, and he had sounded various anti-nuclear notes in the past. It was unclear to anyone – Canadians and their allies – whether Canada would have any nuclear-capable forces in NATO in the near future. British diplomats, for instance, recorded Campbell's adamant insistence that Canada would wish for a seat, but wondered "if, as is widely expected, Canadian forces in Europe give up their nuclear role Canada will wish for or be justified in claiming full membership."[42] Overshadowing the question of Canada's nuclear capability, however, was Canada's relationship to the alliance as a whole. In 1966–67, the Americans, British, and Germans had just barely eked out a plan to avoid American or British troop cuts on the continent. The state of the alliance was precarious, and withdrawal of troops by any state was thought to be a possible first domino in the collapse of the alliance. Trudeau's uncertain trumpet led the other allies to take a delicate approach to the Canadian position.

The allies were on the lookout for signals in the spring of 1969 as to whether Canada really wanted a seat any more. The British High

Commission in Ottawa reported when the issue was raised in the House of Commons. When an MP asked whether Trudeau's proposed plans would make Canada "ineligible for NPG membership," Secretary of State for External Affairs Mitchell Sharp replied that the idea was "completely unfounded." He explained that Canada would and did always sit on the Nuclear Defence Affairs Committee (NDAC), which was open to all; before he could get to Canada's position on the NPG, the Speaker intervened and cut him off. W.N. Hugh-Jones of the High Commission asked around in Ottawa trying to find out just what Sharp might have said if he had not been interrupted – but to no avail.[43]

The British watched the impending showdown for a seat with some worry, and British diplomatic records offer a useful lens through which to view Canadian maneuvering. The British and the Germans were both eager and anxious to support the American line on the NPG, and the American line had been, since McNamara's day, that the smaller, the better. The British worried that if the NPG grew too large the Americans would scrap the Special Committee. It was essential, wrote J.P. Waterfield, the Foreign and Commonwealth Office (FCO) official responsible for the Western Organisations Department, to "secure the postponement of the membership" of either the Dutch, the Norwegians, or the Canadians. In London's analysis, Canada was the "natural candidate to stand down" as, unlike Norway, Canada had already spent time on the NPG. What was more, Canada had "recently declared her intention of running down, if not of abandoning altogether, her nuclear role in Europe."[44]

At the same time, the FCO wanted to avoid the appearance that Canada was "being punished for her decision to reduce her military presence in Europe," and also to avoid the impression that "Europeans are ganging up to exclude Canadians." They preferred to stay in the background and to encourage lobbying in the corridors by the Dutch, Norwegians, and other European allies to convince the Canadians to step down.[45] British officials not directly concerned with the inner workings of NATO, such as P.G. de Courcy-Ireland of the American Department, thought this plan might backfire. Perhaps from a "purely NPG point of view" it was sensible for Canada to be the "odd man out this year." But de Courcy-Ireland worried that something so obviously "bordering on punishment" might cause the Canadians to sour further on NATO. Bringing Canada back into the NPG might help preserve Canadian involvement. The British should "keep right out of this issue and say as little as possible."[46]

Campbell seems to have been personally convinced that Canada must retain its seat on the NPG. Even though Ottawa was likely to give up Canada's nuclear strike role in Europe, that capability would be phased out over a number of years. The next round of the NPG would be crucial as it would cover "discussions about how nuclear forces including our own would be used in war." Looking to the future when the role would be abandoned, he believed Canada would have a "continuing interest as [a] member of [the] alliance in [the] formulation of nuclear strategy."[47] This was very much Campbell's view, as related to External Affairs, rather than the other way around. And while External Affairs supported Campbell's approach, it had not yet taken the issue to cabinet ministers. Campbell was authorized to approach the Americans on the subject but told to "keep in mind [the] Ministerial decision regarding termination of our nuclear role in Europe and implications [that] decision may have with respect to our future attitude towards participation in NPG."[48] It was far from certain in Ottawa whether the Canadian government wished to remain a member of the NPG.

All along, the Nuclear Planning Group, like the Special Committee before it, had been inconsistent with normal NATO practice, which sought to avoid exclusionary groups. While all members of the alliance did not participate in every committee, usually any states that claimed an interest were welcome to take a seat. Nonetheless, Campbell's strategy in Brussels was to press for only a moderate expansion of the NPG from seven members to eight. External Affairs queried him: if NATO practice was to avoid restricted membership, was it not "logical to advocate making NPG open-ended rather than simply increasing membership from seven to eight"?[49] Campbell explained that the issue was one of political practicability. He did not believe that the Americans, with support from the British and Germans, would allow the NPG to be open to all. It was possible that if the Canadians pushed for an open-ended membership rather than an increase of one, they could "destroy [their] chances of regaining membership on NPG."[50]

Campbell was right to think that the Americans were dead set against an open-ended membership for the NPG. Through a private inquiry to Robert Ellsworth, the US Permanent Representative, Campbell learned that Secretary of Defense Melvin Laird believed that seven was already too many and was sure to resist any further enlargement.[51] How to get the Americans to budge? Campbell decided to push for open-ended membership and hoped to bring along a number of smaller states. Then Canada, along with the Belgians, Danes, and Dutch, would offer a fallback position of enlarging the NPG membership by one state every other term. Because of the uneven number of states that sought membership, the membership would first consist of 8, then, 7, then 8 again – what was called the "8-7-8-7" formula.[52]

There was no movement on the issue in September and October. The British reported that the Canadians were "energetically opposing" solutions put forward by the secretary general that would see Canada joining a group of three allies (Denmark and Norway would be the other two) that would rotate on one particular seat, while other pairs of states split their time on the group. The Dutch obviously had firm instructions "to insist that they return to the group" and Campbell had bluffed, convincing others that Ottawa had adopted the same position. The British privately came to believe that the 8-7-8-7 formula was the only solution. If we "do not go nap" on this solution very quickly, the British delegation warned, "the positions of the Netherlands and the Canadians (with the moral support of the Scandinavians) might harden to the point where it might be very difficult to obtain agreement to any solution other than an open-ended one. This would destroy the special nature of the NPG and all that goes with it."[53] By late October, the British worried that the situation was "rapidly approaching deadlock."[54]

The FCO knew that the Canadians, with their insistence that Canada should serve on the Nuclear Planning Group effective January 1, 1970, held "the key" to acceptance of any new scheme of membership in the NPG.[55] The Canadians began to draw the ire of others, both those who wished to preserve the small group and those who wanted to get on the NPG. The Germans, who were displeased with Trudeau's approach to the alliance, "thought that it would be logical, and perhaps salutary, not to bend over backwards to have the Canadians in next time, following their announced decision to give up their nuclear weapons."[56] The Norwegians, eager to ensure their own membership, asked the United States to intercede in Ottawa and ask Canada to abandon its quest for membership in the upcoming cycle.[57] Ellsworth had instructions "to work on the Canadians in order to try to get them to withdraw their candidature," but these instructions resulted in no obvious actions.[58]

Remarkably, and surely not purposefully, the Trudeau government's uncertain – even wobbly – policy on NATO helped insulate Ottawa from greater pressure from Washington and London.[59] American officials declined the Norwegian request, for they "did not want to antagonize us [Canada]."[60] Officials at the British High Commission in Ottawa did "not want to weaken the hands of those" in Ottawa pushing for a continued important role for Canadian Forces in NATO.[61] They seem to have seriously worried that a move to exclude Canada from the Nuclear Planning Group might tip the scales in Ottawa fully against the alliance as a whole.

In fact, they need not have worried. Neither the responsible ministers nor the prime minister had yet made any decision regarding the Canadian position on the Nuclear Planning Group. Indeed, there was little evidence that they had thought about it at all. It was Campbell who almost single-handedly maintained the Canadian hard line in Brussels. Whereas British diplomats thought Campbell may have been "inclined to adopt a somewhat less co-operative attitude in nuclear discussion[s] in NATO than his instructions may have warranted," he had not so much exceeded his instructions as made the very most of the limited authorization he had been given to keep the chance of a Canadian seat alive.[62]

On October 30, when Campbell learned that the issue would finally be put before Trudeau, he sent instructions back to External Affairs. "I need not comment on how you might approach PM," he wrote, before doing just that. Campbell reminded External Affairs of the recent Throne Speech debate in which the prime minister had "expressed considerable interest in NATO strategy." Members of the department, he suggested, should "call attention to the fact that if we wish to have influence over development and refinement of nuclear strategy in this alliance NPG is for all intents and purposes [the] only body where this can be done."[63] Canada had gained its seat on the NPG because of Canada's nuclear capabilities; now it would seek a place to influence debates over nuclear weapons in the alliance even if Canada was giving up its nuclear role.

A few days after Campbell's cable, on November 3, 1969, the British learned just how behind Ottawa was on this issue. The High Commission in Ottawa reported that the Canadians were "only just at the stage of considering whether they wished to remain a candidate for membership of the NPG," with a submission to ministers going in some time that week. The Department of External Affairs would recommend that Canada remain a candidate for a seat. The full nature of the Trudeau government's ambivalence was now obvious: "The main question at the moment is not whether the Canadians want to be on the NPG next year, but whether officials can persuade their ministers to remain a rotational member at all." If Trudeau were to learn that the British and others did "not want Canada on next year," London should "not exclude the possibility that he [Trudeau] would decide to pull out altogether."[64] The FCO reported that, more than a boycott of the NPG, "Canadian Ministers might be led to take an even more difficult line in NATO generally."[65] Given the difficulties the British had recently faced in maintaining their troop commitment to the alliance, they worried that any further Canadian withdrawals could lead to a further unravelling of NATO force levels.[66]

If the British now understood the stakes, there was still no easy resolution to the issue in early November. The deadlock continued, but it was hardly the case of Canada versus all the rest. Many of the other rotating members were growing increasingly frustrated with the US-imposed limits on NPG membership. In one frosty meeting with the secretary general, the Dutch, Belgian, and Danish Permanent Representatives gave voice to "those who expressed lack of comprehension for USA rigidity" over the membership issue. Remarkably, Campbell, who attended, was silent as he had no instructions from Ottawa.[67] With the new term supposed to begin on January 1, 1970, and the membership issue to be settled at the NDAC meeting in early December, there was growing worry among all the delegations that no solution could be achieved.

On November 19, Campbell learned that Trudeau had made his decision. A cable from Ottawa noted that the "PM has agreed that it would be useful for us to seek further period of NPG membership" beginning in January 1970. Going forward, Canada preferred an open-ended membership, but if that remained impossible, then the 8-7-8-7 or 8-member formula was acceptable. The "least satisfactory arrangement" would be one in which Canada was "competing directly for [a] place with [a] friendly country such as Norway."[68] Ottawa asked Campbell if Canadian diplomats should simultaneously pursue the issue in London, Bonn, and Washington, now that the government had decided on a seat. Campbell said yes, but in a revealing warning, noted that he had "carefully avoided" giving any impression that Canada had not always wanted a seat, "so as not to undermine the active part we have always played in . . . the only NATO body where the basic issues of nuclear strategy can be influenced."[69] Campbell's tour de force in Paris in the autumn of 1969 had kept Canada's chances for a seat alive.

Now, with the government all on the same page, Canadian diplomats went to work in the key capitals. The Canadians who visited the State Department sensed sympathy from their counterparts; the Americans suggested that they felt boxed in by Laird's early adamant stance on non-expansion.[70] The British, ever faithful to the better half of their special relationship, noted that as "enlargement of NPG was opposed by USA whose contribution and support were vital to work of NPG,"[71] they did not support expansion. And while the Germans – some of whom had earlier wanted to punish the Canadians – claimed sympathy, they hoped not to expand the membership either, for fear of giving the United States a "pretext for reducing its interest" in the NPG.[72]

A few days after these formal entreaties, Campbell called on Ellsworth, who told him that "he had nothing to say today" and was awaiting instructions. Privately, however, Ellsworth let on that he had recommended the "8-7 or 8 arrangement to Washington and hopes for a positive reply."[73] Two days later, he told the Nuclear Defence Affairs Committee that with "great reluctance," Laird had accepted the 8-7-8-7 formula that would allow alternating eighteen-month terms for all allies who had expressed interest in serving on the NPG.[74] Canada had its seat on the Nuclear Planning Group, even if, very shortly thereafter, it would no longer have nuclear-capable forces.

## CONCLUSION

Canada's early membership on the Nuclear Planning Group harks back to another moment from the historical epoch in which the functional theory was developed. For an exceedingly short period – less than two weeks – at the end of the Second World War, and depending on how one counts ships, the Royal Canadian Navy was briefly the fourth-largest navy in the world.[75] It was during the war that, with so many European states laid low, and

Canada's geography and natural products high in value, the Canadians were elevated to the grand councils of war. But this elevation was largely artificial. The Canadians knew it was temporary, even abnormal. Does the Canadian nuclear-capable period count as one of these hiccups in history? Perhaps, and Campbell recognized the moment. Canada's nuclear history and Canada's nuclear commitments in NATO were hardly a separate sphere of Canadian policy but stayed true to the functionalist form sketched out in the pre-atomic age. For those few years when Canada – a state that had never produced its own nuclear warhead – had the fourth-greatest capacity for launching nuclear destruction in the alliance, it established a position on NATO's Nuclear Planning Group. To argue that Canada "seized" its place would be going too far, but the larger allies sighed and shrugged after the Canadians made their functional principle argument and pulled up their chair to the table.

NOTES

The author wishes to thank Elisabetta Kerr for her research assistance. Thanks, too, to Library and Archives Canada, and especially the staff responsible for processing Access to Information requests. This chapter would not have been possible without their diligent work.

1  Joel J. Sokolsky, "A Seat at the Table: Canada and Its Alliances," *Armed Forces and Society* 16, 1 (1989): 11–35.
2  For the names of the different organizations, see Government of Canada, "Partnerships and Organizations," July 17, 2019, http://international.gc.ca/world-monde/international_relations-relations_internationales/partnerships_organizations-partenariats_organisations.aspx?lang=eng.
3  All quotes from Adam Chapnick, "Canada's Functional Principle: 75 Years On," *International Journal* 72, 2 (June 2017): 271. This article also provides a helpful brief historiography of the "functional principle."
4  This is not to suggest that excellent work on Canada and nuclear weapons has not been written, but only that there is much more work to be done. On the origins of Canada's atomic age, see Robert Bothwell, *Eldorado: Canada's National Uranium Company* (Toronto: University of Toronto Press, 1984); Robert Bothwell, *Nucleus: The History of Atomic Energy of Canada Limited* (Toronto: University of Toronto Press, 1988); Brian Buckley, *Canada's Early Nuclear Policy: Fate, Chance, and Character* (Montreal and Kingston: McGill-Queen's University Press, 2000). On the acquisition of nuclear weapons for Canadian forces, see Matthew Trudgen, "Do We Want 'Buckets of Instant Sunshine'? – Canada and Nuclear Weapons, 1945–1984," *Canadian Military Journal* 10, 1 (2009): 46–55; Sean M. Maloney, *Learning to Love the Bomb: Canada's*

*Nuclear Weapons during the Cold War* (Washington, DC: Potomac Books, 2007); John Clearwater, *Canadian Nuclear Weapons: The Untold Story of Canada's Cold War Arsenal* (Toronto: Dundurn Press, 1998). On the relationship between US nuclear forces and Canadian territory, see John Clearwater, *US Nuclear Weapons in Canada* (Toronto: Dundurn Press, 1999); Timothy Andrews Sayle, "A Pattern of Constraint: Canadian-American Relations in the Early Cold War," *International Journal* 62, 3 (2007): 689–705; David J. Bercuson, "SAC vs Sovereignty: The Origins of the Goose Bay Lease, 1946–52," *Canadian Historical Review* 70, 2 (June 1989): 206–22. On a Canadian approach to nuclear strategy, see Andrew Richter, *Avoiding Armageddon: Canadian Military Strategy and Nuclear Weapons, 1950–1963* (Vancouver: UBC Press, 2011). See the evolution of writing on Canada and the Cuban Missile Crisis in Jocelyn Maynard Ghent, "Canada, the United States, and the Cuban Missile Crisis," *Pacific Historical Review* 48, 2 (May 1, 1979): 159–84, https://doi.org/10.2307/3639271; Peter T. Haydon, *The 1962 Cuban Missile Crisis: Canadian Involvement Reconsidered* (Toronto: Canadian Institute of Strategic Studies, 1993); Asa McKercher, "A 'Half-Hearted Response'?: Canada and the Cuban Missile Crisis, 1962," *International History Review* 33, 2 (2011): 335–52, https://doi.org/10.1080/07075332.2011.555450. For discussion of Canada and nuclear weapons in NATO, see Timothy Andrews Sayle, "Canada, NATO, and the Berlin Crisis, 1961–1962: 'Slow-Boil' or 'Pressure Cooker'?" *International Journal* 68, 2 (June 2013): 255–68; S.M. Maloney, "Berlin Contingency Planning: Prelude to Flexible Response, 1958–1963," *Journal of Strategic Studies* 25, 1 (March 2002): 99–134, https://doi.org/10.1080/714004038; Erika Simpson, *NATO and the Bomb: Canadian Defenders Confront Critics* (Montreal and Kingston: McGill-Queen's University Press, 2001). For the Trudeau era, see Robert Bothwell and J.L. Granatstein, *Trudeau's World: Insiders Reflect on Foreign Policy, Trade, and Defence, 1968–84* (Vancouver: UBC Press, 2017); Susan Colbourn, "'Cruising toward Nuclear Danger': Canadian Anti-Nuclear Activism, Pierre Trudeau's Peace Mission, and the Transatlantic Partnership," *Cold War History* 18, 1 (January 2, 2018): 19–36, https://doi.org/10.1080/14682745.2017.1370456.

5  Sayle, "A Pattern of Constraint"; Bercuson, "SAC vs Sovereignty."

6  "Future NATO Defence Planning in Light of the Effect of New Weapons," Memorandum from Under-Secretary of State for External Affairs to Secretary of State for External Affairs, December 8, 1954, *Documents on Canadian External Relations (DCER)*, vol. 20, *1954*, ch. 3, "North Atlantic Treaty Organization," Document 368, http://epe.lac-bac. gc.ca/100/206/301/faitc-aecic/history/2013-05-03/www.international.gc.ca/depart ment/history-histoire/dcer/details-en.asp@intRefid=519.

7  Under-Secretary of State for External Affairs to High Commissioner in United Kingdom, January 25, 1955, *DCER*, vol. 21, *1955*, ch. 2, "North Atlantic Treaty Organization," Document 168, http://epe.lac-bac.gc.ca/100/206/301/faitc-aecic/history/2013-05-03/ www.international.gc.ca/department/history-histoire/dcer/details-en.asp@int RefId=1193.

8  Ibid. See also Greg Donaghy, "Nukes and Spooks: Canada-US Intelligence Sharing and Nuclear Consultations, 1950–1958," in *Transnationalism: Canada–United States History in the 21st Century,* ed. Michael D. Behiels and Reginald C. Stuart (Montreal and Kingston: McGill-Queen's University Press, 2010).

9  The MLF is, curiously, one organization that Canadians were not eager to join. The best overview of the MLF hijinks remains John D. Steinbruner, *The Cybernetic Theory of Decision: New Dimensions of Political Analysis,* rev. ed. (Princeton, NJ: Princeton University Press, 2002). The NATO element is considered in more detail in Timothy Andrews Sayle, "NATO's Crisis Years: The End of the Atlantic Mystique and the Making of *Pax Atlantica,* 1955–1968" (PhD diss., Temple University, 2014), 285–335, https://digital.library.temple.edu/digital/collection/p245801coll10/id/296731.

10  Numbered Letter N-671 from NATODel [NATO Delegation] to USSEA [Under-Secretary of State for External Affairs], May 5, 1961, RG 25, vol. 5959, file 50219-AL-2-40, pt. 2.2, Library and Archives Canada (LAC). Paul Martin Sr., the Canadian Secretary of State for External Affairs at the time, insisted in his memoir that the decision was the North Atlantic Council's. See Paul Martin, *A Very Public Life* (Ottawa: Deneau, 1985), 386n2, 461. On the plan for demonstrative use and Canadian objections, see Sayle, "Canada, NATO, and the Berlin Crisis."

11  Marc Trachtenberg, *A Constructed Peace: The Making of the European Settlement, 1945–1963* (Princeton, NJ: Princeton University Press, 1999).

12  Patricia I. McMahon, *Essence of Indecision: Diefenbaker's Nuclear Policy, 1957–1963* (Montreal and Kingston: McGill-Queen's University Press, 2009); Simpson, *NATO and the Bomb.*

13  At both ministerials, McNamara broke with secretive American practices and gave speeches with details about the US nuclear commitment to NATO.

14  NATOParis to External 1342, June 29, 1965, RG 24, file S-2-5101-6, pt. 1, LAC.

15  NATOParis to External 1368, June 30, 1965, ibid.

16  NATOParis to External 1341, June 29, 1965, ibid.

17  External to NATOParis DL 1212, July 20, 1965, ibid.

18  Ibid.

19  WashDC to External 2316, July 20, 1965, RG 24, file S-2-5101-6, pt. 1, LAC.

20  NATOParis to External 1543, July 21, 1965, ibid.

21  Ibid.

22  External to NATOParis DL 1336, July 27, 1965, RG 24, file S-2-5101-6, pt. 1, LAC.

23  NATOParis to External 1548, July 22, 1965, ibid.

24  NATOParis to External 1581, July 28, 1965, ibid.

25  NATOParis to External 1543, July 21, 1965, ibid.

26  External to NATOParis G365, August 19, 1965, RG 24, file S-2-5101-6, pt. 2, LAC.

27  WashDC to External 2562, August 12, 1954; NATOParis to External 1711, August 20, 1965, ibid.

28  WashDC to External 2665, August 24, 1965, ibid.

29  NATOParis to External 1702, August 19, 1965, ibid.

30  WashDC to External 2743, August 31, 1965, ibid.

31  WashDC to External 2900, September 15, 1965, ibid.

32  Ibid.

33  WashDC to External 2949, September 17, 1965, RG 24, file S-2-5101-6, pt. 2, LAC.

34  WashDC to External 2975, September 20, 1965, ibid.

35  External to WashDC G399, October 7, 1965, ibid. For Brosio's comments to McNamara, see Circular Airgram from the Department of State to the Posts in the NATO Capitals,

October 26, 1965, *Foreign Relations of the United States (FRUS) 1964–1968,* vol. 13, *Western Europe Region,* Document 105, https://history.state.gov/historicaldocuments/frus1964-68v13/d105.

36 WashDC to External 3211, October 7, 1965, RG 24, file S-2-5101-6, pt. 2, LAC.

37 NATOParis to External 3081, October 18, 1965, ibid.

38 Telegram from the Mission to the North Atlantic Treaty Organization and European Regional Organizations to the Department of State, November 28, 1965, *FRUS 1964– 1968,* vol. 13, *Western Europe Region,* Document 113, https://history.state.gov/historic-aldocuments/frus1964-68v13/d113.

39 UKDelNATO to FCO no. 709, December 20, 1966, Foreign and Commonwealth Office (FCO) 41/429, The National Archives (TNA).

40 CanDelNATO to External 2334, September 4, 1969, RG 24, file S-2-5101-5, pt. 6, LAC.

41 Campbell's personality and role are brought to life in a number of vignettes in Bothwell and Granatstein, *Trudeau's World,* esp. 32, 34, 47–48.

42 UKDelNATO to FCO no. 264, May 9, 1969, FCO 41/428, TNA.

43 W.N. Hugh-Jones to J.P. Waterfield, June 16, 1969, FCO 41/428, TNA.

44 J.P. Waterfield, Western Organisations Department, to A.D.F. Pemberton-Pigott (UKDelNATO), August 15, 1969, FCO 41/428, TNA.

45 Ibid.

46 "Composition of the NPG," Minute by P.G. de Courcy-Ireland, American Department, August 4, 1969, FCO 41/428, TNA.

47 CanDelNATO to External 2334, September 4, 1969, RG 24, file S-2-5101-5, pt. 6, LAC.

48 External to CanDelNATO DN1086, September 11, 1969, ibid.

49 External to CanDelNATO DN1069, September 9, 1969, ibid.

50 CanDelNATO to External 2405, September 10, 1969, ibid.

51 CanDelNATO to External 2625, September 30, 1969, ibid.

52 Ibid.

53 UKDelNATO 161720Z to MoD, September 17, 1969, FCO 41/428, TNA.

54 FCO to UKDelNATO no. 359, October 21, 1969, FCO 41/429, TNA.

55 "NPG: UK Suggested Rotational System," Le Hardy to Alexander, October 22, 1969, FCO 41/429, TNA.

56 "Membership of the NPG," R.J. O'Neill to M.O'D.B. Alexander, September 25, 1969, FCO 41/429, TNA.

57 Oslo to External 580, November 5, 1969, RG 24, file S-2-5101-5, pt. 6, LAC.

58 "Composition of the N.P.G.," C.M. Rose to Waterfield, November 17, 1969, FCO 41/429, TNA.

59 There is no evidence that the issue of Canada's seat on the Nuclear Planning Group entered into the acrimonious and confused debate occurring in Ottawa over Canada's continuing role in NATO. The best account of that debate in Ottawa is available in Bothwell and Granatstein, *Trudeau's World.*

60 Oslo to External 580, November 5, 1969, RG 24, file S-2-5101-5, pt. 6, LAC; "Member-ship of the N.P.G.," Waterfield to Alexander, October 16, 1969, FCO 41/429, TNA.

61 "Nuclear Planning Group," W.N. Hugh-Jones (HICOM Ottawa) to J.P. Waterfield, September 11, 1969, FCO 41/429, TNA.

62 FCO to Ottawa no. 638, October 31, 1969, FCO 41/429, TNA.

63 CanDelNATO to External 2971, October 30, 1969, RG 24, file S-2-5101-5, pt. 6, LAC.

64 Ottawa to FCO no. 1088, November 3, 1969, FCO 41/429, TNA.

65 "Membership of the Nuclear Planning Group," Waterfield to Private Secretary, November 10, 1969, FCO 41/429, TNA.

66 See Sayle, "NATO's Crisis Years," 374–417.

67 CanDelNATO to External 3060, November 6, 1969, RG 24, file S-2-5101-5, pt. 6, LAC.

68 External to CanDelNATO OMD1396, November 19, 1969, ibid.

69 CanDelNATO to External 3187, November 20, 1969, ibid.

70 WashDC to External 3856, November 21, 1969, ibid.

71 London to External 5119, November 21, 1969, ibid. For the British version of events, see FCO to UKDelNATO no. 409, November 21, 1969, FCO 41/429, TNA.

72 Bonn to External 1284, November 21, 1969, RG 24, file S-2-5101-5, pt. 6, LAC.

73 CanDelNATO to External 3228, November 24, 1969, ibid.

74 UKDelNATO to FCO no. 740, November 29, 1969, FCO 41/429, TNA; [Extract of committee minutes] IV. Nuclear Planning Group Membership, undated, FCO 41/429, TNA.

75 Rob Stuart, "Was the RCN Ever the Third Largest Navy?" *Canadian Naval Review* 5, 3 (Fall 2009): 9.

*Part 2*
# POLITICAL POWDERKEGS

# CHAPTER 3

# HOWARD GREEN, DISARMAMENT, AND CANADIAN-AMERICAN DEFENCE RELATIONS, 1959–63

## "A Queer, Confused World"

### Michael D. Stevenson

Traditional appraisals of the political career and legacy of Howard Charles Green, Canada's secretary of state for external affairs from 1959 to 1963, have been largely unsympathetic. Historians frequently stress Green's "simplistic view of the world,"[1] criticize his purported willingness to enable and amplify the erratic nationalism of Prime Minister John Diefenbaker, and marginalize his ministerial contributions by accentuating Diefenbaker's role in formulating Canadian foreign policy.[2] Successive generations of journalists, meanwhile, have characterized Green as Diefenbaker's "charming stooge"[3] displaying a "mulish tenacity"[4] in the pursuit of unrealistic policy aims, and they are also responsible for popularizing scurrilous – and demonstrably false – accounts of Green's supposed unworldliness and detachment from the mainstream of Canadian external relations history.[5] Recent scholarship, however, has begun to challenge these negative evaluations of Green,[6] and a systematic analysis of archival sources, including formerly classified records and previously unexamined documents in Green's personal papers, allows a much more nuanced assessment of his tenure as foreign minister to be formulated.

In particular, Green's handling of the related policy files of disarmament and nuclear weapons acquisition and their impact on Canadian-American relations demonstrates his influence at the helm of the Department of External Affairs. A fundamental personal conviction opposing the spread of nuclear weapons underpinned Green's anti-nuclear activism. Furthermore, political pragmatism augmented his zeal for disarmament, as Green firmly believed that public opinion could be mobilized behind his crusade. General E.L.M. Burns, a privileged member of Green's circle of disarmament advisers, for example, recorded privately in April 1961 that he lobbied against Green's idea for an "advertised and politically proclaimed" disarmament plan. Green proved "impossible to move," however, since he was thinking "more in domestic political terms."[7] Finally, academic accounts painting Green's opposition to nuclear weapons as a misguided policy blunder ignore his position in the mainstream of the burgeoning global disarmament movement. Indeed, before Lester Pearson's road-to-Damascus conversion supporting Canada's acquisition of nuclear warheads in January 1963, the nuclear weapons policy of the opposition Liberals mirrored that of the Diefenbaker government. "As far as I can see," Willis Armstrong, the second-ranking official in the US Embassy in Ottawa, underscored to his State Department superiors in August 1960, "the difference between Mr. Green and his opponents on this issue are hard to find."[8] Although the eventual Progressive Conservative political collapse centred on the issue of nuclear weapons, Green's resolute pursuit of nonproliferation should be viewed sympathetically, as it foreshadowed official Canadian policies adopted in the 1970s that remain entrenched to the present day.

Green experienced two major foreign policy challenges in the first year after his appointment as secretary of state for external affairs in June 1959 that significantly affected Ottawa's relationship with Washington. The first dealt with the question of continental defence cooperation with the United States and the staging of Operation Skyhawk, a joint military exercise to test NORAD's response to a simulated Soviet bomber attack on North America. His personal relationship with the new American secretary of state, Christian Herter, developed smoothly after he met his counterpart during the opening of the St. Lawrence Seaway on June 26. "He is very friendly and gentlemanly," Green remarked, "I am certain that we will get along well together."[9] Nonetheless, storm clouds were gathering on the horizon. Arnold Heeney, commencing his second tour as Canada's ambassador to the United States, worried that Canada-US relations had "worsened materially" since the 1957 federal election due to "a widespread ignorance in Canada of US intentions and habits."[10] Heeney met with Diefenbaker and Green in Ottawa on June 30 following the Seaway opening, and both politicians expressed concern about the number of American requests for defence cooperation. Green, in particular, believed "he had a special responsibility to safeguard Canadian sovereignty," and when considering Washington's defence appeals such as extended Strategic Air Command (SAC) training programs in Canadian airspace, "the United States should be 'held down' and should not be given all they asked for."[11] The discouraged ambassador returned to Washington realizing "that this area is going to be difficult in the months ahead."[12]

Heeney's forecast proved accurate. American and Canadian officials had commenced planning Operation Skyhawk in mid-January 1959 through military service channels, and the joint defence exercise received the personal approval of President Dwight D. Eisenhower nearly seven months later, on August 5. Scheduled to take place sometime between October 2 and 15, the operation was intended to test NORAD's responses by using SAC aircraft to simulate an attack on Canada and the United States. Critically, the use of electronic counter-measures during the exercise also required the grounding of all civilian aircraft in both countries for six hours on the day Skyhawk would occur. By August 15, the Canadian defence minister, the Canadian transport minister, and the civilian air associations in Canada and the United States had been informed about the exercise, yet, remarkably, the Diefenbaker cabinet had not granted formal approval for the exercise to take place. Green himself did not appear to have been aware of Skyhawk until August 25,[13] when a briefing paper about the exercise prepared by Assistant Under-Secretary of External Affairs John Holmes reached him in preparation for a cabinet meeting to be held the next day. Holmes also attached a poorly worded draft press release prepared by the US Department of Defense scheduled to be released on August 31 that unduly emphasized the role of SAC bombers in the exercise approaching Canada through the Arctic; "it appears too obvious," Holmes noted, "that an effort is being made to simulate a Soviet attack." Green's terse margin note on the paper conveyed his view of Skyhawk: "Totally inappropriate and provocative now – Reserve right to consider proposal further."[14]

Diefenbaker and Green led the opposition to Skyhawk during the August 26 cabinet meeting, and the government determined that it was an inappropriate time for the exercise to be held. Canada's rejection of Skyhawk stunned Washington. US ambassador Richard Wigglesworth informed

Diefenbaker during a two-hour conversation at 24 Sussex Drive on August 29 that the Eisenhower administration was "mad as hell" over the decision,[15] and not even a personal entreaty from President Eisenhower to Diefenbaker on September 2 persuaded Canadian ministers to reverse course. Cabinet delegated Green to meet with Wigglesworth to discuss the government's continued firm opposition to Skyhawk. The Canadian foreign minister informed the ambassador that Canada had been placed in an "impossible situation" by the last-minute knowledge of the plan to close Canadian airspace,[16] and Green expressed the greatest concern about the contents of the draft press release that "made his hair stand on end."[17] While Green suggested that Canada might consider a revised version of the exercise that was limited in scope either operationally or functionally and that did not require the grounding of civilian planes, his meeting with Wigglesworth effectively ended the substantive debate about Skyhawk. Ultimately, Wigglesworth passed a message from Eisenhower to Diefenbaker on September 16 in which the president formally announced the cancellation of the exercise. A moderately scaled-down air defence operation named Sky Shield did subsequently take place in the summer of 1960 with the grudging and unenthusiastic support of the Canadian government.[18]

The Skyhawk debacle, Arnold Heeney immediately reflected, "has come closer to doing serious damage to the foundations of Canada–United States relations in joint defence than any other event in my experience."[19] American officials were not inclined to adopt a conciliatory tone in their post-mortem of the affair. "The fact that the Prime Minister and Mr. Green were not informed of this project in an orderly fashion and at a comparatively early date is," Richard Wigglesworth bluntly observed, "clearly the fault of the Canadians," and he identified Green as "playing the key role which resulted in the Canadians turning down Skyhawk."[20] Green, however, remained unapologetic for Canada's decision to thwart Skyhawk. He met Christian Herter in New York on September 21 and admitted that Canada bore partial responsibility for the "procedural failures" that had resulted in Skyhawk's cancellation. But he again highlighted the role of the "distasteful press release" in shaping Canadian views and emphasized "the marked difference in judgment between Ottawa and Washington as to the international and domestic consequences of going ahead" with the exercise.[21] Green maintained this position during the Canada–United States

Ministerial Committee on Joint Defence meetings held at Camp David in November 1959. The Skyhawk affair was "water over the dam," he noted, but Green continued to believe that defence exercises should be "as unprovocative as possible" and that "it did seem to him that the United States government placed more emphasis on the need to impress the Soviet Union with a show of force than did the Canadian government."[22]

Green's second early policy initiative that would similarly concern successive US administrations centred on his advocacy of disarmament. After assuming the external affairs portfolio, he immediately asked his departmental officials to begin drafting the outline of an "impressive and meaty" speech to the upcoming United Nations General Assembly,[23] where he would be making his debut on the international stage. Sparked by the Soviet Union's nuclear testing program, disarmament quickly rose to the top of the agenda of his advisers, and his maiden address to the General Assembly on September 24, 1959, established the primacy of the related issues of nuclear testing, radiation hazards, and disarmament. After securing a seat on the new Ten-Nation Committee on Disarmament, successfully sponsoring a resolution establishing improved mechanisms for monitoring radioactive fallout, and supporting a resolution critical of French nuclear tests in the Sahara, Green took his case to the December 1959 NATO ministerial meeting in Paris and continued to exercise "Canada's new bad-boy role"[24] by emphasizing the need to encourage a thaw in East-West relations. "The Canadian government considers that there is some ground for believing that the basic approach of the Soviet leaders may be in the process of change," Green informed his counterparts, and that "they now desire an amelioration of the relations with the West and possibly some movement towards a measure of real disarmament."[25] Simultaneously, Green also began to muster institutional support within External Affairs for his disarmament initiative. On December 4, 1959, the Canadian government announced the appointment of General Burns as Green's first disarmament adviser. Before the end of the year, Green secured cabinet approval for a significant increase in funding to underpin the creation of a separate disarmament mission in Geneva.[26]

Green's initial expression of "hope and optimism"[27] in the ability of the Ten-Nation Committee on Disarmament to hammer out a comprehensive disarmament agreement proved to be misplaced, as the talks collapsed in

June 1960. Undeterred, he attended the meetings of the Disarmament Committee in August 1960, the only foreign minister to do so. He succeeded in shepherding a strongly worded resolution through to approval by the committee. "We are now out in front on the disarmament question,"[28] he subsequently proclaimed. Charles Ritchie, the head of the Canadian UN mission in New York and no strong admirer of the Diefenbaker government, provided a synopsis of Green's effectiveness in the Disarmament Committee:

> The first morning that I can breathe again after five days of the Minister's presence in New York, during which he pulled off a very neat little ploy on disarmament, sent up his prestige, and got what he wanted by a mixture of toughness and shrewdness that surprised his fellow professional politician, Cabot Lodge, while at the same time stealing the show from him. I think Cabot may have thought he was dealing with a nice old boy from the sticks who was a little slow on the uptake and could be patronized with his usual effortless effrontery – but it did not work out like that.[29]

Green would continue employing "elementary bulldog tactics"[30] in subsequent UN meetings, and further strengthened the departmental disarmament machinery by creating a separate disarmament division within External Affairs.

While Green earned his spurs in the quest for disarmament, he also began to grapple with the question of nuclear weapons acquisitions by Canadian forces. Cabinet first authorized negotiations with the United States to secure nuclear warheads for the Bomarc missile in October 1958, and Diefenbaker made an official policy statement in Parliament on February 20, 1959, following the formal cancellation of the CF-105 interceptor project. "It is our intention to provide Canadian forces with modern and efficient weapons to enable them to fulfil their respective roles," the prime minister announced, while also emphasizing that defensive nuclear weapons could be used "only in accordance with procedures governing NORAD's operations as approved in advance by both governments. Such weapons, therefore, would be used from Canadian territory or in Canadian airspace only under conditions previously agreed to by the Canadian government."[31]

Consultations through military service channels resulted in a draft agreement being circulated among key Canadian government departments in October 1959, and the agreement's revised text, consisting of a draft note and an annex, reached Canadian ministers in December. The draft note stressed the importance of limiting the spread of nuclear armaments and reconfirmed US ownership of all warheads stored on Canadian soil, while the five-section annex laid out general provisions for the construction and oversight of storage sites on Canadian soil. The procedures for the release of nuclear warheads for use by Canadian forces "will be the subject of separate government agreements and will be based on the principles of joint responsibility,"[32] and separate agreement for specific weapons systems would also be negotiated.

Green firmly opposed the apparent growing momentum within cabinet for the conclusion of an acquisition agreement after he became foreign minister. He was buttressed in his anti-nuclear views by Norman Robertson, the departmental under-secretary. "Norman is brilliant," Green observed after their initial meetings, and was "going to be a great help – his knowledge is very extensive."[33] Green's respect for Robertson manifested itself in his habit of telephoning the deputy minister in his East Block office at the far end of the south corridor to personally summon him for consultations,[34] the only courtesy Green did not extend to the other External Affairs officials working in the same corridor, cynically named Killer's Row – "where bright ideas met untimely deaths."[35] Robertson provided a detailed view of his position on nuclear weapons in a July 31, 1959, memorandum stressing that the current strategic philosophy of nuclear deterrence would almost inevitably lead to global annihilation. "The only answer which I can see to this dilemma," he argued, "is the progressive accommodation by non-military means of the interests of the political contestants – at this moment the Western Alliance and the Soviet Union." The first step in this accommodation, Robertson believed, was "to regard all questions connected with nuclear weapons as matters of high policy" and to accept the "obvious risks" that a change in attitude toward nuclear arms "could conceivably undermine the determination of democratic societies to accept the ever-mounting level of defence expenditures."[36]

Robertson's prescriptions for a change in Canadian defence policy shocked Arnold Heeney, who viewed them as a unilateral acceptance of a lower level of preparedness for Canada's military and a deliberate rebuke of American requests for greater cooperative measures for North American security. "If we persist," Heeney warned, "in a policy of delay, refusal, and the imposition of procedural conditions, US authorities are bound to conclude, if they have not already done so, that our attitude derives basically from mistrust of their motives as well as their capabilities."[37] Green closely adhered to Robertson's views, however. In his handwritten comments on the December 1959 draft note and annex governing the acquisition of nuclear weapons, for example, he highlighted the principle of joint custody of the warheads and crossed out a section of the annex that stated that "these procedures will be the subject of separate governmental agreements and will be based on the principles of joint responsibility."[38] Green's expressed reservations about the lack of political oversight of the nuclear weapons deployment process caused Robert B. Bryce, the influential Clerk of the Privy Council, to note ominously: "Nuclear paras. – Green concerned."[39]

Throughout 1960, Green successfully stalled any progress toward the conclusion of a nuclear weapons agreement between Canada and the United States. Ahead of Diefenbaker's visit to Washington to meet President Eisenhower in June, a National Security Council policy paper complained of Ottawa's "reluctance to grant prompt and full support to joint continental defense measures" and of the "closer high-level government scrutiny of projects and consequent efforts to place a somewhat stricter interpretation on defense arrangements with the US."[40] At the meeting of the Canada–United States Committee on Joint Defence held in July at Montebello, Quebec, Green stickhandled around calls for progress to be made in negotiations for the transfer of nuclear warheads to Canadian forces. "The Canadian Government had many questions to resolve before taking a decision on this matter," Green calmly informed his American ministerial guests.[41] The Canadian foreign minister's attitudes toward nuclear weapons only hardened thereafter. Heeney also recorded Green's emotional reaction to the US ambassador's probing questions about nuclear weapons during a meeting in November 1960. "Mr. Green expressed himself as strongly opposed" to accepting US nuclear warheads, since "it would destroy the Canadian position on disarmament and at the UN." Green conceded that permission to store warheads at leased US military bases in Canada might be granted, "but, otherwise, he would not agree to having any nuclear weapons in Canada."[42]

But Green proved unable to continue his delaying tactics by the end of 1960. George Pearkes' resignation as Canada's defence minister enabled his hard-charging successor, Douglas Harkness, to aggressively pursue the consummation of nuclear warhead acquisition agreements with Washington. Furthermore, long-simmering negotiations to secure the transfer of American F-101 interceptors to Royal Canadian Air Force (RCAF) control under a comprehensive triangular transaction were coming to a head, and would, when finalized in 1961, provide Canada with four advanced military platforms – the CF-101 interceptors, the CF-104 strike aircraft in the Air Division operating in Europe, the Bomarc surface-to-air missile, and the Honest John tactical missile batteries – that required nuclear armaments as elsewhere for maximum effectiveness.[43] Finally, the election of John F. Kennedy transformed the plodding, patient approach of the Eisenhower administration into a truculent demand that the Diefenbaker government shoulder its fair share of continental defence responsibilities. The "evolving Canadian attitude of introspection and nationalism" fostered in part by Green's "naïve and almost parochial approach," the Kennedy White House determined, would be challenged.[44]

With Harkness' prodding, the Diefenbaker cabinet on December 6, 1960, approved the resumption of nuclear negotiations "as soon as they can usefully be undertaken," with joint control of the weapons being a "basic principle" of any discussions. A revised version of the initial draft nuclear weapons acquisition agreement was circulated at the ministerial level by the middle of January 1960, and pro-nuclear forces were convinced that there were "no real problems of principle" between Canada and the United States.[45] Ahead of the visit of Diefenbaker and Green to Washington on February 20, 1961, R.B. Bryce counselled the prime minister that the parameters of an acceptable agreement were already in place. "I do not believe that much is to be gained, either internationally or diplomatically," Bryce maintained, "by keeping the Canadian position undefined or fluid. In fact, the Canadian position is reasonably well determined now and needs only some re-affirmation on your part and some defence by your ministers to clear up the confusion in the press and the public which I feel is doing harm to the Government."[46] But Norman Robertson did not share this assessment. Although Diefenbaker's February 1959 statement to the House of Commons represented a "decision in principle" to acquire nuclear weapons, the under-secretary informed Green in a February 14, 1961, memorandum that Diefenbaker's promise that no agreement would be signed while disarmament negotiations were proceeding modified the original policy guidelines. Furthermore, any agreed text of a negotiating draft reached between Green and Harkness should emphasize that the key issue of joint control would apply – and Green underlined this in his notations on Robertson's submission – to the "storage, release from storage, and use" of nuclear warheads, a position opposed to the Department of National Defence's willingness to consider only political controls over the actual use of nuclear armaments.[47]

The course of events continued to move in Harkness' favour after Diefenbaker's visit with Kennedy on February 20. The prime minister, while maintaining the traditional Canadian position on joint Canada-US control over the use of US warheads stored in Canada, informed Kennedy that he was prepared for high-level negotiations to commence that dealt comprehensively with all aspects of nuclear arms within the NORAD structure. "The President expressed appreciation of the position of the Canadian government," Heeney subsequently reported,[48] and Green turned his attention to blunting the zeal of National Defence officials to commence bilateral talks. At the end of March 1961, he demanded changes to the most recent draft of the agreement to acquire nuclear weapons for Canadian forces, since it did not contain storage, release, and use provisions for the specific weapons platforms scheduled to be added to Canada's military arsenal. The draft indicated that the procedures would vary depending on the type of weapon and the operational theatre, and Green insisted that "we know in advance all the implications and obligations involved."[49] Although Harkness believed that Green's approach was "unnecessarily cumbersome," his primary concern was that "we get on with the negotiations."[50] President Kennedy echoed the Canadian defence minister's impatience when he sent "an unusually sensitive message"[51] to Diefenbaker in the first week of August asking for the immediate conclusion of bilateral nuclear weapons agreements, particularly since Kennedy had personally intervened to accede to the Canadian request to complete the F-101 interceptor swap agreement without the inclusion of nuclear-tipped MB-1 rockets for the aircraft.[52]

Diefenbaker responded favourably on August 11: "On receipt of your message, I sent word to our Minister of National Defence to ensure that final preparations were expedited for the negotiation of the agreements to which you referred."[53]

When Harkness circulated a revised draft agreement with schedules for specific weapons, Green set to work to reassert the primacy of political authorities in determining the use of nuclear warheads. In Schedule A dealing with nuclear warheads for use by the RCAF in Canada, the draft text dealing with decisions to use the warheads was vague:

> If advance authorization as indicated above has not been given and the situation is such that in the opinion of CINCNORAD it is necessary for him to have the authority to use the warheads, he may seek approval from the two governments. Normally, such approval will be sought through the Chairmen of the national Chiefs of Staff, but he may simultaneously establish direct contact with the political authorities of both governments.

Green replaced this text with a more pronounced political involvement in the process:

> If advance authorization as indicated above has not been given and the situation is such that in the opinion of CINCNORAD it is necessary for him to have the authority to use the warheads, he shall seek approval from the two governments. Normally, such approval will be sought through the Chairmen of the national Chiefs of Staff, but he may simultaneously establish direct contact with the respective heads of governments.

Similarly, the draft agreement contained vague language about the independence of NORAD's commander:

> CINCNORAD will only be able to issue operational orders to employ the warheads when the necessary release authority has been issued by CINCNORAD to the US release officer at the Combat Operations Centre and the US detachment commander, and the Canadian release

officer and the senior Canadian officer at each site have received the necessary authorization in the manner to be determined by the Canadian government.

Green replaced this opaque text with a clear, definitive statement:

CINCNORAD will only issue operational orders to use the warheads after the heads of government have authorized their release for use as mentioned above.

Ultimately, Green and senior DEA officials maintained that the proposed decision to enter into negotiations "should not be interpreted to mean that Canada has decided to acquire nuclear warheads but rather that it wishes to put itself into a position to do so rapidly if at any time in the future such action should be deemed necessary."[54]

The final version of the memorandum to cabinet containing the full text of the negotiating draft favoured Green's position. New text about the "two-key" procedure for launching Bomarc missiles was included, while Green's text about political approval at the highest levels remained: "CINCNORAD will only issue operational orders to use the warheads after the heads of government have authorized their use."[55] Ministers discussed the proposed draft at three cabinet meetings held on August 22, 23, and 25, but no agreement could be reached. Diefenbaker's inherent political misgivings about nuclear weapons acquisition then resurfaced after an article written by Harold Morrison appeared in the Montreal *Gazette* on September 20, headlined "JFK Presses Canada on Nuclear Warheads," in which he documented President Kennedy's direct personal appeal to Diefenbaker to conclude a nuclear weapons agreement. Cables between Ottawa and Washington crackled with activity about Diefenbaker's potential response, and the State Department received word on October 7 from a trusted source indicating that "Diefenbaker had told close associates that the decision could not be made now 'because it would appear to be a direct response to US pressure'; consequently, Diefenbaker indicated that the 'dust must be allowed to settle.'"[56] Now on the defensive, Harkness attempted to rekindle ministerial discussion of the nuclear weapons issue in November. Meeting minutes for November 21, 1961, note briefly that "Cabinet decided to continue discussion of the matter with the Secretaries absent."[57] On November 30, "the Cabinet agreed to give further consideration at another informal meeting to the proposed negotiations with the United States,"[58] but the momentum in favour of acquisition of US warheads had clearly dissipated.

Confronted with Ottawa's refusal to conclude a nuclear weapons agreement, the Kennedy administration grew increasingly exasperated with the Diefenbaker government by the early months of 1962. Livingston Merchant, the US ambassador on his second tour of duty in Ottawa, reported to Washington in February that the greatest single outstanding problem in bilateral affairs was the Canadian failure to address the nuclear weapons file. Citing Howard Green's prominent opposition to "dirtying Canadian hands and reputation with nuclear weapons under any circumstances," Merchant concluded that the Progressive Conservative government was "virtually paralyzed" and would not deal with defence issues before the next federal election.[59] In a subsequent analysis of debate in the House of Commons about nuclear weapons policy, Merchant upbraided Diefenbaker for his confused responses that stemmed from a "compound of ignorance of a complex subject, profound reluctance to face up to a disagreeable subject, [and an] unfortunate propensity to point to the US as an immovable stumbling block."[60] At the meeting of the Canada–United States Permanent Joint Board on Defence in May 1962, the US section rebuked Canada's position on atomic weapons after the Canadian section attempted to delete the item from the meeting agenda.[61] Even Canadian civil servants were beginning to openly criticize their government's lethargic performance in continental air defence. Meeting with senior diplomats in the US Embassy in Ottawa in August 1962, Dr. J.E. Keyston, vice-chairman of Canada's Defence Research Board, lamented the "disturbingly impaired" relationship with his American counterparts, and noted that the position of RCAF Air Marshal Roy Slemon, the NORAD second-in-command, "had been made disgracefully impossible by the lack of political support from the Diefenbaker government."[62]

Through all of this, Harkness continued to support the conclusion of a nuclear weapons agreement with Washington. He returned to the attack in the first week of October 1962, producing a memorandum for cabinet consideration that called for the negotiation of a general bilateral agreement containing basic principles of atomic stockpiles for Canadian forces before specific schedules were subsequently negotiated covering warheads for each of the four primary Canadian weapons systems requiring them. But Green and the Department of External Affairs remained concerned that Harkness' proposal did not provide a "clear understanding" of the eventual contents of the general agreement. The agreement envisioned by Harkness would provide for the stationing of nuclear weapons on Canadian soil in peacetime. But External Affairs officials reminded their minister that Diefenbaker had indicated several months earlier that Canada was willing "to negotiate only a standby agreement making provision for the acquisition of warheads only in time of actual or threatened emergency."[63] Within these parameters, therefore, the proposal put forward by the Department of National Defence could not be considered a feasible course of action. A draft memorandum to cabinet prepared for Green's signature dated October 19, 1962, formally outlined the External Affairs position supporting a standby arrangement, and further recommended that the general agreement and all acquisition schedules for individual weapons systems be negotiated in their entirety before cabinet would consider approving a comprehensive bilateral covenant.[64]

In normal circumstances, the dueling memoranda prepared for Harkness and Green would have resulted once again in another extensive round of desultory interdepartmental and Cabinet discussions. But the Cuban Missile Crisis punctured the complacency and indecision that had characterized the Diefenbaker government's approach to foreign policy and pushed the issue of nuclear weapons acquisition to the top of the diplomatic agenda. The threat of global nuclear war convinced many wavering Canadian cabinet ministers that nuclear weapons were no longer an abstract policy debate that could be ignored. Diefenbaker's ham-handed response to Washington's call for immediate solidarity with the Kennedy administration's blockade of Cuba announced on October 22, 1962, further inflamed cross-border tensions, most notably in the prime minister's initial refusal to immediately place Canadian NORAD forces on the same DEFCON alert status as their American counterparts – a status Harkness surreptitiously implemented prior to cabinet's eventual sanction. "The Cuban affair," Harkness maintained, "shook the confidence of a number of the Cabinet and the faith of all in him was, I believe, never restored to what it had been."[65] Recent scholarship has painted the Diefenbaker government's response to the Cuban crisis in a more positive light,[66] yet the event represented a difficult time in Canadian foreign policy between 1957 and 1963.

Nonetheless, Green continued to shape Canadian foreign policy and influence international affairs by securing the passage of a major United Nations resolution in November 1962 calling for a moratorium on nuclear tests. This capped the effort he started during his first UN session as secretary of state for external affairs in 1959 to gradually bring nuclear weapons under international arms control. At the autumn 1962 session of the United Nations, the General Assembly debated the issue of an uninspected suspension of nuclear tests, a plan that Douglas Harkness warned Green posed "grave risks" to the Western defence position.[67] Undeterred, Green instructed Canadian officials in New York to accept a potential resolution with an unpoliced testing moratorium clause commencing January 1, 1963, with follow-up agreements to be negotiated to ensure compliance. When neutral countries subsequently submitted an eight-power resolution calling for a moratorium to compete with a resolution sponsored by the United States and the United Kingdom with no moratorium starting date, Canada made no effort to oppose its terms. The Cuban Missile Crisis added fuel to the moratorium debate and widened the divide between Green and Harkness over defence issues, with the defence minister furiously lobbying Diefenbaker to rein in Green and prevent Canada from voting for a testing moratorium without inspection articles.

Green travelled to New York on October 28 to personally handle the testing suspension debate. Nikita Khrushchev's walk-back on Cuba allowed Canada to propose amending the neutral resolution to specifically call for the United States, United Kingdom, and Soviet Union to settle their differences over testing and urge an immediate agreement to ban all tests in the atmosphere, underwater, and in outer space if a complete test ban could not be agreed to by January 1, 1963. Green advised Secretary of State Dean Rusk that the amended resolution was "in as good a shape as it was possibly going to get," and he hoped the United States could at least abstain on the matter.[68] Ultimately, on November 6, the General Assembly passed the neutral resolution with the Canadian amendments with seventy-five votes of support, zero votes against, and twenty-one abstentions. Green's performance at the UN marked the high point of his time as foreign minister, and he received wide praise in Canadian political and press circles. The *Charlottetown Guardian,* for example, noted his "day of triumph" in the face of detractors who regarded him as "a hare-brained idealist," and he "has gotten now, from the world's assembly of nations, an endorsation of his efforts that no power can afford to ignore indefinitely."[69]

Green maintained his important role in the crafting of Canadian foreign policy during the final months of the Diefenbaker government. In November 1962, cabinet attempted to again address the long-simmering question of the acquisition of nuclear weapons by offering to open high-level diplomatic political talks with the United States.[70] Green carefully monitored Canadian negotiators as they attempted to arrange a "missing part" agreement that would conform to Green's wish that complete operational nuclear warheads not be stored on Canadian soil, with an essential element of warheads stored in the United States and moved across the border when an international crisis occurred. But the decision by leader of the Opposition Lester Pearson in January 1963 to commit the Liberal Party to accept US nuclear tips essentially changed the political calculus in the bilateral negotiations between Ottawa and Washington. Green derided Pearson's new approach: "I think it takes us off several hooks and I can't understand why he didn't sit tight and let us stew! Strange fellow – intrinsically a weak sister, I think. He should have stayed with diplomacy!"[71] US officials, however, viewed Pearson's willingness to arm Canadian forces with nuclear warheads as a clear opportunity to rid themselves of Diefenbaker. Although the Progressive Conservative government "is upset, feels that the US has reneged on some implied promises, and probably feels that the US has been working with and for Lester Pearson," the White House decided that that no further negotiations would take place. Any compromise would allow Diefenbaker to claim that he had wrung important concessions from Washington, and "on balance," President Kennedy was advised, "it seems best to stand fast. This course is easy to justify militarily . . . and it could materially enhance Diefenbaker's difficulties" as a possible election approached.[72]

Diefenbaker then made the mistake of revealing the existence of the top secret nuclear negotiations with the United States in a speech to the House of Commons on January 25, 1963. Walton Butterworth, the new US ambassador in Ottawa, labelled the speech a "masterpiece of deception and persuasion ... full of red herrings and non-sequiturs," and he believed that Diefenbaker had been deliberately provocative to "unilaterally change" the Canada-US defence relationship. This was an "important turning point," in the US Embassy's view, and Butterworth stated bluntly that "we have to step in and step in promptly" – if Diefenbaker got away with his "shabby performance," he could only damage NORAD and NATO arrangements.[73] With continued prodding from Butterworth, the State Department issued an unprecedented public rebuke of the Progressive Conservative government through a press release on January 30. Green described this as "the day the State Department did us dirt ... I saw the US press release first when handed it by a Canadian reporter! How on earth the US government expects to hold friends is beyond me – but they may not care. I think this is the time that Canada must stand up to them if she is not to become a satellite."[74] When Douglas Harkness resigned over Diefenbaker's continued refusal to declare Canada's support for the acquisition of nuclear weapons, the government collapsed in early February 1963. During the ensuing election campaign, Green travelled the country and relied heavily on his commitment to disarmament and opposition to nuclear weapons acquisition to argue that voters would decide whether Canada "will be a great nation or a satellite."[75] On this occasion, even many former supporters in his Vancouver Quadra riding turned against him and narrowly returned a Liberal candidate as part of a Liberal minority government. Nonetheless, the veteran Conservative parliamentarian accepted the defeat with grace and simply commented, "That's politics."[76]

An analysis of Howard Green's time as secretary of state for external affairs and his management of the disarmament and continental defence policy files provides important new perspectives on Canadian foreign policy during the Diefenbaker government. Green developed a clear vision of Canada's place in the international arena and the nature of the bilateral tie with the United States, and he wielded considerable influence in the affairs of cabinet. Although he frequently became a polarizing figure for advocating policy positions that often placed him at odds with members of his own government and Canada's Western allies, his influence in shaping Canadian foreign relations from 1959 to 1963 cannot be disputed. In fact, few Canadian foreign ministers in the postwar period have played such a dominant role in determining Canada's foreign policy agenda. Ultimately, writing in November 1962 in the aftermath of the Cuban Missile Crisis, Green provided a personal evaluation of his ministerial tenure at External Affairs that succinctly and accurately encapsulated his political philosophy and experiences:

> What a queer, confused world we live in. And yet the old virtues remain vitally important. Sometimes, I admit, they get badly mixed up with political considerations! It is all exciting and interesting – I wouldn't have missed being in External Affairs these last three years! Anything else will seem rather tame I fear![77]

## NOTES

This research was supported by the Social Sciences and Humanities Research Council of Canada and an Eisenhower Foundation Abilene travel grant.

1  J.L. Granatstein and Norman Hillmer, *For Better or for Worse: Canada and the United States to the 1990s* (Toronto: Copp Clark Pitman, 1991), 200.

2  See Denis Smith, *Rogue Tory: The Life and Legend of John G. Diefenbaker* (Toronto: Macfarlane Walter and Ross, 1995); Patricia McMahon, *Essence of Indecision: Diefenbaker's Nuclear Policy, 1957–1963* (Montreal and Kingston: McGill-Queen's University Press, 2009); and Basil Robinson, *Diefenbaker's World: A Populist in Foreign Affairs* (Toronto: University of Toronto Press, 1989).

3  "Everybody Likes Howard Green but . . .," *Toronto Daily Star*, June 6, 1959.

4  Knowlton Nash, *Kennedy and Diefenbaker: Fear and Loathing across the Undefended Border* (Toronto: McClelland and Stewart, 1990), 81.

5  One widely circulated story involves Congolese leader Patrice Lumumba, who, while visiting Ottawa in July 1960, supposedly requested a woman be sent to his room for sex; "the churchgoing Green," an account maintains, "thought he meant a typist. When the unsuspecting stenographer entered Lumumba's room all hell broke loose"; Lawrence Martin, "Camelot on the Rideau? Don't Wait for It," *Globe and Mail*, February 19, 2013. See also Charles Lynch, *You Can't Print THAT! Memoirs of a Political Voyeur* (Toronto: HarperCollins, 1988), 197, for a more richly embroidered version of this episode. In fact, Green never met Lumumba. He left Ottawa for a fundraiser in Alberta before Lumumba arrived in Canada and returned after Lumumba had departed the nation's capital.

6  See Michael D. Stevenson, "Sidney Smith, Howard Green, and the Conduct of Canadian Foreign Policy during the Diefenbaker Government, 1957–1963," in *Reassessing the Rogue Tory: Canadian Foreign Relations in the Diefenbaker Era*, ed. Janice Cavell and Ryan M. Touhey (Vancouver: UBC Press, 2018), 249–68.

7  E.L.M. Burns diary entry, April 10, 1961, E.L.M. Burns Papers [hereafter ELMB], MG 31 G6, vol. 8, file "Diaries 1961," Library and Archives Canada (LAC).

8  Armstrong to Merchant, August 18, 1960, RG 59, Central Files, box 768, file 742.5/8-360, United States National Archives (USNA).

9  HCG to Lewis Green, June 29, 1959, Howard Charles Green Papers (HCG), series 593-F-1, file 2, City of Vancouver Archives (CVA).

10  Heeney diary entry, March 29, 1959, A.D.P. Heeney Papers (ADPH), vol. 2, file "Memoirs 1959," ch. 15, Diary 1, LAC.

11  "Conversation with the Minister," June 30, 1959, ADPH, vol. 1, file 14, LAC.

12  Ibid.

13  Holmes had also sent a memorandum to Green dated August 21 about Skyhawk, but it is not certain whether it reached Green, who was away from Ottawa at that time. A margin note on this document in Basil Robinson's hand reads "Seen by the Prime Minister." See Holmes to Green, August 21, 1959, in ed. Janice Cavell, Kevin Spooner, and Michael D. Stevenson, *Documents on Canadian External Relations* (*DCER*), vol. 26, *1959*, ch. 4, "Relations with the United States," Document 199, http://epe.lac-bac.gc.ca/100/206/301/faitc-aecic/history/2013-05-03/www.international.gc.ca/department/history-histoire/dcer/details-en.asp@intRefid=11017.

14  Holmes to Green, August 25, 1959, RG 25, vol. 6050, file 50309-D-40, pt. 1.1, LAC.

15  Robinson to Robertson, August 31, 1959, *DCER*, vol. 26, ch. 4, Document 204, http://epe.lac-bac.gc.ca/100/206/301/faitc-aecic/history/2013-05-03/www.international.gc.ca/department/history-histoire/dcer/details-en.asp@intRefid=11022.

16  Ottawa Telegram 155, September 2, 1959, White House Office Files, Office of the Staff Secretary, Records of Paul T. Carroll, Andrew Goodpaster, L. Arthur Minnich, and Christopher H. Russell, 1952–1961, box 23, file "Skyhawk (August-September 1959) (2)," Dwight D. Eisenhower Presidential Library and Museum (DDEL).

17  "Informal Notes of a Telephone Conversation," September 2, 1959, RG 59, Alphanumeric Files Relating to Canadian Affairs, 1957–1963, box 3, file 3-C-3, USNA.

18  See Asa McKercher and Timothy Andrews Sayle, "Skyhawk, Skyshield, and the Soviets: Revisiting Canada's Cold War," *Historical Journal* 61, 2 (2018): 453–75, doi: 10.1017/S0018246X17000292.

19  "Lessons from Skyhawk: Consultations in Canada–United States Defence," September 11, 1959, RG 25, American Embassy Files, vol. 3175, file "Canada-US Defence Relations, 1958–1960," LAC.

20  Wigglesworth to Merchant, October 14, 1959, RG 59, Alphanumeric Files Relating to Canadian Affairs, 1957–1963, box 3, file 3-C-3, USNA.

21  Washington Telegram 2266, September 22, 1959, *DCER*, vol. 26, ch. 4, Document 211, http://epe.lac-bac.gc.ca/100/206/301/faitc-aecic/history/2013-05-03/www.international.gc.ca/department/history-histoire/dcer/details-en.asp@intRefid=11029.

22  Meeting Minutes of Canada–United States Ministerial Committee on Joint Defence, November 8, 1959, H. Basil Robinson Papers (HBR), MG 31 E83, vol. 8, file 12, LAC; reprinted in *DCER*, vol. 26, ch. 4, Document 229, http://epe.lac-bac.gc.ca/100/206/301/faitc-aecic/history/2013-05-03/www.international.gc.ca/department/history-histoire/dcer/details-en.asp@intRefid=11047.

23  Holmes to McCordick, June 16, 1959, RG 25, vol. 7149, file 5475-DW-68-40, LAC.

24  "Canada's New 'Bad-Boy' Role: East and West Find We're Nobody's Satellite," *Maclean's*, December 19, 1959.

25  NATO Telegram MM 11, December 16, 1959, RG 25, vol. 4800, file 50102-X-40, LAC.
26  Cabinet Conclusions, December 30, 1959, Records of the Privy Council Office (PCO), RG 2, LAC.
27  *House of Commons Debates,* March 14, 1960, 24th Parliament, 3rd Session, vol. 2, 2043.
28  H. Green to L. Green, August 23, 1960, HCG, series 593-F-1, file 3, CVA.
29  Charles Ritchie, *Diplomatic Passport: More Undiplomatic Diaries, 1946–1962* (Toronto: McClelland and Stewart, 1981), 122.
30  "Green's Fine Fight," *Vancouver Sun,* December 16, 1960.
31  *House of Commons Debates,* February 20, 1959, 24th Parliament, 2nd Session, vol. 2, 1223–24.
32  Robertson to Green, December 7, 1959, Howard Charles Green Papers (HCG), vol. 10, file 10, LAC.
33  H. Green to L. Green, June 7, 1959, and H. Green to L. Green, June 17, 1959, HCG, series 593-F-1, file 2, CVA.
34  Author interview with Eric Bergbusch, August 17, 2010.
35  John Hilliker and Donald Barry, *Canada's Department of External Affairs,* vol. 2, *Coming of Age, 1946–1968* (Montreal and Kingston: McGill-Queen's University Press, 1995), 49.
36  "Nuclear Weapons – Some Questions of Policy," July 31, 1959, HBR, vol. 11, file "Correspondence and Memoranda, 1957–1962," LAC.
37  Heeney to Robertson, August 31, 1959, HBR, vol. 10, file 10, LAC.
38  Green comments on draft note and annex, January [13–14], 1960, HCG, vol. 10, file "Acquisition of Defensive Nuclear Warheads, 1959–1960," LAC.
39  Untitled notes, January 14, 1960, R.B. Bryce Papers (RBB), MG 31 E59, vol. 8, file 17, LAC.
40  "Discussion Paper on Canada," May 31, 1960, White House Office Files, Office of the Special Assistant for National Security Affairs: Records, 1952–1961, box 26, file NSC 5822, DDEL.
41  Record of Meeting between Canada–United States Committee on Joint Defence, July 12, 1960, *DCER,* vol. 27, *1960,* ch. 3, "Relations with the United States," Document 302, http://epe.lac-bac.gc.ca/100/206/301/faitc-aecic/history/2013-05-03/www.international.gc.ca/department/history-histoire/dcer/details-en.asp@intRefid=12841.
42  Heeney diary entry, November 17, 1960, ADPH, vol. 2, file "Memoirs," ch. 15, Diary 2, LAC.
43  For details of the complex Canada-US swap agreement, see Michael D. Stevenson, "'A Very Careful Balance': The 1961 Triangular Agreement and the Conduct of Canadian-American Relations," *Diplomacy and Statecraft* 24, 2 (2013): 291–311.
44  Rusk to Kennedy, February 17, 1961, President's Office Files, box 113, file "Canada Security, 1961," John F. Kennedy Presidential Library and Museum (JFKPL).
45  "Nuclear Weapons," Bryce handwritten notes, February 12, 1961, RBB, vol. 8, file 19, LAC.
46  Bryce to Diefenbaker, February 15, 1961, HBR, vol. 11, file "Correspondence and Memoranda, 1957–1962," LAC.
47  Robertson to Green, February 14, 1961, HCG, vol. 11, file 3, LAC.
48  Heeney to Green, February 23, 1961, HCG, vol. 7, file 12, LAC.
49  Green to Harkness, March 30, 1961, Douglas Harkness Papers (DSH), vol. 57, file "The Nuclear Arms Question and the Political Crisis which Arose from It in January and February, 1963," LAC.

50  Harkness to Diefenbaker, May 11, 1961, ibid.

51  Bromley Smith comment on routing slip, August 4, 1961, National Security Files, box 20, file "Diefenbaker Correspondence, 1/20/61–8/10/61," JFKPL.

52  State Department Telegram 98, August 3, 1961, ibid.

53  Diefenbaker to Kennedy, President's Office Files, box 113, file "Canada Security, 1961," JFKPL.

54  Draft of negotiating text, HCG, vol. 10, file 11, LAC.

55  Cabinet Document 297/61, August 15, 1961, HCG, vol. 11, file 1, LAC.

56  Ottawa Telegram 386, October 7, 1961, National Security Files, box 18, file "General, 10/61–1/62," JFKPL.

57  Cabinet Conclusions, November 21, 1961, PCO, LAC.

58  Cabinet Conclusions, November 30, 1961, ibid.

59  Ottawa Telegram 807, February 26, 1962, National Security Files, box 20, file "Diefenbaker Correspondence, 10/11/61–10/21/62," JFKPL.

60  Ottawa Telegram 823, February 27, 1962, National Security Files, box 18, file "General, 2/62–3/62," JFKPL.

61  L.D. Wilgress to Bryce, May 11, 1962, DCER, vol. 29, 1962, ch. 3, "United States," Document 216, https://www.international.gc.ca/history-histoire/dcer-drrec/volumes/29/chap_3_united_states.aspx?lang=eng#a3_2a.

62  Memorandum of Conversation, August 30, 1962, RG 59, Bureau of European Affairs, Records Relating to Military Matters, box 2, file 3.42, USNA.

63  Robertson to Green, October 3, 1962, in DCER, vol. 29, ch. 3, Document 227.

64  Ibid., Document 229.

65  "The Nuclear Arms Question," DSH, vol. 57, file "The Nuclear Arms Question and the Political Crisis Which Arose from It in January and February 1963," LAC.

66  See Asa McKercher, "A 'Half-Hearted Response'? Canada and the Cuban Missile Crisis, 1962," International History Review 33, 2 (2011): 335–52.

67  Harkness to Green, October 17, 1962, HCG, vol. 11, file 2, LAC.

68  Bow to Green, November 2, 1962, ibid.

69  "Parliament's Tribute," Charlottetown Guardian, November 7, 1962.

70  For a detailed account of these talks that led ultimately to the collapse of the Diefenbaker government, see Michael D. Stevenson, "'Tossing a Match into Dry Hay': Nuclear Weapons and the Crisis in US-Canadian Relations, 1962–1963," Journal of Cold War Studies 16, 4 (2014): 5–34.

71  H. Green to F. Green, January 13, 1963, HCG, series 593-E-6, file 6, CVA.

72  Legere to Kennedy, January 21, 1963, National Security Files, box 225, file "NATO, Weapons, Cables, Canada, 12/61–11/63," pt. 1, JFKPL.

73  Ottawa Telegram 949, January 27, 1963, National Security Files, box 18, file "General, 10/62–1/63," JFKPL.

74  H. Green to F. Green, February 3, 1963, HCG, series 593-E-6, file 7, CVA.

75  "Canada: Great Nation or Satellite?" Victoria Times, April 5, 1963.

76  "Green's Defeat 'Shocking,'" Edmonton Journal, April 9, 1963.

77  H. Green to F. Green, November 11, 1962, HCG, series 608-F-1, file 1, CVA.

# CHAPTER 4

# NEUTRALISM, NATIONALISM, AND NUKES, OH MY!

## *Revisiting* Peacemaker or Powder-Monkey *and Canadian Strategy in the Nuclear Age*

### Asa McKercher

"Neutralism" is a term rarely associated with Canada. Having taken part in both world wars, Canadians lacked a tradition of neutrality, and during the Cold War, Canada was hardly non-aligned, playing an important role in the foundation of the NATO alliance, dispatching military forces to Korea and Western Europe, and both broadening and deepening its defensive cooperation with the United States. Ottawa even went so far as to accept – albeit grudgingly – tactical nuclear weaponry for its military forces. Furthermore, Canadian foreign policy-makers often looked askance at India, Indonesia, and other proponents of non-alignment. As Robert Bothwell, the dean of Canada's international historians, has pointed out, "at no point were Canadians seriously tempted to jump the fence, turn to neutrality, or abandon the Western side. Public opinion would not have stood for it."[1] This contention is not wrong, particularly in considering the views and actions of foreign policy-makers in Ottawa. Even so, neutralism was in the air in the late 1950s and early 1960s. While Canada hardly ranked as an issue in the 1960 US presidential campaign, a brief on Canada for John F. Kennedy, the Democratic candidate, slammed Republican president Dwight Eisenhower for doing nothing to arrest "an ever-rising tide of neutralism" among Canadians. Appearing on Canadian television in March 1961, Livingston Merchant, newly appointed as Kennedy's ambassador in Ottawa, told his interviewer that he was concerned primarily not with Canadian nationalism or anti-Americanism but with neutralism.[2] Two months earlier, at a national Liberal Party policy convention, party elders had beaten back resolutions calling for Canada to abandon its alliances; leading members of the newly formed New Democratic Party (NDP) did the same at the party's inaugural convention that summer. And in 1960, in its first five months on the market, CBC reporter James Minifie's *Peacemaker or Powder-Monkey* sold over 10,000 copies.

A bestseller, Minifie's book counselled a neutralist foreign policy for Canada. In well-reasoned tones, *Peacemaker or Powder-Monkey* inspired peace activists and other Canadians concerned with the prospect of nuclear warfare, and enraged and alarmed government officials on both sides of the Canada-US border. It even gave hope to Canada's enemies. As late as 1968, *Izvestia* would ask of Canada: "Peacemaker or Ammunition Bearer?"[3] Often referenced by historians but seldom the focus of much attention, Minifie's work was representative of the thinking of a segment of Canadians who questioned Canada's foreign and defence policies in a world in which missile technology and mutual assured destruction (MAD) had revolution-ized the nature of warfare. So, in reconsidering Canadian nuclear history, *Peacemaker or Powder-Monkey* deserves more attention, as does the neu-tralist blip, which, though brief, had a lasting impact on debates over Canadian external relations.

In this chapter, I examine Minifie's *Peacemaker or Powder-Monkey* and trace the responses to his call for Canadian neutralism. This debate over Canadian strategy occurred in the late 1950s and 1960s, partly in response to the development of nuclear missiles. During this period, thanks to the Third World's emergence, neutralism was very *au courant* as a factor in international relations.[4] Within the Canadian context, Minifie has been referenced in relation to three interrelated issues that have dominated the historiography: growing disarmament sentiment, Canada's acceptance of nuclear weaponry, and Canadian independence from the United States.[5] Worth emphasizing at the outset is that calls for Canadian neutralism were often separate from calls for nuclear disarmament, even if the advocates of both positions were in the same choir, or at least singing from the same hymnbook. Nor were Minifie and other advocates of Canadian neutralism pacifists or isolationists – in fact, quite the opposite. Yet, like the supporters of nuclear arms control, Minifie and company challenged the consensus over Canada's Cold War foreign and defence policies. Overall, their long-term impact can be seen in the Canadian embrace of peacekeeping. For neutralism's proponents, peacekeeping emerged as a means for Canada to use its military in more positive ways than in support of the United States and nuclear deterrence.

## MINIFIE AND THE NEUTRALISTS

James Minifie was an unlikely figure to lead a neutralist challenge to the Cold War consensus around Canadian foreign and defence policy. Born in England, he came to Canada as a child and grew up in Vanguard, Saskatchewan. He served overseas with the Canadian Expeditionary Force in the First World War, afterward attending the University of Saskatchewan and winning a Rhodes scholarship upon graduation in 1923. After three years of study at Oriel College, Minifie tried to become a writer, but went broke and so took a job with a European tourist agency. In 1929, after two years of touring the continent, he joined the *New York Herald Tribune,* his employer for twenty-four years, during which time he covered the Spanish Civil War and served as the paper's correspondent in Rome from 1937 to 1940. Once Italy became involved in the Second World War, Minifie went to the *Herald Tribune* office in London and then Washington. Recruited by the US Office of Strategic Services in 1943, he served in Italy and later Austria, conducting psychological warfare operations, for which he received an Order of the British Empire (OBE) and the American Medal of Freedom. Interestingly, given his later status as a Canadian nationalist accused of anti-US views, Minifie became an American citizen, a fact he kept quiet, particularly after 1953, when he left the *Herald Tribune* to become the CBC correspondent in Washington. He held this post until his retirement to Victoria, British Columbia, in 1968, when he became a Canadian citizen. In his unfinished autobiography – he died before completing it – Minifie made a brief mention of his citizenship, noting that during his forty-five years of living in Europe and the United States, "Canada always remained my country."[6]

As Washington correspondent for the *Herald Tribune* and then the CBC, Minifie witnessed a momentous period in American history, and his reporting covered mainly political, military, and foreign affairs. Over the Eisenhower years, he became increasingly disenchanted with US foreign policy, particularly American nuclear strategy, with its emphasis on massive retaliation. The tipping point in his path to neutralism was Ottawa's agreement with Washington to create the North American Air Defense Command (NORAD) in 1957–58, a move linking the Canadian and American air forces and deepening Canada's commitment to the defence of the US nuclear deterrent against an attack by Soviet bombers.[7] This development followed wartime cooperation that outlasted the Nazis as well as the joint construction and operation of a series of radar lines across Canada's north. In late 1958, Minifie denounced the NORAD agreement for committing Canada "automatically where American policy runs afoul of an ally of the Soviets" and even in situations where Ottawa was not consulted over US decision-making. In short, the Canada-US alliance threatened Canadian security and stripped Canada of its independence. His solution was for Canada to become a neutral buffer between the two superpowers, a move that would both strengthen the hand of Americans who rejected the "balance of terror" and "reduce the area from which the Soviets need fear a trans-polar bomber attack."[8] He developed this theme in a weekly column in the *Toronto Telegram,* in a variety of opinion journals, and in speaking engagements in Canadian cities. Neutrality, Minifie told the Montreal Women's Canadian Club, would mean Canada's return to the status of "an equal and autonomous nation" rather than "its present situation as a partially integrated component of the military defence system of a non-Commonwealth power."[9]

It was at one of these speaking events in spring 1959 that Minifie met Hugh Kane, an editor at McClelland and Stewart, who invited him to turn his statements on neutralism into a manuscript. In a subsequent book proposal, Minifie outlined his basic thesis: that the United States and the Soviet Union, locked into mutual assured destruction, had reached a dangerous impasse, and it was left to the middle powers to develop "alternatives" to war and to reduce points of friction between the two superpowers. For Canada, what was required was "a policy of positive neutrality," involving the renunciation of military alliances, more engagement with multilateral bodies such as the United Nations and the British Commonwealth, a shift in the Canadian military's focus toward greater participation in UN peacekeeping missions, and the protection of Canada's sovereignty against both the Soviet Union and the United States.[10] As the manuscript developed, these major points changed little, but the title evolved: Kane nixed Minifie's original title of *Prophet or Powder Monkey?*, suggesting that "prophet" failed to properly connote the alternate role that Canada might play in the world.[11] This move was a good one, for "prophet" smacked of the sanctimony for which Canadian foreign policy-makers were becoming infamous.

Published in March 1960, *Peacemaker or Powder-Monkey Canada's Role in a Revolutionary World* went through five printings and sold 12,066 copies by the end of 1962.[12] In a reflection of the nationalist zeitgeist then gripping English Canadians, Minifie challenged Canada's close economic, cultural, military, and political ties with the United States, expressing a fear that the country's independence was being "swiftly eroded by American military, economic and cultural domination." It was necessary, he counselled, to "free Canada from the taint of satellitism," which damaged its supposed "leadership of the middle and emergent powers" and formed "a serious handicap to the fashioning and preservation of peace." To free the country, he urged Ottawa to issue "a Declaration of Neutralism" followed by the dissolution both of NORAD and of the Canada-US alliance, and Canada's withdrawal from NATO. Next, Canada would enhance its role in the Commonwealth and the United Nations. The latter point was important, for Minifie sought not the "isolating neutralism" of Switzerland but the "positive neutralism" of India, allowing for a "closer identification with internationalism" than was possible through membership in the Western alliance. Judging that this posture would allow greater room for international negotiation, Minifie highlighted the recent experience of the Suez Crisis, which had "established Canadian diplomacy as an important weapon in the armoury of national defence." Yet Minifie was no pacifist. Pointing to Sweden, which maintained a relatively large and well-equipped military, he emphasized that to maintain neutrality and protect sovereignty, military spending was "essential." In this last regard, he even mused about the need for Canada to have the "optimum deterrent," nuclear-armed submarines, an intriguing suggestion glossed over by his fans within the nuclear disarmament movement. Much more palatable was his emphasis that a sizable and well-equipped military would mean that troops would be readily available for UN missions.[13] The basis of Minifie's positive neutralism, then, was neutrality in the Cold War but engagement with postwar internationalism.

Minifie was not alone in urging a neutralist position. Among the Canadian neutralists was Harry Pope, who retired as a major in the Canadian Army in 1959. A highly decorated veteran of the Second World War and Korea, Pope hailed from a distinguished line of civil servants and military officers, making his iconoclasm particularly notable. Over the course of the 1950s, Pope had reached the view, as he explained in the *Canadian Army Journal* shortly before resigning his commission, that Western military strategy had reached a point where there were "only two alternatives: defeat in a conventional war, death in a thermonuclear war." In his resignation letter, he decried the extent to which Canada's armed forces were organized in support of the "suicidal" policies of nuclear warfare, leaving little room for maneuver.[14] Freed from his commission, Pope advocated allowing the Soviets to use the Distant Early Warning (DEW) Line – the northernmost radar line across Canada's north – along with the Americans, thereby providing both nuclear armed neighbours with early warning of an attack. In the missile age, he noted, there was "no defense against nuclear weapons" and so the only recourse was for Canada's defence policy to "aim at preventing war."[15] Like Minifie, Pope held deep doubts about the stark military realities of the nuclear age.

Pope's radical notion of a bidirectional DEW Line flew in the face of the Liberal and Progressive Conservative positions on defence, so Pope signed on with the Co-operative Commonwealth Federation (CCF), becoming executive assistant to party leader Hazen Argue and then, following the creation of the NDP in 1961, to Tommy Douglas. He worked for the party until 1963, even running unsuccessfully as a candidate in the 1962 federal election against Defence Minister Douglas Harkness. Within the CCF/NDP fold, Pope voiced opposition to Canadian defence policy. In a brief authored on behalf of the Combined Universities Campaign for Nuclear Disarmament (CUCND), he emphasized that "defence against thermonuclear weapons is impossible" and advocated withdrawal from NORAD and NATO, two alliances centred on nuclear weapons. Instead, he sought for Canada a "policy of independence and non-alignment," explaining in *Cité Libre*, like Minifie, that by "*neutralisme*" he did not want isolationism but rather "*une role positif en faveur de la paix.*"[16]

Pope was not the only military figure who questioned postwar defence policy. In 1956, Major-General W.H.S. Macklin, recently retired as adjutant general of the Canadian Army, publicly critiqued the "folly" of Canada's strategy. In a display not simply of interservice rivalry – though it is worth noting that both he and Pope were army men – Macklin questioned the huge level of resources being devoted to air defence, observing that since these defences could never be 100 percent effective, the advantage lay with the attacker, and so nuclear strategy had created a situation where modern militaries "cannot buy security." "The great danger," he emphasized at the 1956 Couchiching Conference, was that so much money was being spent in support of nuclear strategy that there was no funding left for more conventional and flexible defence spending. In 1960, Macklin complained of money wasted on obsolete military equipment, emphasizing that Canada should "get out of this immoral and dangerous nuclear strategy, and get back control of our own air force now lost to the United States." A rejigging of spending away from nuclear defences, he joked grimly, would allow the government to "balance the budget and cut taxes while we waited for the nuclear bombs to fall."[17] Pope and Macklin were family friends, and the two men corresponded throughout the 1950s.[18] Moreover, soon after *Peacemaker*'s publication, Macklin commended Minifie: "I hope this book sells a lot of copies because I think it may do a lot of good." Although he rejected neutrality, Macklin agreed with Minifie on the need for a mobile military capable of rapid deployment under multilateral authority for peacekeeping purposes, adding, with considerable emphasis, that this force had to be "TOTALLY INDEPENDENT OF THE UNITED STATES." In response, Minifie explained that he had avoided the term "neutral" and had instead adopted "neutralism," a distinction that, he hoped, dissociated his views "from the notions of pacifism and isolationism which cling to neutrality."[19]

Another notion of neutralism was promulgated by University of Toronto historian Kenneth McNaught. In a series of articles beginning in 1959, he advanced ideas that he hoped would form the basis of a "socialist foreign policy" for Canada. They began from the premises that Canadian foreign policy was constrained by alignment with the United States, and that given the nuclear revolution, Canada was "obsolete as a military nation." McNaught complained of the vast sums spent "in an arms race which we cannot win and which gives us no added influence anywhere." A more fiscally and strategically prudent course, in his view, would be to divert attention from Canada's alliances toward making the United Nations and the Commonwealth into "genuine alternatives to a bi-polar world."[20] In subsequent articles, he underlined the importance of non-alignment as a rational response to "the suicidal arms race." Since Canada's military would accomplish little in an exchange of nuclear arms, the better course, in his view, would be withdrawal from NORAD and the alliance with the United States. As for NATO, Canada's involvement with Western European countries meant involvement with imperial powers, thereby impugning Canada's position with newly independent countries as well as with people still under colonial rule. Better, then, to divert money from the defence budget toward "a serious assault upon the problems of economic and racial inequality and in undeviating support of the principle of a United Nations police force."[21] McNaught's emphasis on peacekeeping and on development spending were key components of the foreign policy proposals of many of neutralism's advocates.

## CHALLENGE AND RESPONSE

Minifie had great timing. His book arrived just as the nuclear disarmament movement was ramping up and a wave of anti-American–tinged nationalism was sweeping over English Canadians, a response to perceived US cultural, economic, and military preponderance. *Peacemaker*, noted cultural critic Robert Fulford, was "'challenging' in the best sense" as it stirred up considerable debate.[22] Although dismissing Canadian neutralists as "misguided," the University of Toronto's James Eayrs admired their "sweeping assault on the very foundation of Canadian policy." A "fresh and fearless re-examination of fundamentals" was needed, he thought, and he himself made the role of gadfly the basis of his career and later became an advocate of Canadian neutralism.[23] In a letter to Minifie, novelist Hugh MacLennan, no fan of the United States, stressed his admiration of Minifie's "thinking and aims," even as he saw little prospect of their coming to fruition, mainly because the United States would not permit "a waverer on its flank." "I reject it," foreign affairs columnist Robert Reford informed Minifie of the latter's thesis. "More on emotional grounds than logic."[24] The emotional aspect was certainly important. On the one hand, historian Frederick Soward identified in the "yearning for neutralism" a "helpless feeling" among Canadians concerned by a "world dominated by superpowers equipped with dreadful and expensive weapons over which they have not the slightest control." On the other hand, John Holmes saw "logical arguments" favouring neutralism, but dismissed them as "too academic." In his view, such a policy failed to account for the fact that "Canadians do not feel or act neutral and could not sustain such a policy."[25]

As *Peacemaker*'s sales figures indicate, there was a ready audience for neutralism, though the book's readership included detractors. A newspaper editor who visited Washington informed Minifie that his work was "well-known to high State Department officials as well as to the Pentagon where a couple of copies have been passed around and read to death."[26] For those who welcomed Minifie's argument, the book, in the words of Frank Underhill, was "a brilliant tract for the times," that confronted that "monstrous immorality of the policies of mass extermination" underpinning nuclear strategy and a defence policy "dependent on some trigger-happy American air-force general."[27] Helen Tucker, of the Voice of Women peace group, told Minifie that *Peacemaker* "did so much" to inspire peace activists.[28] In addition to his fondness for whales and wolves, environmentalist Farley Mowat was a fierce anti-American nationalist, and in the inaugural issue of the CUCND journal *Our Generation Against Nuclear War*, he labelled Canada "Powder Monkey to Pentagon." In May 1960, Mowat founded the Committee for Canadian Independence, a group "dedicated to spread the Minifie doctrine." To Minifie, he explained that for many of the group's founders, *Peacemaker* was "the focal point, the crystallization element, in our own personal concern for and distress about the way things have been developing on the Canadian-US front."[29] Accomplishing little, the short-lived committee signified the popular reception of Minifie's work. After attending meetings of the Canadian Institute for International Affairs in Toronto and Hamilton, Burt Richardson, editor of the *Toronto Telegram*, reported to Minifie that "everyone, it seems, is reading your book and talking about it, so the seed is beginning to take root. I think you have set loose an idea that will greatly change Canadian thinking but whether Parliament would ever adopt a Neutrality Act must be doubtful."[30]

Given its message, *Peacemaker* caused considerable upset among those invested in the status quo. Prime Minister John Diefenbaker castigated Minifie as an "expatriate . . . for whom Canada wasn't good enough." In a wide-ranging discussion with Arnold Heeney, the Canadian ambassador to Washington, over the state of Canada-US relations, the prime minister reported a considerable level of correspondence from the public indicating anger at Canadian-American military cooperation and support for "Canadian 'neutralism' as a desirable policy." Emphasizing that he rejected Minifie's views, Diefenbaker lamented that "they had made an impression upon many Canadians, and were widely shared."[31] No doubt this factor injected a note of caution into the prime minister's thinking about whether Canada should take possession of tactical nuclear warheads, but Diefenbaker made it clear that he had no interest in neutralism. "I have no ear for the lullabies of the neutralist," he told a Kiwanis gathering in July 1961, adding that "Canada's record in two world wars, when freedom was at stake, gives the answer to the neutralist contentions."[32] Douglas Harkness, Diefenbaker's defence minister, issued several public rebukes of Canadian neutralism and the "rantings of some of the armchair strategists or, rather, escapists" who wished to bury their heads in the sand like "ostriches." With the development of nuclear weapons and a variety of delivery systems, he emphasized that no country could "stand on its own feet in defence: It has to have allies."[33] And while a supporter of nuclear disarmament efforts – the focus of Chapter 3 in this volume – Secretary of State for External Affairs Howard Green was careful to emphasize that while he was mindful of the reality of "missiles and hydrogen bombs," Canada was planning neither unilateral disarmament nor the pursuit of neutralism. Such a policy, he thought, "would be out of line with the character of the Canadian people" and would damage relations with countries with which Canada shared interests.[34]

American officials, too, took note of the book. President Eisenhower complained to General Charles Foulkes, the outgoing Chairman of the Chiefs of Staff – the head of Canada's military – that in response to this call for neutralism "Diefenbaker should jam the hard realities down the throats of his people." It "is most important," the president added, that Canada and the United States should "act as solid partners and both make some sacrifices."[35] A National Security Council report on difficulties in the Canada-US relationship highlighted "the much-publicized appearance of a recent book advocating a Canadian policy of neutralism," though it took solace in the fact that Canada's political parties and major newspapers had not endorsed the book's views.[36] As for the incoming Kennedy administration, in December 1960, Adlai Stevenson, soon to be the American UN ambassador, remarked to a Toronto audience that "the worst answer to the problems of U.S.-Canadian relations would be neutralism. For if the broader problem is as serious as he [Minifie] says it is – and it is – it will require not U.S.-Canadian drawing apart but the newer form of allied action which the new circumstances demand."[37] Officials in the Canadian embassy in Washington reported that Minifie's efforts to secure an interview with Dean Rusk, Kennedy's secretary of state, were hampered by State Department authorities mindful of his position "as the leader" of the neutralist movement.[38]

Within the defence and foreign policy community there was considerable opposition to Minifie's views. Freshly retired from Canada's military, Foulkes objected to *Peacemaker* on geographic grounds. Although admitting that neutralism was a "natural" response to MAD, he likened Canada and the United States to Siamese twins, emphasizing that "it is just as impossible to separate the defence of Canada from that of the United States as it would be to separate the Siamese twins and expect them to survive."[39] Former diplomat Peyton Lyon, then emerging as one of the keenest critics of the Sixties brand of anti-American Canadian nationalism, criticized various "Minifie-ite illusions," especially the notion that a neutralist path would automatically improve Canada's influence in the world, rather than damage its standing.[40] Like Diefenbaker and Green, R.J. Sutherland, an adviser to Canada's Department of National Defence, emphasized the cultural and historical affinities binding Canada to Western Europe and the United States, all of which "goes beyond any ordinary conception of common interests." This cultural factor meant that Canadians could not be neutral.[41] "There can be no neutrality for Canada," added the *Globe and Mail*'s Philip Deane, "nor even gestures that smack of neutralism," for there was no equivalence between the United States and the Soviet Union.[42] Offering an American perspective, and with input from the State Department, Melvin Conant of the Council on Foreign Relations published *The Long Polar Watch*, a justification of Canada's role in continental defence that included a dismissal of Minifie's book, "an amalgam of all types of resentments" appealing to readers in search of "an evasion of responsibilities for upholding freedom in the world."[43] If *Peacemaker* accomplished anything, then, it was to force those who supported extant Canadian foreign and defence policy to better define and defend their views.

## POLITICAL FALLOUT

Neutralism resounded with many Canadians, forcing the leadership of Canada's opposition parties to mount their own attacks on it. Liberal leader Lester Pearson, the former foreign minister who had played an important role in steering Canada into its postwar alliances, confronted neutralist sentiment within his own party. In a policy speech in early 1961, he contended that Canada could not contract out of geography, nor was there good reason to break with allied countries when the "aggressive desire of international communism to dominate other countries" remained a threat. The Cold War mattered to Pearson, and in a private memorandum he wrote that a neutral policy "would be to make no distinction between" the two superpowers.[44] In addition to defending the foreign policy he had helped to craft, Pearson sought to beat back neutralist opinion within the Liberal Party. As Jack Cunningham notes in Chapter 5 of this volume, the Liberals sparred over Canada's stance toward nuclear weapons.

At the January 1961 Liberal policy conference, what the press described as a "well-organized group of quasi-neutralists" sought to amend a resolution on Canadian defence policy to demand an end to the country's participation in NATO and NORAD. The objection to NATO membership found little support, but in the meeting of the committee on defence policy, party elders C.M. Drury, Paul Hellyer, and Walter Gordon pushed back against more vigorous calls for Canada to quit NORAD. Instead, they promoted a compromise advanced by Pearson: under a Liberal government, Canada would remain within NORAD but would take part only in the identification – not interception – of Soviet aircraft. The policy was accepted during a last-minute policy session, an effort by the party leadership to limit the time available for neutralists to criticize the status quo. Moreover, the Liberals resolved "not [to] acquire nuclear weapons independently or jointly with U.S.-Canadian control" and to devote more attention to peacekeeping.[45] Soon after the convention Hellyer, the Liberal defence critic, offered the assurance that "this is no time for pacifism or neutralism." Yet to some observers, such as American journalist Stewart

Alsop, it seemed as if "Mike Pearson, once accounted a friend of the US, is now a leading Yankee-baiter, and the whole Liberal party is tending to something that smells very much like neutralism." To an extent, US diplomats agreed with this assessment. Ambassador Livingston Merchant was largely cheered by the results of the Liberal convention. Even so, he noted that Pearson and other Liberals had become "genuinely concerned that anti-Americanism and talk of neutralism – talk which they positively have encouraged – was going so far as seriously to endanger Canadian national interests."[46]

Minifie's influence was not confined to the Liberals. In early 1961, CCF leader Hazen Argue – taking a page from Harry Pope, his executive assistant – contended that in a bid to reduce tension between the nuclear powers, Canada could "become a buffer" between the superpowers by becoming "militarily independent." He also urged the withdrawal of Canada from NATO and the building up of the neutralist bloc in the UN in order to mediate differences between the United States and the Soviet Union.[47] Argue's position was party policy, for although the CCF had supported – somewhat reluctantly – NATO's creation in 1949, in May 1960 the party's National Council had resolved that "Canada's contribution to world peace requires a radical reappraisal of her defence role," involving pulling out of the Atlantic alliance and ending Canada-US military cooperation. At the party's August convention, the rank and file members endorsed this view as well as a resolution calling on the CCF to "take the lead in crystallizing a widespread demand for Canadian Neutrality."[48]

It is little surprise that neutralism resounded with leftists. The problem, however, was that at its 1960 convention, the CCF had also endorsed a merger with the Canadian Labour Congress (CLC) to form what eventually became the New Democratic Party. Strongly anti-communist, the CLC rejected neutralism. "For reasons geographic, economic and historical," the CLC affirmed in its 1961 annual submission to the federal government, "Canada must work in concert with those nations which share her outlook and interests" and should maintain "an effective military establishment which can be useful to herself, to her allies and the United Nations."[49] Furthermore, there were CCF members who opposed the call for neutralism, among them Andrew Brewin, a human rights lawyer who emerged as an influential voice largely supportive of the foreign and defence policy status quo. Neutralists, he contended, suffered from "an immature refusal to face facts," namely, the threat posed by the Soviet Union, and wanted "a shuffling off of responsibility" for collective security. In a debate with Kenneth McNaught on neutralism, Brewin took aim at Minifie and his "deceptive and false" view that cooperating with allied governments ipso facto implied Canadian subservience. Canada, he added, was tied to the United States by geography, a fact that had to be accounted for in its policies.[50]

Through lobbying by Brewin and pressure from the labour wing, at its founding convention in August 1961, and after considerable debate on the issue, the NDP opted, by a four-to-one margin, to stay in NATO. Tommy Douglas, the new party leader, had spoken in favour of the alliance as a means of making the socialists more palatable to voters.[51] Writing to Peyton Lyon soon after, Brewin emphasized the importance of the new party's stance, revealing that while he would have preferred a more glowing endorsement of NATO, "it was quite clear from the debate that the ideas propounded by Mr. Minifee [sic] and Professor McNaught, if I may join two very dissimilar writers . . . have been widely circulated and have attracted a lot of sympathy."[52] Even Pope accepted NATO membership – he opposed participation in NORAD – admitting that it was the price the NDP had to pay to prove to Canadians that the party was not "soft on communism." Harping on the issue, he emphasized, "will doom us to a perpetual inconsequential role in Canada's public life."[53] It was not until 1969 that the NDP rejected NATO membership.

By that point, neutralist ideas were experiencing a renaissance in the welter of the Sixties. Beyond the anti-war activist crowd, there were increasing calls for Minifie-esque policies from within Progressive Conservative and Liberal circles. The Tories' 1967 policy conference saw "spirited debate" over withdrawal from NATO, calls for Canada to "make every effort to strengthen UN peacekeeping and peacemaking capability," and "semantic problems" that prevented any resolution on defence policy from being passed. Addressing the delegates, Dalton Camp, the party's national president and an outspoken Red Tory, referred to the "open secret" of NORAD's "obsolescence" and urged greater involvement in peacekeeping operations. As for NATO, he affirmed that "the solutions of Europe's problems are going to be found by Europeans." In a Toronto speech several months later, Camp stopped short of calling for withdrawal from NATO or NORAD, where Canada's "psychological presence" was helpful. Even so, he stressed that Canadians were "experts in doing in today's world and in the military sense, things that no longer need doing. There is no evidence that our military contribution is now, or can be, significant."[54]

As for the Liberals, several members of the party's left wing gathered at the 1969 "Thinkers" Conference, where they took turns savaging Canada's alliances and emphasizing the need to focus on peacekeeping. "Non-aligned," speculated Lewis Hertzman, "Canada could attempt with some prospect of success to keep itself in a position to talk to all nations, and to help them to talk to each other." For Stephen Clarkson, it was vital to address the threat of "nuclear holocaust" and that meant promoting détente and dealing with "sporadic local wars" that threatened to involve the super-powers; non-alignment would make these tasks easier. And Mel Hurtig judged "that Canada's rejection of a non-aligned role defeats our intended and stated purpose of international de-escalation of tension, reduction of the nuclear balance of terror and the achievement of détente."[55] These figures were representative of the New Nationalists who emerged in the Sixties to challenge the close ties between Canada and the United States and to call for an independent foreign policy.[56] Not all nationalists were neutralists, however. Walter Gordon, an arch economic nationalist, advocated for a defence policy that included peacekeeping, a "useful contribution to NORAD," and a continued if smaller commitment to NATO, even though, as he admitted, "the overwhelming power of nuclear missiles" made Canada's military "somewhat irrelevant."[57]

Oddly, Pearson, as prime minister, seems to have hewed close to the neutralist line on certain points. Not only did he seek to increase aid and development spending but he advocated the creation of a permanent UN peacekeeping force. Moreover, his government's 1964 White Paper on Defence sought in part to create a more mobile military capable of under-taking peacekeeping missions. Pearson toyed with not renewing the NORAD agreement in 1967, and he voiced support for reducing if not withdrawing Canada's military forces deployed to Western Europe under NATO auspices, largely because, with détente leading to warmer East-West relations and with Europe now wealthy and recovered from the Second World War, there was less need for a Canadian military commitment. "We may have to consider," he told an Ottawa audience in February 1965, "new arrangements by which Europe takes responsibility for the security of one side of the Atlantic, North America for the other, with interlocking cooperative arrangements for mutual assistance against attack."[58] Here, however, he was careful to note that he was not neutral, and neither was Canada.

Similar currents led Pearson's successor, Pierre Trudeau, to mull pulling out of NATO in 1968–69. When he arrived in Ottawa that summer, Charles Ritchie, the Canadian high commissioner in London, found the climate "very anti-NATO. There is a great deal of talk of neutrality for Canada based on the Swedish model." As Ritchie recorded, Marcel Cadieux, the under-secretary of state, had told Mitchell Sharp, the new secretary of state for external affairs, that there was "'no expert on neutrality' in the Department."[59] The ensuing fight pitted Sharp and other advocates of the status quo against other ministers such as Eric Kierans, who, in January 1969, mused publicly about NATO withdrawal. A report that formed the basis of the Trudeau government's defence policy rejected non-alignment on the grounds that it would be prohibitively expensive – as with Sweden, huge outlays on defence would be required to enforce Canadian sovereignty – and would diminish Canada's influence not only with the United States and European powers but also with Third World countries, which valued Canada as a bridge to the West. Non-alignment, the report concluded, "would leave the country in a state of semi-isolation in North America."[60] Ultimately, the Trudeau government halved Canada's military commitment in Europe but remained in NATO and in NORAD. Among those who influenced Trudeau in questioning Canadian foreign policy were Clarkson and other members of the "strategic counterculture" that emerged in the Sixties. Questioning the status quo on the "NATO-NORAD Question," these figures took the Minifie-esque position of urging "a foreign policy of moral commitment and military nonalignment."[61]

## CONCLUSIONS

In 1964, James Minifie published a second book on foreign policy, *Open at the Top: Reflections on United States–Canada Relations*. Rehashing much of *Peacemaker,* the book sold far fewer copies than its predecessor and caused much less of a stir.[62] It is tempting to think that neutralism was past its sell-by date, but that same year, John Holmes thought the topic important enough to address it in public comments on the wider ramifications of Canada-US relations. Neutralism remained "an alternative in the back of the Canadian mind," and was not "illogical or unworthy." What mattered, he thought, was that Canadians were "an unneutral people" who were "historically and intellectually allied" with Western Europe and the United States.[63] That indeed, was the nub of the issue, even as a sizable number of Canadians looked for alternatives to a strategic situation that seemingly left Canada with little independence. In a sign of the times, even a young Jack Granatstein was caught up in the neutralist spirit, speculating in 1970 that were Canada to pursue neutralism, it would lead other NATO and Warsaw Pact members to follow suit. "If Canada can persuade others to follow her example," he gushed, "we could conceivably be on the threshold of a golden era in foreign policy."[64]

That Canadian advocates of neutralism had such high hopes should not come as a surprise. Their ideas, aired most prominently by Minifie, were a direct counterpoise to the grim realities of the nuclear age. Peacekeeping had the same lofty promise, and it is no coincidence that Minifie juxtaposed powdermonkey and peacemaker. Indeed, it is important to keep in mind that *Peacemaker* appeared less than four years after the Suez Crisis, and so it arrived in print just as growing numbers of Canadians, dissatisfied with the Cold War status quo surrounding NATO and the Canada-US alliance, were looking for new outlets for internationalism. In the end, whether through non-alignment or peacekeeping, these Canadian neutralists sought a way out of the straitjacket of a foreign and defence policy bound to American nuclear deterrence.

# NOTES

For his helpful comments on a draft of this paper, I thank Jack Granatstein. My thanks, too, to the editors, to the reviewers, and to my fellow participants at the Canada's Nuclear Histories symposium.

1   Robert Bothwell, *The Big Chill: Canada and the Cold War* (Toronto: Irwin Publishing, 1998), xii.
2   Briefing book: "Africa, Air Pollution, Airlift, Arab States and U.S. Policy, B-70 Bomber, Belgian Congo, Budget Policies, Canada, Child Welfare, Civil Defense, Communist China and Formosa, Conflict of Interest, Conventional Weapons and Non-Nuclear Deterrence," Pre-Presidential Papers, Presidential Campaign Files, 1960, box 993, John

F. Kennedy Presidential Library and Museum (JFKPL); Transcript, "Close-up," March 14, 1961, Livingston Merchant Papers, box 19, folder "Speeches, Statements, Testimony, 1961," Seeley Mudd Manuscript Library, Princeton University.

3  "Peacemaker or Ammunition Bearer?" *Izvestia,* January 18, 1968, in *Current Digest of the Soviet Press* 20, 3 (1968): 20–21.

4  Peter Lyon, "Neutrality and the Emergence of the Concept of Neutralism," *Review of Politics* 22 (1960): 255–68; Michael Brecher, "Neutralism: An Analysis," *International Journal* 17 (1962): 224–36. Historians have accorded neutralism and non-alignment increasing attention: "Beyond and between the Cold War Blocs," *International History Review* 37, special issue (2015): 901–1013; Sandra Bott, Jussi M. Hanhimäki, Janick Marina Schaufelbuehl, Marco Wyss, eds., *Neutrality and Neutralism in the Global Cold War: Between or within the Blocs?* (Abingdon, UK: Routledge, 2015); Natasa Mišković, Harald Fischer-Tiné, and Nada Boškovska, eds., *The Non-Aligned Movement and the Cold War: Delhi-Bandung-Belgrade* (Abingdon, UK: Routledge, 2014).

5  Erika Simpson, *NATO and the Bomb: Canadian Defenders Confront Critics* (Montreal and Kingston: McGill-Queen's University Press, 2001), 159; Jamie Glazov, *Canadian Policy toward Khrushchev's Soviet Union* (Montreal and Kingston: McGill-Queen's University Press, 2002), xix; Andrew Richter, *Avoiding Armageddon: Canadian Military Strategy and Nuclear Weapons, 1950–63* (Vancouver: UBC Press, 2002), 175n43; Robert Teigrob, *Living with War: Twentieth-Century Conflict in Canadian and American History and Memory* (Toronto: University of Toronto Press, 2016), 129; Matthew Trudgen and Joel Sokolsky, "The Canadian Strategic Debate of the Early 1960s," *International Journal* 67 (2012): 183–94.

6  James M. Minifie, *Expatriate* (Toronto: Macmillan, 1976), 1.

7  NORAD was renamed North American Aerospace Defense Command in 1981.

8  James M. Minifie, "Neutrality for Canada?" *Canadian Commentator,* October 1958.

9  "Canada Urged Get Out of NORAD," *Montreal Gazette,* March 19, 1959.

10  Minifie to Hugh Kane, July 2, 1959, McClelland and Stewart Fonds (M&S), series A, box 44, McMaster University Archives [MUA].

11  Minifie to Kane, November 16, 1959, and Kane to Minifie, November 24, 1959, James Minifie Fonds, vol. 3, file "Correspondence re Peacemaker or Powder-Monkey," Library and Archives Canada (LAC).

12  Memo from Hugh Kane, n.d., M&S, file BA Dk1 BSB-47, MUA.

13  James M. Minifie, *Peacemaker or Powder-Monkey Canada's Role in a Revolutionary World* (Toronto: McClelland and Stewart, 1960), 4–5, 164–65, 78, 87.

14  W.H. Pope, "Problems of Future War," *Canadian Army Journal* (April 1959): 56; W.H. Pope, *Leading from the Front: The War Memoirs of Harry Pope* (Waterloo, ON: Laurier Centre for Military, Strategic, and Disarmament Studies, 2002), 234. Pope's paper was reprinted in the *Australian Army Journal* 126 (1959): 17–36, and was read by Basil Liddell Hart: Basil Liddell Hart Papers, 15/5/289, Liddell Hart Military Archives, King's College London.

15  W.H. Pope, "Let the Russians Use the DEW Line," *Maclean's,* December 5, 1959.

16  W.H. Pope, *Let Canada Lead: A New Defence Policy* (Montreal: CUCND, 1961); W.H. Pope, "Le Canada et le Neutralisme," *Cité Libre* (March 1961).

17  W.H.S. Macklin, "The Costly Folly of Our Defense Policy," *Maclean's,* February 18, 1956; W.H.S. Macklin, "Canadian Defence Policies," in *Texts of Addresses Delivered at the 25th Annual Couchiching Conference, 1956* (Toronto: Canadian Institute on Public Affairs, 1956), 76, 77; W.H.S. Macklin to the Editor, *Globe and Mail,* March 30, 1960.

18  J.L. Granatstein, *The Generals: The Canadian Army's Senior Commanders in the Second World War* (Toronto: Stoddart, 1993), 216; Pope, *Leading from the Front,* 224.

19  Macklin to Minifie, April 11, 1960, and Minifie to Macklin, April 18, 1960, Minifie Fonds, vol. 3, file "Correspondence re Peacemaker or Powder-Monkey," LAC.

20  Kenneth McNaught, "The Dilemma of Our Defense Policy," *Maclean's,* March 28, 1959; Kenneth McNaught, "Canada: An Opportunity for Leadership," *Saturday Night,* October 10, 1959; Kenneth McNaught, "Foreign Policy: The Search for Status," *Saturday Night,* August 29, 1959.

21  F. Andrew Brewin and Kenneth McNaught, *Debate on Defence* (Toronto: Woodsworth Memorial Foundation, 1960); Kenneth McNaught, "Canada Must Get Out of the Arms Race," *Saturday Night,* June 10, 1961.

22  Robert Fulford, "A Radical Challenge for Canada," *Toronto Star,* March 28, 1960.

23  James Eayrs, "Canadian-American Relations, 1939–1960," in *Second Seminar on Canadian-American Relations at Assumption University* (Windsor, ON: Assumption University Press, 1960), 28, 29.

24  MacLennan to Minifie, December 21, 1960, and Reford to Minifie, April 22, 1960, Minifie Fonds, vol. 3, file "Correspondence re Peacemaker or Powder-Monkey," LAC.

25  F.H. Soward, "On Becoming and Being a Middle Power: The Canadian Experience," *Pacific Historical Review* 32 (1963): 125; John W. Holmes, "The Unequal Alliance: Canada and the United States," in *Fourth Seminar on Canadian-American Relations at Assumption University* (Windsor, ON: Assumption University Press, 1962), 257.

26  Minifie to McClelland, June 24, 1960, M&S, series A, box 44, MUA.

27  Frank Underhill, "Review of *Peacemaker or Powder-Monkey*" *International Journal* 15 (1960): 249–50.

28  Tucker to Minifie, January 23, 1962, Minifie Fonds, vol. 2, file "CBC Correspondence and Memoranda," LAC.

29  Farley Mowat, "Powder Monkey to Pentagon: Canada Joins the Club," *Our Generation against Nuclear War* 1, 1 (1961): 10–14; Pierre Berton, "Farley Mowat and the New Idealism," *Toronto Star,* June 14, 1960; Harry Allen, "Free-Canada Body Wants Neutrality," *Toronto Telegram,* May 21, 1960; Mowat to Minifie, May 12, 1960, Minifie Fonds, vol. 3, file "Correspondence re Peacemaker or Powder-Monkey," LAC.

30  Richardson to Minifie, April 4, 1960, Minifie Fonds, vol. 2, file "CBC Correspondence and Memoranda," LAC.

31  Heeney to file, "Memorandum of Conversations with the Prime Minister in Ottawa, Tuesday, August 30, 1960, and Wednesday, August 31, 1960," n.d., Arnold Heeney Fonds, vol. 1, file 15, LAC.

32  Canada, Department of External Affairs (DEA), *Statements and Speeches,* 61/7, July 3, 1961.

33  "Neutralists Are Likened to Ostriches," *Globe and Mail,* February 11, 1961; John Bird, "New Defence Chief 'a Man of Action,'" *Toronto Star,* October 21, 1960; *House of Commons Debates,* 24th Parliament, 4th Session, vol. 2, January 31, 1961, 1570.

34 Speech by Hon. Howard Green on *The Nation's Business*, April 21, 1960, Howard Green Fonds, vol. 12, LAC.

35 Memorandum of Conference with the President, May 9, 1960, White House, Office of the Staff Secretary, International series, box 2, folder Canada (2), Dwight D. Eisenhower Presidential Library and Museum (DDEL).

36 James Lay, "Memorandum for the National Security Council," May 24, 1960, and attached paper, "Certain Aspects of United States Politico-Military Relationships with Canada," White House, Office of the National Security Advisor, NSC series, Policy Papers, box 26, folder NSC 5822, DDEL.

37 USIS Text, December 3, 1960, RG 25, vol. 5089, file 4901-40, pt. 13, LAC.

38 Farquharson to Robertson, March 30, 1961, A.E. Ritchie Fonds, vol. 2, file "Correspondence with Norman Robertson – 'F,'" LAC.

39 Charles Foulkes, "The Defence Dilemma Facing Canada," *Canadian Commentator*, May 1961; Charles Foulkes, "Canadian Defence Policy in a Nuclear Age," *Behind the Headlines*, May 1961, 10.

40 Peyton V. Lyon, "The Truth about U.S.-Canadian Relations," *Canadian Commentator*, June 1961.

41 R.J. Sutherland, "Canada's Long Term Strategic Situation," *International Journal* 17 (1962): 205.

42 Philip Deane, "Alliances Shows the Strains of Age," *Globe and Mail*, November 7, 1960.

43 Melvin Conant, *The Long Polar Watch: Canada and the Defense of North America* (New York: Harper, 1962), 114.

44 "Defence of Peace," Address to the Annual Banquet of the Ontario Secondary School Teachers' Federation, January 21, 1961, Lester Pearson Fonds, series N6, vol. 42, file "Nuclear Defence," LAC; Lester Pearson, Memorandum Re. Neutralism in the Cold War, February 2, 1960, Lester Pearson Fonds, series N2, vol. 88, file "Neutralism," LAC.

45 D.C. Thomson, "Liberals Settle for the Middle Road," *Saturday Night*, February 4, 1961; Bruce Macdonald, "A Creep, Not a Leap, to the Left for the Liberals," *Globe and Mail*, January 13, 1961; National Liberal Rally Proceedings, January 11–13, 1961, Paul Hellyer Fonds, vol. 51, file "Liberal Proceedings," LAC; Summary of Liberal Resolutions at the National Rally 1961, Walter Gordon Fonds, vol. 13, folder 15, LAC.

46 *House of Commons Debates*, 24th Parliament, 4th Session, vol. 2, January 31, 1961, 1600; Alsop to Sommers, February 2, 1961, Stewart Alsop Papers, box 30, folder 5, Library of Congress; Merchant to White, April 4, 1961, RG 59, Bureau of European Affairs, Office of British Commonwealth and Northern European Affairs, Alpha-Numeric Files Relating to Canadian Affairs, box 1, folder "Nationalism, Neutralism and Anti-Americanism, 1960–1962," US National Archives and Records Administration (NARA).

47 Hazen Argue, "The CCF and Its Pursuit of Peace," *Canadian Commentator*, April 1961.

48 Bruce Macdonald, "Scrap Norad, Bomarc CCF Council Urges," *Toronto Star*, May 17, 1960; Panel Reports, National Convention, 1960, Tommy Douglas Fonds, vol. 1, file "National Convention," LAC; Report, Sixteenth National Convention, August 9–11, 1960, CCF Fonds, vol. 372, file "National Council CCF," LAC.

49 "CLC Opposes Neutralism," *Canadian Labour*, February 1961.

50 F. Andrew Brewin, "Canada Foreign Policy: The Need for Maturity," *Canadian Forum*, February 1961; Brewin and McNaught, *Debate on Defence*.

51  "New Party Decides Stay in NATO, 4 to 1," *Toronto Star*, August 4, 1961; "Convention Ponders NATO Abandonment," *Globe and Mail*, August 4, 1961; "Douglas Averts A-Arms, NATO Splits," *Toronto Telegram*, August 4, 1961.

52  Brewin to Lyon, August 21, 1961, F. Andrew Brewin Fonds, vol. 8, file 17, LAC.

53  W.H. Pope, "NATO after Nassau," January 9, 1963, Tommy Douglas Fonds, vol. 125, file "External Affairs and National Defence," LAC.

54  "Canada and the World" Policy Session and "Address by Dalton Camp," in Progressive Conservative Policy Advisory Conference, *Report on the Montmorency Conference*, August 7–10, 1967 (Progressive Conservative Party of Canada, 1967); "Keep Military Alliances but Be a Peacekeeper, Camp Urges Canada," *Globe and Mail*, November 7, 1967.

55  Lewis Hertzman, "Model for a New Course in Canadian Foreign Policy"; Stephen Clarkson, "Canada's Role in Long-Term Perspective"; and Mel Hurtig, "Alternatives in Canada Foreign and Defence Policy," in Liberal Party Conference, November 21–23, 1969, Part II, *Task Force on International Relations* (Liberal Party of Canada, 1969).

56  Stephen Clarkson, ed., *An Independent Foreign Policy for Canada?* (Toronto: McClelland and Stewart, 1968); Lewis Hertzman, John Warnock, and Thomas Hockin, *Alliances and Illusions: Canada and the NATO-NORAD Question* (Edmonton: Hurtig, 1969); Thomas Axworthy, "Soldiers without Enemies: A Political Analysis of Canadian Defence Policy, 1945–1975" (PhD diss., Queen's University, 1978).

57  Walter Gordon, *A Choice for Canada: Independence or Colonial Status* (Toronto: McClelland and Stewart, 1966), 13.

58  DEA, *Statements and Speeches*, 65/3, February 10, 1965; Greg Donaghy, "Domesticating NATO: Canada and the North Atlantic Alliance, 1963–68," *International Journal* 52 (1997): 445–63.

59  Charles Ritchie, *Undiplomatic Diaries, 1937–1971* (Toronto: McClelland and Stewart, 2008), 530.

60  Special Task Force on Europe, "Canada and Europe: Report of the Special Task Force on Europe," February 1969, Cabinet Document 158–69, RG 2, vol. 6342, LAC.

61  Louis Hertzman, "Canada and the North Atlantic Treaty Organization," in Hertzman, Warnock, and Hockin, *Alliances and Illusions*, 5; Mary Halloran, "'A Planned and Phased Reduction': The Trudeau Government and the NATO Compromise, 1968–1969," in *Transatlantic Relations at Stake: Aspects of NATO, 1956–1972*, ed. Christian Nuenlist and Anna Locher (Zurich: Center for Security Studies and Conflict Research, 2006), 125–43; Michel Fortmann and Martin Larose, "An Emerging Strategic Counterculture? Pierre Elliott Trudeau, Canadian Intellectuals and the Revision of Liberal Defence Policy Concerning NATO (1968–1969)," *International Journal* 59 (2004): 537–56; J.L. Granatstein and Robert Bothwell, *Pirouette: Pierre Trudeau and Canadian Foreign Policy* (Toronto: University of Toronto Press, 1990).

62  James M. Minifie, *Open at the Top: Reflections on United States–Canada Relations* (Toronto: McClelland and Stewart, 1964).

63  John W. Holmes, "The Relationship in Alliance and in World Affairs," in *The United States and Canada* (Englewood Cliffs, NJ: Prentice Hall, 1964), 114–15.

64  J.L. Granatstein, "A World without War?" in *Visions 2020*, ed. Stephen Clarkson (Edmonton: Hurtig, 1970), 45.

# CHAPTER 5

# THE ROAD TO SCARBOROUGH
## Lester Pearson and Nuclear Weapons, 1954–63
### Jack Cunningham

On Saturday, January 12, 1963, Canada's leader of the Opposition, Lester Pearson, stood before a lunchtime meeting of the York-Scarborough Liberal Association and announced a change in the Liberal Party's defence policy. Public and press attention had focused on the inability or unwillingness of John Diefenbaker's Progressive Conservative government to follow through on commitments to accept nuclear weapons for the Canadian military, and on its seeming reluctance to support the United States during the recent Cuban Missile Crisis. The question confronting Pearson's Liberals was whether they would abandon their previous opposition to equipping the Canadian forces in NATO and NORAD with nuclear weapons and honour the commitments Diefenbaker had made. Addressing his Scarborough audience, Pearson announced that they would, while seeking to negotiate future non-nuclear roles. "Until the present role is changed," he concluded, "a new Liberal government would put Canada's armed services in the position to discharge fully commitments undertaken for Canada by its predecessor."[1] A little less than a month later, Diefenbaker's government lost two no-confidence motions in the House of Commons, precipitating a general election that was held on April 8. Pearson and the Liberals won a minority government that was dependent upon the support of the left-wing New Democratic Party to pass legislation.

Past accounts of Pearson's Scarborough speech primarily assess it within the context of his electoral contest with Diefenbaker. Pearson himself denied in his memoirs that his shift in stance was prompted by political considerations, though he later remarked to political scientist (and Diefenbaker biographer) Denis Smith that it was only with the Scarborough speech "that I really became a politician."[2] While Pearson was attentive to electoral factors, his thinking and decision-making on the nuclear question were sophisticated. His thinking reflected important continuities, notably a preoccupation with the question of nuclear control and how a decision to use the weapons would be made. He consistently approached the possession of such weapons as a matter of prudence rather than one of morality, but he reserved the right to change tack if circumstances changed.

## NUCLEAR DISCONTENTS

Pearson's first major public comment on nuclear strategy and questions of control came in 1954. During the Korean War (1950–53), the Truman administration (despite one instance of public musing by the president about their availability for use) effectively ruled out resort to atomic arms. It seemed impossible to identify suitable targets, to employ nuclear weapons without escalating the conflict to a wider war, or to release the weapons without enraging or demoralizing key allies. Indeed, nuclear arms seemed useless for any purpose other than deterring nuclear attack. After the 1952 election, the incoming Eisenhower administration, particularly the new secretary of state, John Foster Dulles, sought to increase the political utility of nuclear weapons by normalizing their use to some degree and making them available as tools of compulsion in limited conflicts. In a January 12, 1954, speech to the Council on Foreign Relations, Dulles warned that taking nuclear weapons off the table emboldened aggressors to exploit local superiority and attack where it might prove decisive. "The way to deter aggression," he concluded "is for the free community to be willing and able to respond vigorously at places and with means of its own choosing."[3] Dulles' speech laid out the administration's nuclear strategy: the doctrine of massive retaliation.

Two months later, Pearson, then secretary of state for external affairs in Louis St. Laurent's government, delivered his response at the National Press Club in Washington. He conceded that "this new defence concept . . . may turn out to be the best deterrent against aggression," but it made diplomacy more important, not only to reduce East-West tensions but also to harmonize the Western allies' position "so that 'our choosing' will mean an agreed collective decision, without prejudicing speedy and effective action in an emergency."[4]

While Pearson's warning seems to have made little impact among Eisenhower's inner circle, the new administration found atomic realities as intractable as its predecessor. Eisenhower and Dulles found it difficult to translate nuclear superiority into diplomatic leverage during the administration's first years, as nuclear weapons did little to bring about an end to the Korean War or shape events in Indochina, particularly as the French forces were besieged at Dien Bien Phu in 1954.[5] Eisenhower seems to have been genuinely ambivalent about the potential use of nuclear weapons, occasionally thinking aloud about their utility to end localized aggression but rarely seriously considering their employment.[6] By the late 1950s, massive retaliation came under fire, as critics dismissed the idea that the United States would resort to strategic nuclear weapons in response to a local crisis halfway around the globe. In various formulations, they called for more flexible options to respond, such as stronger conventional forces and tactical nuclear weapons.[7]

Pearson was to echo some of the same themes in his 1958 William Clayton Lectures at the Fletcher School of Law and Diplomacy at Tufts University in Massachusetts, along with a plea for greater consultation within NATO regarding nuclear and non-nuclear strategy. As long as NATO conventional forces were dramatically inferior to those of the Eastern Bloc, he lamented, "the alternative is to rely excessively on those unlimited weapons, such as H-bombs, unsuitable for defense except in one contingency and, in any case, completely outside collective control."[8] Reviewing the published lectures, Senator John F. Kennedy noted that Pearson "argues convincingly that we have shuttered diplomacy . . . 'coalition diplomacy' and collective action in NATO require not merely policy clearance and routine exchange of views but the machinery for policy-making."[9]

Following Diefenbaker's election victory of 1957, Pearson, now leader of the Opposition, criticized the new government's handling of the NORAD agreement. It had been haphazardly concluded, Pearson charged, without proper cabinet consultation or preparation of orders-in-council before Canadian forces were placed under US command.[10] In a 1959 defence debate, he criticized the Diefenbaker government for not encouraging the kind of far-reaching debate that had occurred in both the United States and Britain following the launch of the Soviet satellite Sputnik. He also took the Conservatives to task for scrapping production of the CF-105 Avro Arrow interceptor, as well as the decision to acquire Lockheed Starfighters, Bomarc B missiles, and the SAGE system from the United States. Defensive systems, he argued, would do little against intercontinental ballistic missiles (ICBMs).[11] As Pearson wrote to his son Geoffrey, a Foreign Service Officer stationed in Paris, "nine CF 100 squadrons don't make any sense to me as a symbol of Canadian power and prestige or as protection for Canadian cities or, indeed for anything else."[12]

The two discussed ideas for collective control of NATO nuclear weapons. Placing nuclear weapons under collective control was, the younger Pearson wrote, "the way NATO thinking is now moving." Secretary General Paul-Henri Spaak had already suggested that NATO's nuclear powers "pool" control of nuclear armaments while building up their conventional capabilities.[13] In late 1960, Pearson met Spaak during a visit to Europe. Their meeting included a discussion of Spaak's concept of a "nuclear pool."[14] Already, Pearson's thinking reflected a sense of skepticism about air defences along with an acute interest in shared control of nuclear weapons.

## KINGSTON AND AFTER

After the Liberals' twin defeats in the 1957 and 1958 elections, Pearson took the risky step of reshaping the party's policy platform. He instigated a "thinkers' conference" at Kingston in September 1960, followed by a National Liberal Rally in January 1961, aimed at developing an unusually activist and detailed policy platform for a future Pearson government. To do so, he turned to Tom Kent, formerly of the *Manchester Guardian* and *The Economist,* and more recently editor of the *Winnipeg Free Press,* and Walter Gordon of the accounting firm Clarkson Gordon. The result was a marked shift to the left.[15] The Kingston Conference focused mainly on domestic policy, and in his speech to the conference banquet Pearson stressed domestic reforms, managing only a few words about defence and foreign affairs. "Here again," he remarked, "new and basic thinking is essential – both in relation to national policy and international collaboration." With the advent of the ICBM and in the aftermath of Sputnik, "everything changed, especially for smaller powers. Canadian policy has not changed with it – and there is no sign that those responsible see any need for change."[16] The main presentation on defence was a speech by James Eayrs, a political science professor at the University of Toronto. Eayrs echoed Pearson's earlier calls for greater consultation regarding the disposition of NATO's nuclear arms, speaking out in favour of a committee composed of NATO's current nuclear powers and rotating membership for the non-nuclear ones that would consult with NATO's Supreme Allied Commander on the use of nuclear weapons.[17]

Shortly after the Kingston Conference, a memorandum by Toronto banker R.M. MacIntosh noted that both Eayrs and economist Harry Johnson, whose remarks called for closer economic integration with the United States, had sounded strong pro-American notes, somewhat at odds with the "anti-U.S. sentiment which is gaining such currency in Canada." "The *sentiment* for disengagement from the United States," MacIntosh noted, "is a political fact of importance, and by itself would seem to preclude a positive program directed towards complete defence integration or complete economic integration."[18]

Anti-American impulses shaped the Liberals' rally in January 1961. At a policy session on January 11, some delegates agitated for discussion of foreign policy and defence in order to pass a resolution calling for Canadian withdrawal from NORAD. Gordon, who was presiding over the rally, refused on the grounds that most Policy Committee members were absent. He did call a session for later in the afternoon, which adjourned for the rally banquet and reconvened afterwards, "with everybody talking in their sleep about 11:30 p.m." The leadership's preferred resolutions were ultimately adopted, though only after a heated debate.[19]

The defence resolution rejected the acquisition or manufacture by Canada of nuclear weapons under Canadian control or joint control with the United States. "Membership in the nuclear club," the resolution asserted, "should not be extended beyond the three countries which now possess such weapons. Canada cannot arm her forces with her own or American nuclear weapons and, at the same time, deny them to others." It called for enhanced and more mobile Canadian conventional forces, as well as a re-examination of NATO strategy to reduce "reliance on strategic nuclear retaliation outside

NATO control." Since the Soviet Union was equipping its own forces with tactical nuclear weapons, if a re-examination of NATO policy concluded that NATO's conventional forces should be reinforced by tactical nuclear arms, "then Canadian forces under NATO command should possess such weapons." But these tactical weapons should be solely for defensive use by NATO forces and not under national control by any NATO members save the United States.[20]

According to the defence resolution, Canada should continue to cooperate with the United States in conventional defence. Crucially, this did not require the use of nuclear weapons or integration into NATO as then constituted. The Canadian role in air defence should be limited to detection, identification, and warning, with systems appropriate to this role.[21] A note by Pearson from around the same time reaffirmed his view that NATO needed to re-examine its strategy and structure, and that there had to be "greater unity of policy among the members" and "greater authority given the Council."[22]

At the January rally, Pearson had deflected internal calls for Canada's withdrawal from NORAD, but at the cost of coherence in the Liberals' position. It had, Pearson wrote to his son, "left us in some confusion on defence. That was inevitable with the various points of view voiced and the short time in which to reconcile them." His own task was to clarify party policy, "and I think I can do that in a way which will not mean a default on our obligations to NATO."[23] But the incoherence in policy did not go unnoticed. A few weeks after the Liberal rally, John Gellner, a former Royal Canadian Air Force Wing Commander and foreign editor of the *Canadian Commentator*, ridiculed the Liberal position on NORAD. If this policy were adopted, Gellner wrote in the *Commentator*, "we would warn the Americans that the enemy was coming, we would tell them who he is, we would fix and track him, but then we would virtuously withdraw and let the Americans do the killing." This was "a solution worthy of Pontius Pilate."[24]

Gellner said that Canada did its part in protecting the American deterrent against pre-emptive attack through early warning and the provision of refuelling bases for Strategic Air Command's bomber fleet, but it had done so before NORAD and could readily do so after leaving. Gellner noted the failed effort of the so-called Young Turks at the Liberal rally to pass a resolution calling for withdrawal from NORAD altogether. "Such a resolution," he wrote, "would not have been an expression of silly anti-Americanism, but rather of good sense."[25]

Two months later, Paul Hellyer defended Liberal policy in the *Canadian Commentator*. His justification echoed some of Gellner's earlier logic, arguing that Canada should continue to protect the US deterrent posture through warning and detection systems. Doing so could, Hellyer wrote, "be performed by us whether we're in NORAD or out." And it did not require nuclear weapons. Hellyer contended that the world was safer with nuclear weapons restricted to those states that already had them, and for Canada to equip its forces with nuclear arms would weaken its voice in support of non-proliferation and nuclear disarmament. He held out the possibility of Canada's adoption of nuclear weapons if circumstances changed. He reiterated Pearson's view that NATO strategy should reduce reliance on nuclear weapons, but that if nuclear weapons remained essential, Canada should acquire them "provided the decision to use the weapons is subject to NATO control rather than the control of any one nation."[26]

In his interest in collective control of NATO nuclear weaponry, Pearson lent support to ideas that would be included in President Kennedy's speech to the Canadian Parliament on May 17. Kennedy noted the desire of allies for a voice in nuclear decision-making and reiterated Eisenhower's earlier offer of five Polaris submarines (and more as they came on-stream) to NATO command and looked toward a multilateral force of surface ships under collective ownership and control "once NATO's non-nuclear goals have been achieved."[27]

Pearson gave the most sustained exposition of his thinking about nuclear weapons in the House of Commons on September 14, 1961, during a supply debate on national defence. He acknowledged that Canada produced the uranium that made nuclear defence and deterrence possible, so "it is therefore not because of any superior moral considerations ... that we take our stand." Echoing major strategic debates of the day, he suggested that with strategic nuclear forces dispersed or hardened, "the temptation would be removed to bring about victory through some kind of sneak attack." He remarked that he was aware that NATO planning assumed the early use of nuclear weapons in the event of Soviet attack, including the possible use of tactical nuclear weapons, leading to all-out war. He cited Henry Kissinger on the danger that NATO would eventually face Soviet aggression and the choice between yielding or escalating to all-out nuclear war. The solution, at least as Pearson saw it, was to build up the alliance's conventional defences and bring nuclear arms "under some form of collective control."[28]

Pearson distinguished between custody and control of nuclear weapons. If decisions pertaining to their potential use were "brought under NATO control," Pearson cared little about whether the weapons remained in US custody. The alternative was for NATO to have both custody and control, with the United States, United Kingdom, and France – the alliance's three nuclear powers – relinquishing control of their respective national forces. "If Canadian forces had nuclear weapons as part of such an arrangement," it would not expand the nuclear club because some members would be "giving up their own national control to a collective organization." If NATO were to enhance its conventional capabilities and an attack were to take place, "we would have time to determine whether the NATO council would authorize nuclear weapons to be used." In the event of a Soviet missile attack on North America, of course, it would not matter what mechanism NATO had in place.[29] Rather than respond to Pearson's analysis, Defence Minister Douglas Harkness referenced Gellner's characterization of Liberal defence policy as worthy of Pontius Pilate, claiming "truer words were never spoken."[30] In his effort to clarify Liberal nuclear policy, Pearson still had some distance to go.

## IN SEARCH OF CLARITY

In early 1962, Pearson tried to put together a pamphlet on nuclear weapons and defence. He consulted widely with trusted advisers, including Hellyer, Gordon, Kent, Douglas LePan (a former External Affairs official now teaching English at Queen's University), and Maxwell Cohen (Dean of Law at McGill University). All agreed that there was no protection against missile attack; the only option was deterrence based on retaliation by US strategic nuclear forces. Canada did not need to contribute to this deterrent directly, but could help ensure its invulnerability through early warning systems, patrol and surveillance squadrons, and air-refuelling arrangements. As such, the Bomarc should be scrapped. There was, of course, the possibility that the United States might develop an effective anti-missile system in the future, in which case circumstances would have changed and, as Kent put it, "make it necessary to locate modern and effective nuclear weapons in Canada." For now, the acquisition of nuclear weapons by Canada would not materially add to Canadian or Western security, and would weaken Canadian credibility in advocating for non-proliferation or the renunciation of nuclear weapons by others.[31]

Pearson's advisers also agreed that collective control of NATO nuclear weapons would create a different set of conditions, though they disagreed on whether it was a realistic option or how control might work. Gordon believed that Kennedy would never share control of nuclear weapons. LePan favoured a general agreement in NATO covering the control and custody of all nuclear weapons for the alliance. Cohen argued that a NATO nuclear force would be useless unless new command and control procedures were put into effect. There was "general agreement that the NATO alliance must have both nuclear and conventional forces, that at present there is a necessity, amounting to a priority, to build up the conventional forces so that there need not be reliance on nuclear weapons exclusively to deal with every attack."[32]

Diefenbaker's position on nuclear arms had gone through a number of contortions by the time he entered the fourth year of his 1958 mandate. Not only had he scrapped the Avro Arrow interceptor in 1959 in favour of the Bomarc missile but he had also committed to acquiring CF-104 Starfighters and Honest John artillery for Canadian forces in Europe. The former was scheduled for a strike-reconnaissance role in the event of hostilities and both were designed to carry nuclear warheads. In November 1960, Diefenbaker told an Ottawa gathering that he would not make a firm decision on the acquisition of nuclear weapons as long as there was measurable progress toward nuclear disarmament. A few months later, in his first meeting with Kennedy, he indicated that as long as the disarmament talks continued in Geneva he would not acquire nuclear warheads for the systems requiring them. Instead, he promised to decide quickly in the event of war.[33]

In late 1961 and early 1962, Diefenbaker indicated again that he would acquire the warheads at the outbreak of war; in February 1962, he told the House of Commons that "the nuclear family should not be increased so long as there is any possibility of disarmament among the nations of the world." He also promised that the warheads (if acquired) would be under dual control arrangements similar to the two-key arrangement the British had. Liberal external affairs critic Paul Martin noted statements by Kennedy that seemed to rule out dual control, and asked if this did not make acquisition of the warheads impossible. Diefenbaker responded that until the United States accepted dual control, "we do not intend to go further than we have unless war breaks out," and contrasted his alleged clarity with Pearson's "evasions."[34]

Behind the scenes, Diefenbaker's nuclear policy was even more chaotic. Minister Willis Armstrong of the American Embassy visited his old friend Douglas LePan in Kingston in mid-February, and reported on Diefenbaker's policy. According to Armstrong, when Diefenbaker last saw Kennedy, he undertook to prepare Canadian opinion for the acquisition of nuclear weapons. No steps had been taken. Ambassador Livingston Merchant had already visited Diefenbaker, suggesting that it would be prudent to draw up draft agreements in anticipation of Canadian acceptance of nuclear weapons. Diefenbaker had agreed, but "nothing has been done, and it would seem that nothing further has been done for the present."[35] Pearson raised the issue in the House, denouncing Diefenbaker's position as one "which approaches the ludicrous. They will take nuclear warheads when it will be too late for them to be of value to anybody." Pearson's Liberals were hardly more coherent, however. Pearson acknowledged that he had not yet put his thoughts on these nuclear and defence questions together as a pamphlet around which the Liberal Party could unite and go to the voters.[36]

In March, with an election likely in the very near future, Pearson gave an interview to the broadcaster Mavor Moore on the Canadian Broadcasting Corporation program *The Nation's Business*. Moore opened by describing the Liberals' policy on nuclear weapons as "murky." Pearson denied this, arguing that it was Liberal policy not to acquire nuclear weapons or possess them under joint control with the United States. "Now, that's clear cut," he summed up. Pearson then went on to attack the Diefenbaker government for making commitments that could not be honoured without acquiring nuclear weapons. Diefenbaker had then wavered, as the government did not acquire the weapons or withdraw from the commitments. "Now, surely," Pearson concluded, "that is a weak policy. It's a policy of indecision, and I think it's a dangerous policy." Diefenbaker had indicated that the warheads could be acquired in an emergency, and "has even given the impression that this could be done in from thirty minutes to an hour – but, of course, I don't think this makes any sense at all." He did not explore the possibility of collective control of nuclear weapons within NATO, but did say that it was unwise for an Opposition to dogmatize on such questions, since conditions changed rapidly and the Opposition did not have access to all the pertinent information.[37] He gave little hint of what he would do in office.

Pearson conceded the difficulty of taking a definite stand on nuclear weapons while in opposition. His task, as he remarked to one correspondent, had been made more difficult by Diefenbaker's refusal to set up a select defence committee. "So far as nuclear warheads are concerned," he wrote, "I have tried to avoid being final and dogmatic (and have gotten into a good deal of political trouble as a result) and have been careful in my choice of words." For instance, he had said that Canadian policy should not "'require' us to use nuclear warheads, which is, of course, less definite than to say that we will *never* use nuclear warheads in any circumstances." He reiterated that he saw problems in acquiring nuclear warheads under present circumstances, not least that it would undercut Canadian advocacy of non-proliferation. He concluded that if collective control of NATO nuclear warheads did come about, Canada should participate.[38] Those seeking clarity could be forgiven for thinking there was little difference between Diefenbaker and Pearson. And that may have been the electorate's conclusion in the June 18 election, when it returned Diefenbaker, albeit with a minority government. The Canadian nuclear debate would enter a new phase with the Cuban Missile Crisis later that year, however.

## RESOLUTION

In October, Diefenbaker was briefed by former Ambassador Merchant that the United States had discovered offensive nuclear weapons in Cuba and was going to impose a blockade to compel their removal. Diefenbaker delayed giving authorization to place Canadian forces in NORAD on enhanced alert, though Harkness went ahead without prime ministerial or cabinet approval. As the prime minister dithered, Canadian officials worked behind the scenes to provide intelligence, use what leverage they had over Cuba, and offer support to the United States.[39]

On October 30, after the acute phase of the crisis had passed, cabinet agreed to resume negotiations with the United States on accepting warheads for Canadian forces. It did so, however, on the familiar – and impractical – basis of keeping the warheads (or at least a missing component) in the United States, to be flown in should an emergency occur.[40] Pearson gave an address on *The Nation's Business* in which he noted Kennedy's failure to consult with Canada and others on his response to the missiles in Cuba, but acknowledged that the rapid pace of events had made consultation almost impossible. He indicted Diefenbaker for "getting the worst of both worlds; taking the wrong course in the first place, then refusing either to change it or follow it." The Cuban Missile Crisis had shown "our inability to play the part in continental defence that we had, rightly or wrongly, accepted." He reiterated his call for a reassessment of NATO strategy and said that Canada should "now adapt our contribution to changing circumstances and changing conditions after the fullest consultation with our allies."[41]

Meanwhile, Hellyer had asked John Gellner, who had been consulting with him and a defence committee of MPs that Pearson had established in 1962, to help formulate a defence policy for the next election. Gellner warned him not to let the government "get away with explaining the acceptance of nuclear arms with the Cuban (or the Berlin) crisis – giving nuclear arms to Canadian troops would not solve the one or the other. They should be made to say frankly why we must have them – there are rational grounds for it, you know."[42] Hellyer noted Gellner's warning, fearing a potential shift in the government's policy.[43] Hellyer's concerns proved unfounded – Diefenbaker did not move. At Pearson's suggestion, Hellyer invited Gellner to put together his thoughts as a draft "'Liberal white paper' on defence," though he could not guarantee it would become party policy, especially before the election.[44] Hellyer then headed off to the NATO parliamentarians' conference in Paris, accompanied by two other Liberal MPs, Judy LaMarsh and Ross Macdonald.

When Hellyer returned from Paris, he informed Gellner that the trip had helped shape his thinking.[45] Diefenbaker's indecision, it seemed clear, had frustrated many NATO military and civilian personnel as well as parliamentarians from across the alliance. Hellyer was now convinced that the Liberals should change tack and announce that they would honour the commitments Diefenbaker had already made.[46] Canada's NATO ambassador, George Ignatieff, had managed with difficulty to prevent the North Atlantic Council from censuring Canada for defaulting on its commitments. Supreme Allied Commander Lauris Norstad met with Hellyer and showed him which targets, earmarked for Canadian Starfighters, were not covered as a result of Ottawa's policies.[47]

To get Pearson to change course, Judy LaMarsh insisted that the best approach would be to make the case for "a right-about-face *at this time.* This will cost us ban-the-bomb support and make a hero out of [External Affairs Minister and anti-nuclear crusader Howard] Green. If the Govt. should go along, it won't help us."[48] Hellyer tried to convince Pearson of the dire consequences of inaction. He noted that the official American view at the conference in favour of flexible response would minimize the risk of nuclear escalation, as Pearson had long advocated. So far only the United States had met its conventional force commitments. Even so, Canada was an obvious laggard. Norstad was counting on the Canadians to carry out a strike-reconnaissance role, and "if we do not fulfill our commitment, there will be intense pressure on us to withdraw and turn the facilities over to others. Our influence in NATO will be reduced to negligible."[49]

Hellyer then argued that acquiring nuclear weapons under a bilateral agreement with Washington did not constitute proliferation, as the United States retained ultimate ownership and a veto. Canada would only be joining other allies, including Britain, West Germany, Holland, Italy, Turkey, Belgium, and Norway – none of whom, save Britain, were considered nuclear powers. "If we decide to fulfill those commitments which we have undertaken in NATO," he went on, "I cannot see why we should not do the same in NORAD." He had not changed his mind about the inutility of air defences, but "if there is one thing that is more useless than an armed Bomarc it is an unarmed Bomarc." He concluded that most Canadians would want their government to honour its commitments, and that the Liberals would be safe politically, having "consistently recommended a different course at a time when a different choice was feasible."[50]

Hellyer managed to convince Gellner to switch position and endorse nuclear weapons in his long memo of late December, though Gellner took the view that these nuclear commitments should be renegotiated as quickly as possible. Gellner argued that air defences were of limited use and that nuclear weapons did nothing but deter nuclear war. For other purposes, stronger, more mobile conventional forces were what NATO needed and what Canada should supply. He advocated a stronger, more mobile Canadian presence in Europe, unified at the headquarters and command levels, and capable of being withdrawn to deal with brushfire conflicts or engage in UN peacekeeping missions.[51] Pearson circulated the memorandum to key aides and advisers, including veteran parliamentarian J.W. Pickersgill, Kent, and his press secretary, Dick O'Hagan. Hellyer had forwarded the memo to Pearson with the observation that it was written as a guide to thinking for the Liberal Party, not as a publishable campaign document. Using it as it stood would "open up new misunderstandings."[52]

Pickersgill viewed the Gellner paper with skepticism. It was too preoccupied with what would follow acceptance of the nuclear roles, and with the specifics of the conventional role Gellner envisaged for the Canadian military. "There is only one defence question," Pickersgill argued, "that enters the realm of *practical politics,* nuclear weapons," where voters saw both government and Opposition as unclear. Pearson had already decided on the course to follow with no dissent in caucus, "but let it be said simply and decisively and without any qualifications about trying to get out of it." If Pearson were to qualify his acceptance of nuclear commitments with a proposal to renegotiate them, Pickersgill warned of "another morass" ahead. "The average person just cannot grasp subtle and constantly qualified positions and the average MP or candidate can't explain them either." He urged Pearson to be clear that "Canada is not and will not ever become a nuclear power on its own."[53]

O'Hagan also encouraged Pearson to keep it simple. The Liberals needed a straightforward answer to the question of whether Canada would accept nuclear weapons. Pearson's response should be "a model of simplicity and decisiveness, even – and I say this advisedly – at the risk of some oversimplification." O'Hagan, unsurprisingly given his role as press secretary, also homed in on the question of timing. Pearson had two suitable speaking engagements, one on January 12, another on January 18, 1963. Speaking on the former – a Saturday – he would not reap the benefits of immediate press coverage, but if he waited until the latter, he might end up being scooped by Diefenbaker, who was scheduled to address a Tory gathering that morning.[54] Pearson went with January 12.

On January 3, Norstad visited Ottawa as part of his farewell tour of allied capitals prior to retiring. Responding to a journalist's query, he indicated that Canada had failed to honour its NATO obligations. The Canadian chief of staff, Air Marshal Frank Miller, at his side, audibly agreed. Liberal Party president Major General Bruce Matthews warned Pearson that Norstad's press conference "gave me the impression that clarification would have to be forthcoming at an early date and that the P.M. might feel obliged to make a statement earlier than the P.C. Association meeting." Matthews urged Pearson to make a strong statement himself.[55] Tom Kent prepared a draft for Pearson that emphasized the inconsistencies and evasions of the Diefenbaker government on nuclear weapons but stopped short of urging acceptance of the weapons.[56]

Pearson took some of O'Hagan's and Pickersgill's advice, but not all. He indicated that he would accept the nuclear role for Canadian forces and then attempt to renegotiate it. He did not go into detail about Gellner's (and by now Hellyer's) plans for reshaping the Canadian military. He rejected the notion that there was any moral question involved in the possession of nuclear weapons as such; rather, he said, the question was political. Custody could remain in American hands, with control shared with another country, each having a veto over the weapons' use. "But that does not," he went on, "make the second country a nuclear power, through manufacture or ownership of nuclear weapons." He also reiterated his familiar observation that Canada should support any move in the direction of a genuinely multilateral deterrent within NATO.[57]

Before giving his speech, Pearson had the opportunity to review polling data suggesting that in the battleground provinces of Ontario and Quebec there was strong support for acquiring nuclear weapons, and that defence had risen in importance as an electoral issue.[58] And in the wake of the Scarborough speech, Pearson appeared to reap increased public support and editorial approval.[59] Diefenbaker now tried to outflank the Liberal leader. On January 25, he announced in the House of Commons that the recent Kennedy-Macmillan talks at Nassau (where he had formed an unwanted third) and the resulting proposal for a seaborne Polaris multilateral force raised the question of whether Canada needed to honour its nuclear commitments in NATO. He also indicated that secret negotiations with Washington on acquiring nuclear weapons were under way, and that accepting the weapons – even under joint control – would constitute proliferation.[60]

Those at the American Embassy in Ottawa concluded that Diefenbaker's motive was to slow if not stop "the momentum towards a clarification of Canadian defence policy which began as a popular movement after the Cuban crisis, and which reached a high point in Liberal leader Pearson's speech earlier this month." They recommended clarifying the situation with a press release that pointed out the exploratory nature of the discussions, highlighting that the Canadians had not proposed an arrangement sufficiently practical to merit serious consideration and that dual-key arrangements did not constitute proliferation.[61] Undersecretary of State George Ball issued the press release on January 30, prompting Diefenbaker to eye an immediate election on the theme of Canadian independence from US tutelage.[62] Pearson was mildly critical of the American intervention, but noted that the Kennedy administration had been sorely tried by Diefenbaker's evasions.[63] Then Defence Minister Douglas Harkness and two other cabinet members resigned. Other key members of the prime minister's team chose not to run again. His position severely damaged, Diefenbaker entered the campaign following a no-confidence vote on February 5. Liberal National Director Keith Davey predicted accurately that Diefenbaker would "attempt to paint the Liberal Party as apologists for the Americans," and was happy to wage the battle on that terrain.[64]

Yet Diefenbaker on the stump proved a sometimes compelling figure, and his rhetorical stress on Canadian independence and old-fashioned oratorical stemwinders appealed to many voters, particularly the older, the self-consciously British, and the rural. Pearson lacked Diefenbaker's rhetorical gifts and proved a less than enthralling stump speaker. As well, voters' memories of past Liberal failings in government, Pearson's lacklustre performance as leader of the Opposition, and the fact that he entered the campaign as the front-runner and therefore the target of the other parties all undermined his hopes of a decisive victory. After the polls closed, it became clear that Pearson had managed only 129 seats, just shy of a majority. In government, he faced pressure from some ministers, notably Walter Gordon and some of the key francophones, to move quickly to renegotiate

Canada's nuclear role, but he honoured Diefenbaker's commitments and indeed took a step in the direction of nuclear consultation with the formation of NATO's Nuclear Planning Group. In the end, he navigated the shoals of nuclear politics well enough to have a hold, albeit tenuous, on power.

## NOTES

1 "Defence Policy," text of an address by the Honourable Lester B. Pearson delivered at a luncheon meeting of the York-Scarborough Liberal Association, Toronto, Ontario, January 12, 1963, Tom Kent Papers, box 2, file "January-February 1963," Queen's University Archives (QUA).

2 *Mike: The Memoirs of the Right Honourable Lester B. Pearson*, vol. 3, *1957–1968*, ed. John A. Munro and Alex I. Inglis (Toronto: University of Toronto Press, 1975), 69–75; John English, *The Worldly Years: The Life of Lester Pearson*, vol. 2, *1949–1972* (Toronto: Alfred A. Knopf Canada, 1992), 262. English notes the importance of polling data while also acknowledging Pearson's genuine interest in matters nuclear (244–52). Patricia I. McMahon, *Essence of Indecision: Diefenbaker's Nuclear Policy, 1957–1963* (Montreal and Kingston: McGill-Queen's University Press, 2009), 156–62, also stresses the political considerations, comparing Pearson's reliance on sophisticated polling to Diefenbaker's on his fabled mailbag. Isabel Campbell, "Pearson's Promises and the NATO Nuclear Dilemma," in *Mike's World: Lester B. Pearson and Canadian External Affairs*, ed. Asa McKercher and Galen Roger Perras (Vancouver: UBC Press, 2017), 275–96, explores Pearson's thinking about nuclear weapons but is concerned primarily with his tenure as prime minister.

3 John Foster Dulles, "The Evolution of Foreign Policy," speech to the Council on Foreign Relations, January 12, 1954, *Department of State Bulletin*, Issue 30, February 11, 1954, 107–10.

4 "A Look at the 'New Look,'" text of address by Pearson to National Press Club, March 15, 1954, *Statements and Speeches*, No. 54/16, Information Division, Department of External Affairs.

5 See, for example, William I. Hitchcock, *The Age of Eisenhower: America and the World in the 1950s* (New York: Simon and Schuster, 2018), 102–7, on Korea; and Fredrik Logevall, *Embers of War: The Fall of an Empire and the Making of America's Vietnam* (New York: Random House, 2012), 498–500, on Indochina.

6 John Lewis Gaddis, "The Origins of Self-Deterrence: The United States and the Non-Use of Nuclear Weapons, 1945–1958," in *The Long Peace: Inquiries into the History of the Cold War* (Oxford: Oxford University Press, 1987), 104–46.

7 See Henry A. Kissinger, *Nuclear Weapons and Foreign Policy* (New York: Harper and Row, 1957); James M. Gavin, *War and Peace in the Space Age* (New York: Harper and Row, 1958); and Maxwell D. Taylor, *The Uncertain Trumpet* (New York: Harper and Row, 1960).

8 Lester B. Pearson, *Diplomacy in the Nuclear Age* (Cambridge, MA: Harvard University Press, 1959), 71.

9   John F. Kennedy, "The Terrain of Today's Statecraft," *Saturday Review*, August 1, 1959, 19–20. Kennedy also noted Pearson's championship of non-military cooperation under NATO's Article II. For Pearson's efforts along these lines, see John C. Milloy, *The North Atlantic Treaty Organization, 1948–1957: Community or Alliance?* (Montrea and Kingston: McGill-Queen's University Press, 2006), 14–44.

10  *House of Commons Debates*, 23rd Parliament, 1st Session, vol. 1, October 22, 1957, 242, and November 13, 1957, 1001, 1061–62. On this issue, see Joseph T. Jockel, *No Boundaries Upstairs: Canada, the United States, and the Origins of North American Air Defence, 1945–1958* (Vancouver: UBC Press, 1987), 107–17.

11  *House of Commons Debates*, 24th Parliament, 2nd Session, vol. 4, July 2, 1959, 5360–62. The Bomarc could attack only bombers, and SAGE was an air defence control system of doubtful reliability. See Joseph T. Jockel, *Canada in NORAD, 1957–2007: A History* (Montreal and Kingston: McGill-Queen's University Press, 2007), 43–49.

12  Pearson to Geoffrey Pearson, April 1, 1959, Geoffrey Pearson Papers, box 46, file "LBP to GAHP, April 1, 1959," Carleton University Archives (CUA).

13  Geoffrey Pearson to Lester Pearson, October 1960, Geoffrey Pearson Papers, box 46, file "GAHP to LBP (from Paris-copy), October 1960," CUA. Spaak's ideas are outlined in brief in his "New Tests for NATO," *Foreign Affairs* 37, 3 (April 1959): 357–65. As Geoffrey Pearson noted in the letter cited above, he had edited the English-language version of the piece.

14  Pearson to Geoffrey Pearson, November 24, 1960, Geoffrey Pearson Papers, box 46, file "LBP to GAHP, November 24 1960," CUA.

15  English, *The Worldly Years*, 212–38.

16  Address by Pearson at the banquet of the Kingston Conference, Queen's University, September 6, 1960, Tom Kent Papers, box 6, file "Study Conference on National Problems, Kingston, September 1960 (3)," QUA.

17  James Eayrs, "Defending the Realm: A National Security Policy for Canada in the 1960s," Tom Kent Papers, box 6, file "Study Conference on National Problems, Kingston, September 1960 (4)," QUA.

18  MacIntosh memo of October 4, 1960, Tom Kent Papers, box 6, file "Study Conference on National Problems, Kingston, September, 1960 (1)," QUA.

19  Gordon to Kent, January 16, 1961, Tom Kent Papers, box 6, file "National Liberal Rally, January, 1961 (1)," QUA. On Pearson's authorship of the foreign policy and defence resolutions brought forward for consideration at the rally, see November 25, 1960, "Status" note on drafts, Tom Kent Papers, box 6, file "National Liberal Rally – drafts, January, 1961 (2)," QUA.

20  "Defence Policy," n.d., ibid.

21  Ibid.

22  Note by Pearson, February 1, 1961, "Foreign Policy," Tom Kent Papers, box 6, file "National Liberal Rally – drafts, January, 1961 (2)," QUA.

23  Pearson to Geoffrey Pearson, February 11, 1960, Geoffrey Pearson Papers, box 46, file "LBP to GAHP, February 11 1961," CUA.

24  John Gellner, "The Liberals and NORAD," *Canadian Commentator*, February 1961, 2–4.

25  Ibid.

26 Paul Hellyer, "The Liberal Party and National Defence," *Canadian Commentator*, April 1961, 5–6, 9.

27 Address before the Canadian Parliament, Ottawa, May 17, 1961, in *Public Papers of the Presidents: John F. Kennedy, 1961* (Washington, DC: Government Printing Office, 1962), 385. On the building up of conventional forces in Europe and US openness to nuclear sharing, see Francis J. Gavin, "The Myth of Flexible Response: United States Strategy in Europe during the 1960s," *International History Review* 23, 4 (December 2001): 847–75. At least since Sputnik had foreshadowed the possible decoupling of North American and European nuclear defences, NATO's European members had chafed at the American nuclear preponderance within the alliance. The Multilateral Force (MLF) was an American proposal for a fleet of nuclear-armed vessels with crews drawn from a number of participating NATO states. Disagreements over basing modes and financing were among the reasons the proposal, in its various iterations, never came to fruition. See Marc Trachtenberg, *A Constructed Peace: The Making of the European Settlement, 1945–1963* (Princeton, NJ: Princeton University Press, 1999), 146–200 and passim, and Jack Cunningham, "Nuclear Sharing and Nuclear Crises: A Study in Anglo-American Relations, 1957–1963" (PhD diss., University of Toronto, 2010).

28 *House of Commons Debates,* September 14, 1961, 24th Parliament, 4th Session, vol. 8, 8350–52. For the early emergence of mutual assured destruction (MAD) thinking among Canadian officials and strategists, see Andrew Richter, *Avoiding Armageddon: Canadian Military Strategy and Nuclear Weapons, 1950–63* (Vancouver: UBC Press, 2002), 59–79.

29 *House of Commons Debates,* 24th Parliament, 4th Session, vol. 8, September 14, 1961, 8350–52.

30 Ibid., 8352.

31 Untitled Pearson memo on defence, February 27, 1962, Papers of Lester B. Pearson, vol. 49, file "Nuclear Policy," pt. 1, Correspondence Series, 1958–63, Leader of the Opposition, Library and Archives Canada (LAC).

32 Ibid.

33 J.L. Granatstein, "When Push Came to Shove: Canada and the United States," in *Kennedy's Quest for Victory: American Foreign Policy, 1961–1963,* ed. Thomas G. Paterson (Oxford: Oxford University Press, 1989), 91–92.

34 *House of Commons Debates,* 24th Parliament, 5th Session, vol. 2, February 26, 1962, 1250.

35 LePan to Pearson, February 21, 1962, Papers of Lester B. Pearson, vol. 49, file "Nuclear Policy," pt. 1, Correspondence Series, 1958–1963, Leader of the Opposition, LAC.

36 Ibid.

37 Transcript of Pearson interview on *The Nation's Business*, March 28, 1962, file National Defence, Nuclear Defence, vol. 113, "Papers of Lester B. Pearson, vol. 113, file 'National Defence, Nuclear Defence,'" LAC.

38 Pearson to Air Marshal W.A. Curtis, April 5, 1962, Papers of Lester B. Pearson, vol. 49, file "Disarmament, Correspondence Series, 1958–63, Leader of the Opposition," LAC.

39 Asa McKercher, "'A Half-Hearted Response?' Canada and the Cuban Missile Crisis, 1962," *International History Review* 33, 2 (2011): 335–52.

40 McMahon, *Essence of Indecision*, 151–52.

41 Text of Pearson broadcast, October 31, 1962, Papers of Paul Hellyer, vol. 72, file "Liberal Defence Committee," LAC.

42 Gellner to Hellyer, October 22, 1962, ibid.

43 Hellyer to Gellner, October 25, 1962, ibid.

44 Hellyer to Gellner, November 7, 1962, ibid.

45 Hellyer to Gellner, November 27, 1962, ibid.

46 Hellyer memorandum to Pearson and the Liberal Defence Committee, "Following the NATO Parliamentary Conference Held in Paris, November 1962," n.d. but evidently late November 1962, Papers of Paul Hellyer, vol. 75, file "NATO Parliamentarians Conference, Paris, 1962," LAC.

47 George Ignatieff, *The Making of a Peacemonger*, prepared with the assistance of Sonja Sinclair (Toronto: University of Toronto Press, 1985), 208–9; interview with Paul Hellyer by Antony Anderson, July 31, 1996, courtesy of Antony Anderson.

48 LaMarsh to Hellyer, n.d. but late November 1962, Papers of Paul Hellyer, vol. 72, file "Liberal Defence Committee," LAC.

49 Gellner to Hellyer, October 22, 1962, ibid.

50 Ibid.

51 Gellner to Hellyer, December 21, 1962, and enclosed "Proposals for a Liberal Defence Policy," Paul Hellyer Papers, vol. 72, file "John Gellner, 1961–62," LAC. In the letter to Hellyer, Gellner wrote that there was nothing new in his document, except "I have insofar yielded to your (very persuasive) arguments that I now believe we should make good on our commitments to NORAD and NATO until we can change them through renegotiation."

52 Hellyer to Pearson, December 31, 1962, Papers of Lester B. Pearson, vol. 49, file "Disarmament, Correspondence Series, 1958–63, Leader of the Opposition," LAC.

53 Pickersgill to Pearson, January 3, 1963, ibid.

54 O'Hagan to Pearson, January 7, 1963, ibid. O'Hagan was concerned about Pearson's distrust of rhetoric and his proclivity for presenting policy with all the pertinent qualifications. Conversation with Dick O'Hagan, August 20, 2018.

55 Matthews to Pearson, January 7, 1963, Papers of Lester B. Pearson, vol. 49, file "Nuclear Policy, Part 1, Correspondence Series, 1958–63, Leader of the Opposition," LAC.

56 Kent, "Defence Note," January 7, 1963, Tom Kent Papers, file "January-February 1963 (1)," box 2, QUA. There is some controversy as to precisely when Pearson decided to accept the weapons. Pickersgill's note suggests that he had already decided to do so as early as January 3. McMahon suggests that he had not done so as late as O'Hagan's letter, which she suggests deals with the question of whether, not when and how, to accept the weapons. This seems to misread the letter's focus on what the question is from the standpoint of the public. See McMahon, *Essence of Indecision*, 158. The memoir literature does little to help. Pearson chalks up his change of tack to the Cuban Missile Crisis and Hellyer's letter of late December, as does Hellyer. Pickersgill reiterates that Pearson had made up his mind by early January. Kent downplays the difference between his rejected draft and what Pearson actually said at Scarborough. See Text of Pearson broadcast, October 31, 1962, Papers of Paul Hellyer, vol. 72, file "Liberal Defence Committee," LAC, 69–75; Paul Hellyer, *Damn the Torpedoes: My Fight to Unify Canada's*

*Armed Forces* (Toronto: McClelland and Stewart, 1990), 25–26; J.W. Pickersgill, *The Road Back: By a Liberal in Opposition* (Toronto: University of Toronto Press, 1986), 53; and Tom Kent, *A Public Purpose: An Experience of Liberal Opposition and Canadian Government* (Montreal and Kingston: McGill-Queen's University Press, 1988), 187–95. It is difficult to be sure, not least because Pearson, according to his teaching assistant at Carleton University in the last years of his life, was deflective, and allowed people to assume that because he had listened to them he was in agreement. Conversation with Norman Hillmer, August 2, 2018.

57  "Defence Policy," text of an address by the Honourable Lester B. Pearson delivered at a luncheon meeting of the York-Scarborough Liberal Association, Toronto, Ontario, January 12, 1963, Tom Kent Papers, box 2, file "January-February 1963," QUA.

58  Penetration Research, "A Survey of the Political Climate of Ontario and Quebec," January 10, 1963, Tom Kent Papers, file "January-February 1963 (1)," box 2, QUA.

59  McMahon, *Essence of Indecision,* 161–62.

60  *House of Commons Debates,* 25th Parliament, 1st Session, vol. 3, January 25, 1963, 3125–39. The Nassau conference was related to the American abandonment of the Skybolt missile, on which Prime Minister Harold Macmillan had pinned his hopes for continuing Britain's deterrent. See Trachtenberg, *A Constructed Peace,* 359–67.

61  Memo from Tyler to Ball, January 29, 1963, "Proposed Press Statement on United States–Canadian Negotiations Regarding Nuclear Weapons," *Foreign Relations of the United States, 1961–1963 (FRUS),* vol. 13, *Western Europe and Canada* (Washington, DC: Government Printing Office, 1994), 1193, https://history.state.gov/historicaldocuments/frus1961-63v13/d443.

62  Department of State Press Release No. 59, "United States and Canadian Negotiations Regarding Nuclear Weapons," January 30, 1963, ibid., 1195–96, https://history.state.gov/historicaldocuments/frus1961-63v13/d444; McMahon, *Essence of Indecision,* 165.

63  See Kent draft for Pearson, untitled, January 31, 1963, Tom Kent Papers, file "January-February 1963 (1)," box 2, QUA.

64  Davey to Pearson, Gordon, and Kent, January 31, 1963, ibid. On the campaign, see McMahon, *Essence of Indecision,* 165–69, and Asa McKercher, *Camelot and Canada: Canadian-American Relations in the Kennedy Era* (New York: Oxford University Press, 2016), 197–203. On Pearson's handling of nuclear issues in office and the Nuclear Planning Group, see Campbell, "Pearson's Promises and the NATO Nuclear Dilemma," 280–92, and Chapter 2 in this volume. Of course, in the face of the rising costs of a nuclear role in NATO sizable enough to confer much influence, Pearson and Hellyer also initiated a greater emphasis on peacekeeping, where small powers are at an advantage, given the political objections to great power intervention. On this, see Jon B. McLin, *Canada's Changing Defense Policy, 1957–1963: The Problems of a Middle Power in Alliance* (Baltimore: Johns Hopkins University Press, 1967), 208–9.

*Part 3*

# IN SEARCH OF NUCLEAR
# TASKS AT HOME
# AND ABROAD

# CHAPTER 6

# WHO'S GOING TO INVADE ARCTIC CANADA, ANYWAY?

## Debating the Acquisition of the Nuclear Submarine in the 1980s

Susan Colbourn

I n June 1987, Brian Mulroney's Progressive Conservative government released a new Defence White Paper, *Challenge and Commitment: A Defence Policy for Canada*. Canada's first comprehensive defence review in sixteen years, it envisioned a three-ocean navy befitting a three-ocean nation. Critics slammed it as outdated, steeped in the logic of the Cold War. "The estimate of the Soviet forces and the Soviet threat in the White Paper," one MP bemoaned, was "even more exaggerated than the estimates in the Pentagon's propaganda."[1]

Peace groups across the country mobilized against what they termed the White Paper's "Ramboization of Canadian defence thinking."[2] Voice of Women dismissed it as "propaganda, couched in advertising terms, attempting to sell the Canadian people a perilous policy."[3] Operation Dismantle took aim at the White Paper's projected spending figures, arranging a mock bake sale on Parliament Hill, complete with the sale of $35 million muffins.[4] At a rally in Nanaimo, British Columbia, one protestor put it plainly, marching with a placard that read "Mulroney's white paper" – with a roll of toilet paper perched atop the sign.[5]

The White Paper's most controversial recommendation was the purchase of ten to twelve nuclear-powered submarines (also known as SSNs or hunter-killer submarines). Canada had deployed submarines previously, though not nuclear-powered ones. The *Globe and Mail's* Jeffrey Simpson warned that a national debate was "coming as surely as you're reading this."[6] Simpson was right: even before the White Paper had been released, the

Canadian Centre for Arms Control and Disarmament spoke out against the submarines.[7]

For such a high-profile defence program, little has been written about the Canadian Submarine Acquisition Program (CASAP).[8] Mulroney's extensive memoirs make no mention of the submarines, and neither does the most recent survey of the prime minister's foreign policy.[9] The submarines surface, albeit briefly, in larger narratives tracing disputes over Arctic sovereignty, the transformation of Canadian defence policies at the end of the Cold War, and the evolution of Canada's submarine program.[10] Perhaps the lack of interest is easily explained: the submarines never materialized; the dog did not bark. But between 1987 and 1989, the Mulroney government expended considerable time and energy negotiating to purchase the submarines, and the debates surrounding the acquisition hinted at the complexities and contradictions at play in Canada's relationship with nuclear technologies and its own murky status as a nuclear nation without nuclear weapons.

Using recently released materials from Library and Archives Canada, this chapter highlights the major debates over the submarines – those within the Mulroney government, among Canadians, and between Ottawa and the potential suppliers – and revisits traditional arguments, such as the program's links to Arctic sovereignty and the White Paper's inflated estimate of the Soviet threat. The arguments made, both for and against the submarines, extended far beyond the acquisition itself: they tackled much broader questions about Canada's place in the global nuclear order and its responsibilities as a non–nuclear weapons state. For some, the prospect of acquiring an SSN fleet flew in the face of Canada's stated commitment to nuclear non-proliferation and threatened to upset international norms that Ottawa had long championed. To others, there was an obvious distinction: nuclear-powered submarines were not nuclear weapons, and Canada had a tradition of nuclear research dating back to the 1940s that justified the program. As Canadians debated the merits of the nuclear submarines, they tried to make sense of their own complicated nuclear past.

## "WE'RE NOT A BUNCH OF NUCLEAR YOKELS"

CASAP emerged out of a study begun in the early 1980s, designed to replace the existing diesel-electric Oberons.[11] Initially, the process had considered other diesel-electric options, but in 1985 Minister of National Defence Erik Nielsen pushed for a feasibility study on SSNs. By 1986, the idea had been endorsed by the Cabinet Committee on Foreign and Defence Policy and the Priority and Planning Committee. This is not to suggest that all were enthusiastic about the proposal. At the Department of External Affairs, many were critical of the proposed submarines. Nuclear submarines, one official concluded, were "appealing . . . as a macho trip with great-power hardware. Derring-do under the ice and all that has its attractions." In practical terms, they made little sense for Canada. Frank Griffiths suggested that a study be conducted on the conventional force options available to defend the Arctic waters.[12]

Once the decision was made to pursue the nuclear-powered option, the Canadians had two options: the British Trafalgar class and the French Rubis/Amethyste class. (US submarines were ruled out: the 7,000-ton Los Angeles class did not suit the Canadians' needs and no smaller option was available.) Between the Trafalgar and the Rubis/Amethyste, the French submarine seemed preferable on paper. It cost less and was composed entirely of French technologies. The Trafalgar, by comparison, required approval from the United States, as it incorporated US technologies whose transfer was restricted under existing nuclear arrangements between the United States and the United Kingdom. Most submariners, however, tended to prefer the British Trafalgars, as much of their equipment was compatible with the submarines already in the Canadian fleet.[13]

Another layer of complication was the product of the submarines' nuclear propulsion. Canada did not possess its own enrichment facility and, as a result, would require a foreign supplier for the enriched uranium needed to fuel the submarines. Likely, this enriched uranium would be supplied by France, the United Kingdom, or the United States. Taken together, this translated into a complex web of bilateral negotiations necessary to acquire the submarines. Some existing agreements on nuclear cooperation would need to be renegotiated; most had been concluded in the 1950s and the language often treated "military applications" and use in nuclear weapons production as interchangeable. For the Canadians, who were planning a "military application" but not the production of a nuclear weapon, the distinction needed to be made clear.

Before a British bid for a submarine contract could even be considered competitive, the Canadians needed to secure agreement from the United States that it would approve the necessary technology transfer. British submarines, after all, relied on restricted US technology. Initial reactions in Washington were hardly promising. The nuclear submarine acquisition plans were met with skepticism – and a healthy dose of condescension. In July 1987, at one meeting with Minister of National Defence Perrin Beatty and Secretary of Defense Caspar Weinberger, the higher-ups at the US Navy laughed at the idea. "They want us to act like a little boy," Allan Gotlieb, the Canadian ambassador in Washington, confided in his diary after the meeting, "not a big one."[14] Time and again, representatives from the US Navy disparaged Canadian technical know-how. There was no way the Canadians possessed the skills necessary to manage a fleet of nuclear submarines, they insisted. They were "treating us like a Third World country," Gotlieb bemoaned after another meeting that September.[15]

Much of the US Navy's opposition boiled down to self-interest. They were not keen to see the "SSN fraternity" grow.[16] Already, they worried that environmental objections could kill the US nuclear submarine program – a fear exacerbated by the high-profile nuclear accidents at Three Mile Island in 1979 and Chernobyl in 1986. Naval reactors were the only nuclear reactors still being built in the United States. "The last thing the U.S. Navy wants," one Canadian briefing summed up the opposition, "is a proliferation of amateurish nuclear navies." The note's author went on to point out that the United States had turned down previous requests for assistance, including one from "such a traditional (and hardly amateurish) seafaring nation as the Netherlands."[17] The US Navy's strategy seemed straightforward, at least from Ottawa's vantage point. They would lay out a long laundry list of all the problems and dangers ahead, offer little to no help resolving them, and dissuade Congress and US businesses from supporting the program.[18]

The Navy may have been the most vocal, but critics could be found throughout Washington. On Capitol Hill, some members of Congress worried about the export of sensitive technologies and the precedent such a transfer would set.[19] At the Pentagon, Assistant Secretary of Defense Frank Gaffney lamented that the Canadians had not come to discuss the scheme earlier. Those in Ottawa responded, noting that they had tried but that their attempts had been ignored in Washington.[20]

Before considering the requisite negotiations (and the associated inter-agency battles), officials in Washington wanted evidence that the Canadians were serious about the submarine program. The Americans worried that the program was politically motivated and assumed that Ottawa would not follow through on a defence program of that size and scope.[21] Colin Powell, the deputy national security adviser, warned that the Canadians were "stepping into a financial morass."[22] Similar doubts surfaced in the United Kingdom. The Defence Export Services Organisation of the Ministry of Defence expressed doubts so plainly in one letter that Rear Admiral John Anderson opened his response, remarking that "under normal circumstances I would consider the matter of being subject to this line of questioning to be inappropriate." He went on to outline Canada's qualifications and experience as "a world leader in high technology" with experience in manufacturing commercial nuclear reactors, managing nuclear power stations, and maintaining a strong safety record.[23]

Canadian officials often tried to demonstrate the country's qualifications by highlighting Ottawa's earlier involvement in nuclear programs. Justifications pointed to a long lineage of nuclear research, dating back to the 1940s.[24] Others echoed Anderson's arguments, playing up Canada's experience with civilian nuclear reactors. This approach, the British warned, was hardly helping the Canadian case. The Office of Naval Reactors in the United States refused to hire individuals with civilian reactor experience. References to Canadian experience with civilian reactor technologies had the opposite effect intended in many cases, strengthening the Americans' belief that Canadian officials did not appreciate the magnitude or scope of the task ahead.[25]

Throughout the second half of 1987 and into the new year, Allan Gotlieb campaigned on CASAP's behalf in Washington. Meeting with Secretary of Defense Frank Carlucci, Weinberger's successor, in April 1988, Gotlieb insisted that the issue could do long-lasting damage to bilateral defence relations. The nuclear submarines constituted the most important Canadian defence initiative since NORAD, the ambassador argued. He warned that if the Reagan administration refused to support it, any reasoning the administration offered would undoubtedly offend their counterparts in

Ottawa. Either Washington would be saying that the Canadians were incapable or that the United States wanted to dominate the Arctic. Carlucci responded, pointing to another rationale for opposing the Canadian nuclear submarines: the scheme was simply "a bad one" that did little to improve Western defences.[26]

## AT WHAT COST?

As the Mulroney government worked to ensure that there were two viable, competitive bids for the submarines, opposition to the entire program grew at home. As with so many defence procurements, some opponents fixated on the price tag. Government estimates put the total purchase cost at $8 billion, but many insisted that those estimates were far too conservative. Alternative figures suggested that the program would cost upward of $14 billion or, in the words of one peace group, "a stack of one-dollar bills over 2200km ... high."[27] Often, critics appealed to a common refrain: that money could be better spent elsewhere.[28]

Some argued that the same results could be achieved at a much lower price point. Canada could, for example, acquire a surveillance network to monitor US and Soviet maritime forces in the Arctic.[29] Instead, the director of the Canadian Centre for Arms Control and Disarmament argued, those at the Department of National Defence had come under the spell of "a vision of Canada as 'Rambo of the North': muscular, independent, ready to take on all comers."[30] *The Economist* dismissed the Mulroney government's planned purchase as "astonishing." Canadian dollars would be better spent on building up the country's existing forces stationed in the Federal Republic of Germany.[31] Others wondered whether the financial costs mattered at all. An editorial in the *Edmonton Sun* cast a stark choice: Canadians could pay for the defence of the second-largest country on the planet or they could "free ride on the coattails of their allies, and to heck with the consequences for our sovereignty – not to mention our self-respect."[32]

But much of the debate boiled down to the intangible costs. The acquisition would, as no shortage of domestic critics of the program argued, do considerable damage to Canada's reputation as a champion of arms control and disarmament. Part of their concern stemmed from the technology involved: the highly enriched uranium needed for the submarines' nuclear propulsion could also be used to produce a nuclear weapon. Under Article 14 of the safeguard agreement between the International Atomic Energy Agency (IAEA) and signatories of the Nuclear Non-Proliferation Treaty (NPT), a non–nuclear weapons state could remove highly enriched uranium from safeguards for use in non-explosive military purposes. But no state had done this before: Canada would be the first state to actually invoke Article 14 if the government went through with the acquisition.

The Canadian Centre for Arms Control and Disarmament, one of the program's fiercest critics, accepted the Mulroney government's argument that the submarines were not inconsistent with Canada's non-proliferation policy or its existing obligations as a signatory to the NPT. Even so, it argued that the decision would set a negative precedent, undermining the global non-proliferation regime and weakening IAEA safeguards. "No one, of course, expects Canada to mislead the IAEA," John Lamb, the centre's executive director, and Tariq Rauf, a senior research associate, argued in one *Globe and Mail* article, "much less divert nuclear materials to manufacture bombs. But can we really say Canada is setting a good precedent unless we are equally confident in a comparable bilateral safeguards agreement between France and, say, Iraq or Brazil?" The prospect of purchasing French submarines was singled out as a particular problem. France was not a signatory of the NPT, and its record as a nuclear supplier could be charitably described as spotty. Paris had sold a nuclear reactor and weapons-grade uranium to Iraq, offered support to the Israeli nuclear program, and undercut a US embargo on the sale of nuclear fuel to South Africa. Canada would be the first to purchase French nuclear-powered submarines. Doing so, Lamb and Rauf concluded, would make Ottawa "an accessory to France's irresponsible and widely despised policy."[33]

Anxieties about the potential damage to global norms and the nuclear non-proliferation regime were made worse by vague language that blurred the lines between nuclear power and nuclear weapons. One editorial in the *Toronto Star*, for instance, argued that the submarines could fire nuclear missiles.[34] The government's briefing note, drafted in response to the *Star*'s claims, acknowledged that this was in fact possible. But, as the memo put it, "the Canadian Forces possess many systems that could theoretically fire or deliver nuclear weapons (from CF-18s to 155mm howitzers) – the point is that the Canadian Government has a policy not to acquire nuclear weapons."[35] Repeatedly, the Mulroney government issued reminders that a nuclear-powered submarine was not a nuclear weapon; it was just a propulsion system.[36]

As in earlier debates over the country's nuclear policies, opponents of the submarines argued that the decision to acquire them would deal a severe blow to Canada's international image.[37] "It seems grotesque," one critic argued in the *Bulletin of the Atomic Scientists'* special feature on Canadian defence policy, "that Canada should now be the first non-nuclear country – and the first non-nuclear party to the Non-Proliferation Treaty of 1968 – to advocate the production, conversion, and/or transfer of peaceful fissionable material to military purposes."[38] Who might be emboldened if Canada were to set a new precedent?

Internal government studies reflected these same concerns about the potential damage to Canada's image worldwide. David Karsgaard, director of the Defence Relations Division, emphasized the prospect of undercutting "the 'human face'" of Canadian diplomacy. Pointing to Canada's foreign aid and assistance programs, its traditional role as a "helpful fixer," and what he (and others) saw as an "absence of imperial tradition," Karsgaard argued that these factors had long shaped Canada's international reputation. All of this would change with the nuclear-powered submarines, he worried. "We may not be regarded as being as benign as we once were, or as disinterested." Canada would instead be joining a new circle of uncertain status, a conclusion underscored by reactions to India's recent acquisition of nuclear-powered submarines.[39] When Pakistan's ambassador to India, for instance, outlined his (predictable) opposition to the Indian nuclear-powered submarines, his critique was far broader than the Indian program. "To my mind," he remarked in one interview, "nuclear military power is not restricted to nuclear bombs but also includes the use of nuclear energy for other weapons short of war."[40] Similar arguments could easily be made about the Canadian acquisition.

## SECURITY AND SOVEREIGNTY

For many, the nuclear submarines were an Arctic issue. Certainly, the Defence White Paper evoked this association. The cover illustration of *Challenge and Commitment* showed a globe focused on the Arctic Circle.[41]

Many of the arguments in favour of SSNs underscored these Arctic dimensions. Nuclear propulsion offered a clear advantage over diesel-electric options, at least in part because it would enable the submarines to operate under the ice.[42] "The decision to replace Canada's aging diesel subs with nuclear-propelled subs reflects strategic realities," one briefing insisted. "The Soviet Navy has grown rapidly and it now has some 375 submarines, 160 of them nuclear-powered." Each constituted a potential threat, or so readers were meant to conclude.[43] A memorandum prepared for Secretary of State for External Affairs Joe Clark in the spring of 1987, months before the government released the Defence White Paper, admitted that National Defence's marketing strategy seemed based on "playing up a potential Soviet threat."[44] But the government's own assessments offered a competing interpretation, as contemporary requests under the Access to Information Act made clear to the public. One request yielded a National Defence internal study confirming that there was no Soviet submarine presence in the Canadian Arctic. Worse still, at least from the perspective of the submarines' champions, the department concluded that a threat remained unlikely in the future.[45]

Recent developments on the world stage left many skeptical that the threat emanated from Moscow. The Cold War atmosphere had thawed visibly, as Soviet General Secretary Mikhail Gorbachev advocated the complete elimination of nuclear weapons by the year 2000. "No doubt," the president of Veterans Against Nuclear Arms acknowledged, "some of these measures have a one-upmanship element in them to present the Soviet Union as more peace-loving than NATO," but Gorbachev's initiatives were still cause for optimism, as he seemed to be on the hunt for a way "to get the disarmament race started."[46] Others pointed to Gorbachev's policies of *glasnost* and *perestroika* as evidence that the times were changing. Soviet representatives, for instance, now acknowledged that a famine had ravaged Ukraine during the 1930s – something they had refused to admit for decades.[47] Seventy-one percent of Canadians, according to a 1988 poll by the Canadian Institute for International Peace and Security, believed Gorbachev to be trustworthy on arms control.[48] Real breakthroughs in US-Soviet relations reinforced this sense of optimism. In December 1987, after seven years of on-and-off negotiations, the United States and the Soviet Union signed the Intermediate-Range Nuclear Forces Treaty, abolishing an entire category of nuclear weapons for the first time in history. "Is this the time to rearm?" one letter to the editor in *Maclean's* wondered in early 1988.[49]

Skeptical that the Soviet threat justified the procurement of nuclear submarines, many viewed the program as a response to another threat: the erosion of Canadian sovereignty. In the summer of 1985, a US icebreaker, the USCGC *Polar Sea,* travelled through the Northwest Passage. The Canadian government had been notified in advance of the voyage. Few saw it as a source of concern: the *Polar Sea* needed to conduct a supply run and transiting through the Northwest Passage shaved a month off the journey, making it possible for the icebreaker to complete the supply run and return in time for a scheduled mission. But the *Polar Sea* reignited domestic debates over Canadian sovereignty, as critics seized on the issue as further evidence that Mulroney was subservient to the Americans.[50] In the wake of the *Polar Sea's* voyage, Canada's sovereignty in the Arctic remained a preoccupation. "We do not at the moment have any military capability in our own North," Peter C. Newman lamented in the pages of *Maclean's* in January 1987. "If there were any incursion we could literally do nothing – except maybe send out a Mountie on a Ski-Doo to dispense parking tickets."[51] Gotlieb summed up the current arrangements between Canada and the United States succinctly: "It's our Arctic, but they protect it."[52]

Douglas Frith, the Liberal Party's defence critic, saw the nuclear-propelled submarines as a misguided response to the *Polar Sea* incident. The Mulroney government, he concluded, hoped to assuage fears that they had failed to stand up for Canadian sovereignty, but if the core problem was a legal one, a military response made little sense. "Suppose our sub in the Arctic runs into an American or a Soviet or a British submarine," Frith wondered, "and we say 'You're in Canadian waters,' and they say, 'No, we're in international waters.' What do we expect the sub to do about this anyway?" NDP defence critic Derek Blackburn concurred: the submarine was more symbolic than strategic. Purchasing nuclear-powered submarines was nothing more than "a way of showing that we're prepared to 'stand up to the Yanks' over our disputed Northwest Passage, and even to pay a lot of money to wave that flag up there."[53]

Critics repeatedly returned to the theme of showing the flag as evidence that the submarine acquisition was an ill-conceived boondoggle. "You can't show the flag with an SSN," one former British submariner argued. "The whole point of a hunter-killer [submarine] is that nobody knows you are there, so you can't go waving your periscope around with a flag on it and playing The Maple Leaf Forever."[54] A protest song, set to the tune of The Beatles' "Yellow Submarine," picked up the same theme:

If, God Forbid, a war should come
Would the subs we have-serve us well?
They'd fly the flag-beneath the ice
While the rest of us are blown to Hell!
We won't fight with nuclear submarines . . .[55]

The Canadian Centre for Arms Control and Disarmament insisted that the submarines would do nothing to encourage the United States – and the US Navy – to respect Canadian sovereignty in the Arctic, while dealing a severe blow to Ottawa's non-proliferation policies.[56] Canadians were not alone in assuming that the submarine acquisition was motivated by Arctic sovereignty disputes. When Gotlieb called on Weinberger with a copy of the White Paper, Weinberger demanded to know whether the submarines related to Canada's claims to the Arctic waters.[57]

At the Department of National Defence, many continued to believe that these appeals to sovereignty were the most compelling argument in support of the submarines. The Defence White Paper sought to redress imbalances in Canada's defence posture, closing the gap in the country's perennial "commitment-credibility dilemma."[58] Canada would be in a far better position to defend its own territory; the three-ocean country would finally have a three-ocean navy. The submarines, in particular, were billed as "the only proven vehicle . . . capable of sustained operation under the ice."[59] Asserting Canadian sovereignty was the only justification for the program that appealed to those who objected to the acquisition on anti-nuclear or environmental grounds.[60] If Canada purchased nuclear-powered submarines, the question remained, how would they be used?

Paradoxically, the answer left some convinced that Canada's sovereignty would be further eroded by the submarine acquisition. NATO lacked an established maritime strategy beyond a few documents, outlining basic principles like "forward defence" and "containment." These ideas were left vague: "How far forward?" one Canadian official wondered.[61] Opponents of the submarines charged that Canada would be drawn into US maritime strategy, a strategy they considered to be needlessly provocative and destabilizing.[62] They pointed to provisions calling for attacks on Soviet submarines still in Soviet coastal waters as particularly escalatory.[63] Others feared that Canada would be drawn into another defence arrangement with the United States at sea—a "wet NORAD" of sorts.[64] The *Ottawa Citizen,* for instance, ran a story under the headline "'NORAD of the Sea' Price for Nuke Subs." Citing a naval attaché at the US Embassy in Ottawa, the article insisted that Canada would need to support a joint maritime strategy in order to secure support for the submarines in Congress.[65] (The attaché's comments were disavowed by the US Embassy.[66]) Even if a new maritime NORAD did not emerge, peace activists insisted that Canadians were being left in the dark about "water management" – a burden-sharing scheme of patrols to ensure that allies did not waste time tracking one another.[67] "As long as Canada stays in NATO," Steve Shallhorn, the disarmament coordinator of Greenpeace Canada's Nuclear Free Seas campaign, concluded, "it will have no independent submarine operations."[68]

To some opponents, recent developments illustrated the pressures for Canada to integrate further with the United States: cruise missile testing, the Air Defense Initiative, the Strategic Defense Initiative, and the North Warning System were all offered up as evidence that Canada was being dragged into Washington's orbit.[69] Obstacles in the path of the submarines themselves, such as the need for US approval for the transfer of British technologies, chafed. The *Toronto Sun* likened the situation to being a colony once more.[70] The fact that these conversations took place in tandem with a heated national debate over the benefits and dangers of a free trade agreement with the United States added fuel to the fire, stoking fears that Canada might be subsumed by its more powerful southern neighbour.

## SINKING THE SUBS

Negotiations dragged on as Canada sought a draft memorandum of understanding with France and the United Kingdom in advance of a final decision on the submarines' country of origin. These talks encompassed an array of complicated issues, including nuclear safety, training, security, operations, maintenance, liability, and nuclear safeguards. Agreements were finally reached in February 1988. Two months later, in April, the State Department publicly announced that the United States would support the request if Canada decided to move forward with the British Trafalgars.[71] A decision seemed to be on track. Exploratory talks went ahead with the IAEA that spring, laying the groundwork for further talks on safeguards once the submarines' country of origin was selected. A consortium conducted a ten-day, ten-city tour across Canada in April, as representatives involved with the Trafalgar met with counterparts in Canadian industry to discuss the advantages of the British submarine.[72]

The same arguments against the submarines continued to circulate in Canada. Parliamentary debates repeatedly highlighted the proposal's unpopularity. When would "the cold warriors in the Government listen," one MP wondered.[73] Calls for a denuclearized zone in the Arctic gained traction, as both the Liberals and the NDP spoke out in favour of such a proposal.[74] On May 12, 1988, Operation Dismantle launched a nationwide campaign against the nuclear submarines, dubbed the S.O.S. campaign. It hit some early obstacles: the mayors recruited to speak out against the submarines were not the critics Operation Dismantle had hoped for. "We have to have a sovereignty presence in the Arctic," Thunder Bay's Jack Masters remarked during the news conference to launch the campaign, "and if we have to use nuclear subs, fine."[75] In light of the increased media attention, Defence Minister Beatty circulated talking points on the submarines to all cabinet ministers the following month.[76]

In July 1988, a group of former politicians, businesspeople, and academics launched the Committee for a Sovereign and Effective Naval Defence, dedicated to supporting the government's nuclear submarine plans. The proposed acquisition received support from an array of organizations, including the Business Council on National Issues, the Canadian Nuclear Association, the Canadian Shipbuilding and Ship Repair Association, and the Conference of Defence Associations. The *Globe and Mail* offered its endorsement. "Canada is one of the leading nuclear-power states," it noted, "and there is no reason in principle why our submarines should not be propelled by the same original energy source as heats toaster ovens in Toronto."[77] Polling done by the Canadian Institute for International Peace and Security, for instance, showed that some 55 percent of respondents still favoured the submarine acquisition.[78]

The Mulroney government deferred a decision until after the upcoming federal election, scheduled for November 1988. Presuming that the Progressive Conservatives would carry the election, Paul Dick, the associate minister for national defence, indicated that a debate on the purchase would take place in February 1989. The government's first priority, however, would be the Canada-US Free Trade Agreement.[79] Even though the Liberals and the NDP opposed the acquisition, none of the three parties wished to make defence an election issue. The Progressive Conservatives hoped to keep the issue "submerged." With polls showing that some 80 percent of Canadians supported the country's membership in NATO, the NDP had little interest in reminding voters that its platform called for Canada to leave the North Atlantic Alliance. The Liberals, for their part, "had little else to say on defence except the cancellation of the submarine project."[80] The 1988 election centred on free trade to the exclusion of most other questions, the submarines included.

CASAP's fate was sealed in the spring of 1989. Perrin Beatty was removed from the defence portfolio in a cabinet reshuffle, replaced by a relative unknown, William McKnight. But the biggest problems were financial. Already, the Mulroney government faced acute pressure to reduce expenditures and bring down the deficit. Then, as part of the April 27 budget, massive cuts to National Defence funding were announced, totalling some $2.74 billion over five years.[81] With its funding gutted, the writing was on the wall. Sixty-six percent of respondents in one June 1989 poll took no issue with the Mulroney government's "decision" to abandon the nuclear-powered submarines. A further 15 percent reported that they were "not very upset." The poll's structure underscored what kind of issue it was: the submarines were included in a series of questions dealing with the national debt.[82]

## CONCLUSION

The demise of CASAP, which was quietly shelved after its funding dried up, leaves a major question unanswered. Why did the Mulroney government go to so much trouble – negotiating draft memoranda of understanding with the British and the French, seeking Washington's approval, and reopening decades-old nuclear agreements – only to walk away from the plan entirely? Was it the case, as many Americans assumed, that Ottawa had neither the will nor the wherewithal to see such a massive defence expenditure through? To be sure, the financial obstacles were considerable. Canadian federal finances were in ruin, and the cuts announced in the spring of 1989 extended far beyond the submarines.[83] But the financial costs of such a program were obvious from the outset, something that countless US interlocutors had underscored.

Other perspectives on the failed program remain difficult to explore. There are few non-Canadian records available on the submarine acquisition at present. How did Canadian allies – particularly the three implicated directly in the scheme, France, the United Kingdom, and the United States – view the proposed acquisition? What did they think of the decision to shelve the submarines? Already, the available Canadian records point to considerable frustration. French officials complained constantly that their bid was nothing more than a decoy, designed to make sure that a "real" decision was taken. US complaints about the lack of seriousness on the part of Ottawa shine through clearly, be it in Allan Gotlieb's diaries or the cables sent back from his colleagues in Washington. Ample research remains to be done on how – if at all – the Mulroney government's waffling on the submarines impacted relations with some of the country's key allies. Timing almost certainly helped the Canadians mitigate any long-term damage, as the fundamental transformations that marked the end of the Cold War took over the agenda as 1989 wore on.

Though the program never came to fruition, CASAP's history and the debates it provoked speak to broader themes in Canadian nuclear history. As in other debates, such as those over the Bomarc missile in the 1960s or cruise missile testing in the 1980s, some Canadians appealed to the country's non-nuclear status as a central aspect of Canada's international reputation. Peace groups and champions of arms control pointed to a Canadian commitment to nuclear non-proliferation and the regime of international norms and institutions designed to prevent the spread of nuclear weapons as a prime reason to oppose the submarines, though this rationale did little to sway the Mulroney government's views on the project. But the arguments marshalled in favour of the submarines spoke to a more complicated Canadian nuclear past. Canadian officials might have been misguided, as their counterparts south of the border suggested, but they weren't wrong when they harked back to a long lineage of Canadian nuclear research and the country's experience in building and exporting civilian reactors. That both these arguments were true speaks, yet again, to the complexity of Canada's relationship with nuclear technologies.

## NOTES

I would like to thank Simon Miles for his comments on an earlier draft, as well as the anonymous reviewers for their suggestions and recommendations. Thanks also go to the staff at Library and Archives Canada, particularly the Access to Information analysts without whom this project would not have been possible.

1 *House of Commons Debates,* 33rd Parliament, 2nd Session, vol. 11, March 11, 1988, 13664.
2 Jennifer Ramsay and Larry Ross, "This Country Must Stay Nuclear-Free," *Peace Magazine,* February-March 1988, 12.
3 Voice of Women pamphlet, "Canada's White Paper on Defence: A Reply," May 1988, Ursula M. Franklin Papers, box 039, folder "VOW Muriel Duckworth and Others 1981–1983," University of Toronto Archives and Records Management Services (UTARMS).
4 "Peace Groups React to White Paper," *Canadian Peace Alliance News* 2, 2 (Summer 1987): 3, in box 140019, folder "Canadian Association of Municipal Nuclear Weapons Free Zones (2)," City of Toronto Archives (CTA).
5 *Pacific Tribune* photograph, "Nanaimo demonstration against Mulroney on nuke subs [nuclear submarines], free trade," July 11, 1987, image MSC160-1491_20, SFU Digital Archives, http://digital.lib.sfu.ca/pt-4160/nanaimo-demonstration-against-mulroney-nuke-subs-nuclear-submarines-free-trade.
6 Jeffrey Simpson, "Those Costly Subs," *Globe and Mail,* May 22, 1987.
7 "Nuclear Subs Called Waste of Money," *Globe and Mail,* April 30, 1987.
8 A notable exception is Adam Lajeunesse, "Sovereignty, Security and the Canadian Nuclear Submarine Program," *Canadian Military Journal* 8, 4 (Winter 2007–08): 74–82, http://www.journal.forces.gc.ca/vo8/no4/lajeunes-eng.asp.
9 Brian Mulroney, *Memoirs: 1939–1993* (Toronto: McClelland and Stewart, 2007); Fen Osler Hampson, *Master of Persuasion: Brian Mulroney's Global Legacy* (Toronto: Signal, 2018).
10 See, for example, Julie H. Ferguson, *Through a Canadian Periscope: The Story of the Canadian Submarine Service* (Toronto: Dundurn, 1995), 309–28; Adam Lajeunesse, *Lock, Stock, and Icebergs: A History of Canada's Arctic Maritime Sovereignty* (Vancouver: UBC Press, 2016), 280–86; Sean M. Maloney, "Better Late Than Never: Defence during the Mulroney Years," in *Transforming the Nation: Canada and Brian Mulroney,* ed. Raymond Benjamin Blake (Montreal and Kingston: McGill-Queen's University Press, 2007), 139–42.
11 The title of this section – "We're Not a Bunch of Nuclear Yokels" – is from the November 12, 1987, diary entry in Allan Gotlieb, *The Washington Diaries, 1981–1989* (Toronto: McClelland and Stewart, 2006), 505.

12  Griffiths to SSEA [Secretary of State for External Affairs], "Nuclear-Powered Subma-
    rines in Political Context," December 12, 1986, RG 25, vol. 26931, file 27-1-1-3-2-CASAP,
    pt. 1, Library and Archives Canada (LAC).
13  "Acquisition of Nuclear Powered Submarines," September 3, 1987, RG 25, vol. 26931,
    file 27-1-1-3-2-CASAP, pt. 2, LAC.
14  Gotlieb diary entry, July 8, 1987, in Gotlieb, *Washington Diaries,* 470.
15  Gotlieb diary entry, September 21, 1987, in ibid., 484.
16  Washington to External Affairs, "Cdn Defence Policy: Submarine Acquisition Pro-
    gram (CASAP)," July 24, 1987, RG 25, vol. 26931, file 27-1-1-3-2-CASAP, pt. 1, LAC.
17  Washington to External Affairs, "Cdn Nuclear Submarine Pgm: Trouble Ahead,"
    November 27, 1987, RG 25, vol. 19453, file 27-1-1-3-2-CASAP, pt. 3, LAC.
18  "An Analysis of USA Export Controls on Nuclear Submarine Technology," RG 25,
    vol. 26931, file 27-1-1-3-2-CASAP, pt. 1, LAC.
19  Washington to External Affairs, "CASAP Invitation to Secretary Herrington and Amb
    Call on Deputy Secty Taft," October 18, 1987, RG 25, vol. 26931, file 27-1-1-3-2-CASAP,
    pt. 2, LAC.
20  Washington to External Affairs, "Cdn SSN Program," September 10, 1987, RG 25, vol.
    26931, file 27-1-1-3-2-CASAP, pt. 2, LAC.
21  Washington to External Affairs, "Cdn SSN Programme – Mtg with Ikle," September
    16, 1987, RG 25, vol. 26931, file 27-1-1-3-2-CASAP, pt. 2, LAC.
22  Gotlieb diary entry, September 21, 1987, in Gotlieb, *Washington Diaries,* 484.
23  Anderson to Husk, October 1, 1987, RG 25, vol. 26931, file 27-1-1-3-2-CASAP, pt. 2, LAC.
24  Beatty to Herrington, November 1987, RG 25, vol. 19453, file 27-1-1-3-2-CASAP, pt. 3,
    LAC.
25  Washington to External Affairs, "USA," November 27, 1987, RG 25, vol. 19453, file 27-1
    -1-3-2-CASAP, pt. 3, LAC.
26  Gotlieb diary entry, April 15, 1988, in Gotlieb, *Washington Diaries,* 550.
27  Ish Theilheimer, "The Trouble with Subs," *The Dismantler,* Spring 1988, 4, in MG 28 I
    445, vol. 40, folder "Operation Dismantle Promotional Dismantler Originals 1987–88,"
    LAC.
28  "Dismantling Nuclear Submarines," *Peace Magazine,* June-July 1988, 27; *Pacific Tribune*
    photograph, "Stop the subs rally, Robson Square with EAR [End the Arms Race],
    church groups," June 28, 1988, image MSC160-1645_12, SFU Digital Archives, http://
    digital.lib.sfu.ca/pt-4300/stop-subs-rally-robson-square-ear-end-arms-race
    -church-groups.
29  Al Rycroft, "Surveillance Makes More Sense," *The Dismantler,* Spring 1988, 5, in MG
    28 I 445, vol. 40, folder "Operation Dismantle Promotional Dismantler Originals
    1987–88," LAC; Oldham to Clark, August 26, 1987, RG 25, vol. 26931, file 27-1-1-3-2
    -CASAP, pt. 2, LAC.
30  John M. Lamb, "Roiling the Arms Control Waters," *Bulletin of the Atomic Scientists* 4,
    11 (October 1987): 18.
31  Gregory Wirick, "Report from the Hill," *Peace and Security* 3, 2 (Summer 1988): 13.
32  "Submarine Acquisitions Project," in *International Canada,* 45, supplement to *Inter-
    national Perspectives: The Canadian Journal on World Affairs* XVII, 5 (September/
    October 1988).

33  John M. Lamb and Tariq Rauf, "Canada Sets Sail in Dangerous Water: Nuclear Safeguards Simply Too Weak," *Globe and Mail,* May 12, 1988.
34  "Arctic Choice: Subs or Peace Zone," *Toronto Star,* February 14, 1988.
35  Department of External Affairs House of Commons book briefing note, "Canadian Nuclear-Powered Submarines: Allegation That They Would Be Equipped with Nuclear Missiles," February 19, 1988, RG 25, vol. 19453, file 27-1-1-3-2-CASAP, pt. 5, LAC.
36  Peter Gizewski, Michael Holmes, and Francine Lecours, *A Guide to Canadian Policies on Arms Control, Disarmament, Defence and Conflict Resolution 1987–1988* (Ottawa: Canadian Institute for International Peace and Security, 1988), 97.
37  On the nuclear debates of the early 1960s, see Chapter 4 in this volume. For similar debates in the early 1980s, see Susan Colbourn, "The Elephant in the Room: Rethinking Cruise Missile Testing and Pierre Trudeau's Peace Mission," in *Undiplomatic History: The New Study of Canada and the World,* ed. Asa McKercher and Philip Van Huizen (Montreal and Kingston: McGill-Queen's University Press, 2019), 253–76.
38  William Epstein, "New Stance Tarnishes Canada's Reputation," *Bulletin of the Atomic Scientists* 4, 11 (October 1987): 11.
39  IDR to IFB, "Defence Issues and Canadian Nuclear-Powered Submarines (SSN)," March 4, 1988, RG 25, vol. 19453, file 27-1-1-3-2-CASAP, pt. 5, LAC.
40  Rone Tempest, "Nuclear-Powered Submarine Fuels Controversy over India's Intentions," *Los Angeles Times,* February 20, 1988.
41  *Challenge and Commitment: A Defence Policy for Canada* (Ottawa: Department of National Defence, 1987).
42  Perrin Beatty, "Why Canada Needs Nuclear Subs," *Globe and Mail,* June 6, 1987.
43  "Canada Opts for Nuclear Subs," RG 25, vol. 19453, file 27-1-1-3-2-CASAP, pt. 5, LAC.
44  Memorandum for the Secretary of State for External Affairs, "Defence White Paper: Maritime Strategy," March 31, 1987, RG 25, vol. 26931, file 27-1-1-3-2-CASAP, pt. 1, LAC.
45  Ish Theilheimer, "Momentum Gathers to Sink the Nuclear Subs Proposal," *The Dismantler,* Fall 1988, 1, in MG 28 I 445, vol. 40, folder "Operation Dismantle Promotional Dismantler Originals 1987–88," LAC.
46  C.G. Gifford, "Gorbachev's Vision: A 'Post-Nuclear Age,'" *Peace Magazine,* August-September 1987, 10.
47  Alan Maxwell letter, "No Longer Anti-Soviet," *Peace Magazine,* April-May 1988, 5.
48  Michael Driedger and Don Munton, "Security, Arms Control and Defence: Public Attitudes in Canada," Canadian Institute for International Peace and Security Working Paper 14 (December 1988), 9.
49  U. Paul Ronald letter, *Maclean's,* February 29, 1988, 4.
50  Lajeunesse, *Lock, Stock, and Icebergs,* 255–61.
51  Peter C. Newman, "About-Face in Defence Strategy," *Maclean's,* January 12, 1987, 28.
52  Gotlieb diary entry, July 8, 1987, in Gotlieb, *Washington Diaries,* 470.
53  Barry Stevens, "The Defence White Paper: Six Comments," *Peace Magazine,* August-September 1987, 24, http://peacemagazine.org/archive/v03n4p24.htm.
54  Paul Koring, "Defence Expert Says Nuclear Subs Ill-Suited to Meet Canada's Goal," *Globe and Mail,* June 5, 1987.
55  "Don't Sink Money into Nuclear Submarines," *The Dismantler,* Fall 1988, 9, in MG 28 I 445, vol. 40, folder "Operation Dismantle Promotional Dismantler Originals 1987–88," LAC.

56  *House of Commons Debates*, 33rd Parliament, 2nd Session, vol. 12, May 11, 1988, 15341.
57  Gotlieb diary entry, June 8, 1987, in Gotlieb, *Washington Diaries*, 465.
58  Michael Tucker, "Canadian Security Policy," in *Canada among Nations 1988: The Tory Record*, ed. Brian W. Tomlin and Maureen Appel Molot (Toronto: James Lorimer, 1989), 65–70.
59  *Challenge and Commitment*, 52–53.
60  Cook to Moher, "CASAP/SSN Multibranch Exercise Kingston, October 13–14, 1987," October 19, 1987, RG 25, vol. 26931, file 27-1-1-3-2-CASAP, pt. 2, LAC.
61  IDR to IFB, "Defence Issues and Canadian Nuclear-Powered Submarines (SSN)," March 4, 1988, RG 25, vol. 19453, file 27-1-1-3-2-CASAP, pt. 5, LAC.
62  Tariq Rauf and Marie-France Desjardins, "Canada's Nuclear Submarine Program: A New Proliferation Concern," *Arms Control Today* 18, 10 (December 1988): 14; William M. Arkin and Steve Shallhorn, "Canada Even More under U.S. Thumb in Sub Plan," *Globe and Mail*, July 7, 1987; John M. Lamb, "Roiling the Arms Control Waters," *Bulletin of the Atomic Scientists* 4, 11 (October 1987): 18.
63  IDR to IFB, "Defence Issues and Canadian Nuclear-Powered Submarines (SSN)," March 4, 1988, RG 25, vol. 19453, file 27-1-1-3-2-CASAP, pt. 5, LAC.
64  Memorandum for the Secretary of State for External Affairs, "Canadian Submarine Acquisition Program (CASAP): Issues Expected to Arise," February 5, 1988, RG 25, vol. 19453, file 27-1-1-3-2-CASAP, pt. 4, LAC.
65  Iain Hunter, "'NORAD of the Sea' Price for Nuke Subs," *Ottawa Citizen*, November 19, 1987.
66  "U.S. Embassy press line on Captain Hofford's Comments as dictated at 12:19 hrs November 19," RG 25, vol. 19453, file 27-1-1-3-2-CASAP, pt. 3, LAC.
67  Steve Shallhorn, "Canada Does Not Have Its Own Submarine Strategy," *Peace Magazine*, August-September 1987, 35.
68  Steve Shallhorn, "Standing Up to the United States," *Bulletin of the Atomic Scientists* 4, 11 (October 1987): 17.
69  "The Liberal Defence Policy: Douglas Frith Answers Questions," *Peace Magazine*, August-September 1988, 6. For detail on the controversy over cruise missile testing in the early 1980s, see Colbourn, "The Elephant in the Room"; Susan Colbourn, "'Cruising toward Nuclear Danger': Canadian Anti-Nuclear Activism, Pierre Trudeau's Peace Mission, and the Transatlantic Partnership," *Cold War History* 18, 1 (2018): 19–36. Little has been written in-depth on Canadian opposition to the Strategic Defense Initiative, but overviews can be found in Nelson Michaud and Kim Richard Nossal, "The Conservative Era in Canadian Foreign Policy, 1984–93," in *Diplomatic Departures: The Conservative Era in Canadian Foreign Policy, 1984–93*, ed. Kim R. Nossal and Nelson Michaud (Vancouver: UBC Press, 2002), 14–15. A broad overview of public discussion of these defence issues can be found in Ann Denholm Crosby, "The Print Media's Shaping of the Security Discourse: Cruise Missile Testing, SDI, and NORAD," *International Journal* 52, 1 (Winter 1996–97): 89–117.
70  "Submarine Acquisitions Project," in *International Canada*, 43, supplement to *International Perspectives: The Canadian Journal on World Affairs* XVII, 4 (July/August 1988).
71  Department of State statement, "Canadian Acquisition of Nuclear-Powered Submarines," April 27, 1988, *Department of State Bulletin*, July 1988, 61.

72  Allan to Clark, June 2, 1988, RG 25, vol. 19454, file 27-1-1-3-2-CASAP, pt. 9, LAC.

73  *House of Commons Debates,* 33rd Parliament, 2nd Session, vol. 12, April 21, 1988, 14691.

74  By 1987, Manitoba, Ontario, and the Northwest Territories had declared themselves to be nuclear weapons–free zones, along with hundreds of municipalities across the country. Some 60 percent of Canadians, according to one estimate, lived in a nuclear weapons–free zone: "169 Nuclear Weapons Free Zones in Canada!" *Canadian Peace Alliance News,* Summer 1987, 12, in box 140019, folder "Canadian Association of Municipal Nuclear Weapons Free Zones (2)," CTA.

75  "Anti-Sub Lobby Runs Aground," *Canadian Defence Update* 2, 5 (June 1988): 4.

76  Beatty to all Cabinet ministers, June 27, 1988, RG 25, vol. 19454, file 27-1-1-3-2-CASAP, pt. 9, LAC.

77  "Choosing Submarines," *Globe and Mail,* June 21, 1988.

78  Michael Driedger and Don Munton, "Security, Arms Control and Defence: Public Attitudes in Canada," Canadian Institute for International Peace and Security Working Paper 14 (December 1988), 9.

79  Ken Romain, "Submarine Decision Unlikely before February," *Globe and Mail,* October 27, 1988.

80  "Submarine Acquisitions Project," in *International Canada,* 43, supplement to *International Perspectives: The Canadian Journal on World Affairs* XVII, 4 (July/August 1988).

81  Kenneth Calder, "The Federal Budget: Defence and Foreign Policy," *Peace and Security* 4, 2 (Summer 1989): 4.

82  Decima Quarterly 38, June 1989. Earlier polls framed the issue similarly: Decima Quarterly 36, December 1988; Environics Focus Canada 1989-2, March 1989.

83  The budget also included the closure of seven bases and the scaling back of operations at seven more, as well as reductions in plans to purchase tanks, light-armoured vehicles, and communications systems: "Canada Canceling Plan to Purchase Atom Submarines," *New York Times,* April 28, 1989.

# CHAPTER 7

# "BAPTISM BY FIRE"

## Canadian Soldiers and Radiation Exposure at Nevada and Maralinga

*Matthew S. Wiseman*

A t 5:10 a.m. PDT on May 5, 1955, Squadron Leader W. Greensword of the Royal Canadian Air Force (RCAF) crouched down in the bottom of a four-foot trench, his eyes closed and one forearm tightly pressed against his face. The trench was 3,500 yards from a 500-foot tower constructed as the base for Apple II, a forty-kiloton yield atomic bomb. Positioned alongside a tri-service contingent of Canadian personnel, Greensword waited, not knowing what to expect. Then it happened. "The flash was brighter than gazing at the sun," Greensword later recalled, despite having his back to the explosion. "The ground shock wave arrived almost instantaneously. The ground rocked slowly at first then with increasing speed and severity. The trench caved in a little. This feeling of an earthquake was the most perturbing feature of the explosion." At forty kilotons, the estimated force of Apple II was about twice the yield of Fat Man, the atomic bomb dropped on Nagasaki in August 1945. Greensword described hearing a "giant thunderclap" before rising to observe the final stages of the fireball that preceded the mushroom cloud. Hot gases produced a pink and purple mass, and the blast showered "considerable quantities of loose earth . . . into the trench and a pall of dust covered the area."[1] After the explosion, Greensword climbed out of the trench, dusted off, and went for breakfast. His day had only just begun.

At 8:30 the same morning, just three hours and twenty minutes later, Greensword observed a specially trained unit of the Canadian Army enter the blast zone. Thirty personnel of No. 1 Radiation Detection Unit (1 RDU), wearing protective clothing and standard issue respirators, entered the contaminated area to plot and measure radioactivity near ground zero. The unit spent six hours and thirty minutes monitoring radiological contamination, allegedly free of any substantial danger. "No significant radiation was received either from the flash or from residual contamination, which was very light," Greensword reported. "The operation was completely successful, but the lack of heavy contamination tended to give a false picture of the results of a ground burst." The height of the bomb tower minimized the fireball's impact, according to representatives from Atomic Energy of Canada Limited (AECL). Founded as a Crown corporation in 1952, AECL researched and developed peaceful uses of nuclear energy.[2] The Apple II test provided an excellent opportunity to observe an atomic explosion and record scientific data. The bomb tower stood on an area of asphalt measuring 600 feet in diameter, which reduced the quantity and spread of contaminant. "As a result of these precautions, and the nature of the dry dusty area," Greensword concluded, "there was only negligible contamination of personnel, vehicles and equipment, and little was learned of the problem of decontamination."[3]

Greensword's vivid account survived because Group Captain Kenneth Maclure, RCAF member of the Canadian Joint Special Weapons Committee (JSWC), asked for a report about the value of Exercise Sapling, the secret Canadian operation conducted in conjunction with the detonation of Apple II.[4] Between April 20 and May 11, 1955, 1 RDU monitored, surveyed, and plotted a large field of radiation at the Nevada Test Site, both before and after the Apple II test.[5] Fifty-eight Canadians participated, including ten headquarters and administrative staff and eighteen personnel from detachments of the RCAF and the Royal Canadian Navy (RCN).[6] The thirty soldiers of 1 RDU entered the contaminated area alone, using Geiger counters and related instruments to detect and measure radiation following the detonation of Apple II. Having undergone extensive technical training at radiological facilities in Canada, the exercise provided an opportunity to test the specially trained unit under conditions produced by the actual detonation of a nuclear bomb.

Exercise Sapling was part of a series of military experiments designed to prepare the Canadian armed services for atomic warfare. Military officials in Ottawa established 1 RDU in March 1950 to assess radiological hazards for the three services and study the problems associated with managing the residual effects of atomic explosions.[7] The unit was a product of the early Cold War, established and maintained as a practical response to new developments in warfighting and the fear associated with a global nuclear conflict. Operational between 1950 and 1959, the unit carried out decontamination work at Chalk River and radiological monitoring during atomic weapons trials at the Nevada Test Site and the Maralinga Range in southern Australia.[8] The history of 1 RDU is valuable for investigating Canada's official position on atomic weapons activities and radiation science during the nuclear age.

Recently declassified records suggest that Canadian military officials exposed personnel of 1 RDU to unsafe levels of radiation during training and operational duty. The same concerns that motivated the creation of 1 RDU influenced how military leaders understood the role and value of specially trained radiological soldiers, the term applied to describe soldiers thought capable of operating safely in irradiated areas. Despite the health and safety risks associated with monitoring and surveying radiation in highly contaminated areas, the Canadian armed services subjected 1 RDU to extremely hazardous conditions. Operating under flawed assumptions about radiation tolerance in the human body, the officials who created 1 RDU permitted unit personnel to be exposed to abnormally high radiation levels during decontamination work and nuclear weapons trials. The desire to obtain military knowledge about the immediate and residual effects of radiation trumped health concerns for the individual and collective safety of unit personnel, a stark reality of the Canadian experience with radiation science and atomic warfare research during the early Cold War.

Tracing the history of 1 RDU allows for a deeper appreciation of Canada's official involvement in nuclear affairs prior to the 1963 Partial Nuclear Test Ban Treaty, which prohibited atmospheric nuclear weapons tests.[9] While Canadian involvement in nuclear weapons trials dates to 1946, no government or military representative actively participated in an atomic weapons test prior to the formation of 1 RDU. Canadian personnel had observed atomic trials from a distance at Bikini Atoll in the Marshall Islands, but the Apple II test in Nevada marked the first live trial involving Canadian soldiers on the ground. By functioning as a mobile radiological field lab, the unit assessed nuclear toxicity at blast sites in both the United States and Australia. Personnel also coordinated and carried out the testing and evaluation of technological equipment under nuclear test conditions, and trained civil defence workers in Canada. Yet 1 RDU has received scant attention in historical scholarship about the Canadian experience with atomic weapons trials and radiation science. Outside the work of historians John Clearwater, Sean Maloney, and Andrew Godefroy, the origins and activities of 1 RDU remain largely untold.[10] This chapter draws upon the few published military sources and recently declassified records, adding to narrative accounts of 1 RDU at Nevada and Maralinga by calling attention to medical and ethical considerations about the employment and experience of unit personnel exposed to unusually high radiation levels during training and operational duty.[11]

## FORMATIVE YEARS OF 1 RDU

In early March 1950, Lieutenant-General Charles Foulkes wrote to Minister of National Defence Brooke Claxton proposing the formation of a special unit of the Canadian Army regular force to be designated No. 1 Radiation Detection Unit, Royal Canadian Engineers. "Owing to the likely use of atomic bombs in any future war," wrote Foulkes, "it is considered that immediate steps should be taken to perfect measures for handling an atomic bomb disaster in any city or area. There is a need for specially-trained personnel who can assist in solving the radioactivity problems associated with any attack."[12] An experimental unit, he argued, would serve as a medium to test Canada's defence organization, procedures, personnel, and equipment. Claxton authorized Foulkes' proposal on March 13, formally establishing 1 RDU.[13]

Canadian officials considered 1 RDU to be unique, the world's first radiological military unit formed under the looming threat of an atomic war. "The task of No 1 RDU is to study all aspects of radiation detection as they affect the Canadian Army," stated a report prepared by Lieutenant-Colonel R.A. Klaehn. "Since No 1 RDU is working in a field in which no experience is available as a guide, either from Canadian sources or from other countries, its officers require considerable experience and ability."[14] The unit trained in Ottawa and Kingston near research facilities operated by the scientific and technical research branch of Canada's Department of

National Defence, the Defence Research Board (DRB).[15] Unit personnel trained to identify and manage radioactive contamination by conducting mock exercises under simulated nuclear-attack conditions, exercises deemed valuable for Canadian security and national defence in the event of an actual atomic war.

The challenge of preparing for nuclear war meant having soldiers trained to operate on the radioactive or toxic battlefield. One of Canada's earliest experiences with radiological military training occurred in October 1952, when the Canadian Army participated in Exercise Medical Rubicon, a British initiative designed to develop capabilities in dealing with the threat of tactical atomic bombs.[16] Fifteen months later, the Royal Canadian Army Medical Corps held its own exercise called Medical Broad Front II at Camp Borden. Soldiers of the First Canadian Corps took part in a simulated attack involving a mock twenty-kiloton yield atomic bomb, which produced an estimated 10,000 casualties resulting from blast, burn, and radiation.[17] Later field trials emphasized the practical value of civil defence and the importance of military preparations for handling a targeted nuclear attack against a highly populated Canadian city.

The first experience of 1 RDU with live radiation occurred at Chalk River, an atomic pile and nuclear research facility located on the Ottawa River, approximately 180 kilometres northwest of Canada's capital.[18] On December 12, 1952, the NRX reactor, owned and operated by AECL, suffered a partial meltdown from a leak of radioactive material. An explosion occurred the next day while workers tested the effluent, and the accident contaminated the reactor and equipment in the pile building.[19] Workers on site flooded the pile to prevent a fire, resulting in a large pool of contaminated water in the reactor's basement. AECL Chalk River requested military assistance on December 14, and all three services subsequently participated in a large cleanup operation that occurred at the reactor building through October 1953.

For Canadian military officials, the accident at Chalk River represented a training opportunity. Immediately upon request for assistance, the armed services sent personnel to support the cleanup effort, knowing that all workers on site would receive instruction in radiological safety and valuable first-hand experience for any future decontamination duty. The army's radiation detection unit received special instructions, however. Under the code name Exercise Charity, 1 RDU personnel undertook a detailed site survey of the entire plant area, monitored on-site workers and their supplies for traces of radioactivity, and mopped up the contaminated water in the reactor's flooded basement.[20] Dressed in heavy underwear, white coveralls, rubber boots, respirators, caps, and elbow-length rubber gloves, 1 RDU personnel worked in pairs for ten-minute shifts, cleaning the basement on a rotational basis. Each soldier had film badges and pocket dosimeters that monitored individual exposure levels. The basement cleanup took approximately one hour during the afternoon of December 17, resulting in one reported incident involving a man who fell in the water and received immediate scrubbing as part of a decontamination process. The existing records do not describe the decontamination process for the accident victim, although standard practice included the removal and discarding of uniform and clothes, full-body washing, medical examination with urinalysis and radiological readings, and removal from active duty.

Charity was a three-part exercise. The initial accident was much worse than initially predicted and the cleanup lasted for months, prompting military officials to redeploy 1 RDU for additional assistance in February 1953. The unit's return to Chalk River provided much-needed support and critical information about the existing dangers for on-site workers. AECL wanted to dismantle the entire reactor, but radiation monitoring showed that maintenance workers had received dangerously high doses in short periods. In some cases, on-site personnel received their maximum permitted daily dose within a few minutes. Military officials returned 1 RDU to the accident site under the assumption that unit personnel had the training and skills necessary to decontaminate the area under controlled conditions. "Personnel of 1 RDU [will] be employed to aid in the decontamination of material at Chalk River," one exercise report explained, "and they [will] be permitted to incur a radiation dosage of up to 5 roentgens per man over a period of about a month."[21] At the time, the International Commission on Radiological Protection (ICRP) set the international safety standard for bodily exposure to radiation. The recommended external radiation level in 1953 was a maximum of 0.3 roentgen per working week for whole-body exposure.[22] Named for the German physicist Wilhelm Röntgen and adopted in 1928 as the first international unit for measuring the quantity of ionizing radiation, the roentgen enabled scientists to monitor exposure to X-rays and gamma rays for protection against unsafe levels of radioactivity.[23] At 5 roentgens per month, Canadian military officials permitted 1 RDU personnel to reach individual radiation exposure levels approximately four times higher than the recommended international safety standard.

Decontaminating the reactor at Chalk River exposed 1 RDU personnel to radiation doses considered abnormally high by medical authorities in the Canadian armed services. On April 10, 1953, the director general of medical services, Brigadier K.A. Hunter, expressed concern over individual radiation exposures and requested complete physical examinations, blood counts, and radiological recordings for all members of the unit. "Personnel of No. 1 Radiation Detection Unit (RDU) RCE are presently employed on a decontamination task at Chalk River, involving a possible exposure to 5 roentgens of ionizing radiation per man over a period of a month, which is a greater exposure than is commonly encountered," Hunter wrote in his letter requesting the individual medical examinations.[24] Eleven days later, medical officer Colonel S.G.U. Shier sent a follow-up request for specific information about the level of radiation exposure experienced by the entire unit. "These personnel have been exposed to possibly 5 roentgens of ionizing radiation over a period of a month," Shier told Army Headquarters (HQ), before requesting individual dosimeter readings for the entire unit.[25] Whether Army HQ fulfilled Shier's request is unclear, but the safety concerns raised by medical authorities prompted changes to the monitoring of 1 RDU at Chalk River.

During Exercise Charity III from June to October 1953, 1 RDU personnel received medical examinations prior to dispatch and upon return home. Pre-work examinations included differential blood count and urinalysis, and post-work examinations included full urinalysis to check for the presence of radioisotopes. Participating soldiers also received a second complete physical examination after returning to their home station. Nonetheless, military officials permitted 1 RDU personnel to reach higher radiation exposure levels despite medical advice to the contrary. "Because personnel are only exposed to radiation for a two week period they can receive a much higher radiation count per week than is allowable for plant personnel," stated the report for Exercise Charity III. "It is estimated that one service personnel is the equivalent of six plant personnel in this regard."[26] In other words, military officials deliberately exposed 1 RDU personnel to abnormally high doses of radiation at Chalk River under the assumption that participating soldiers could receive monthly and yearly permitted doses in a truncated period. This flawed understanding of radiation exposure in the human body remained with 1 RDU throughout the 1950s, retrospectively underscoring the health risks incurred by unit personnel during subsequent nuclear weapons trials in the United States and Australia.

## NUCLEAR TRIALS AT NEVADA AND MARALINGA

Canadians first participated at an atmospheric nuclear weapons trial in mid-1946 when a delegation attended Operation Crossroads to observe a pair of atomic explosions conducted by the United States at Bikini Atoll. Canadian participation in American trials ceased thereafter, until 1954, when a revision to the US Atomic Energy Act of 1946 (McMahon Act) allowed for foreign activities.[27] In the interim, Canadian officials struggled for access to scientific information about the defensive aspects of nuclear war preparations. In February 1953, the chair of Canada's Defence Research Board, Omond Solandt, urged senior officials in Ottawa to ask the US government to permit Canadians to participate in atomic weapons trials.[28] Knowing that the McMahon Act prevented foreign participation, the Chiefs of Staff Committee decided against making a request on Solandt's behalf. Charles Foulkes informed those in attendance that he expected the American position to change within a year, and Solandt received the committee's permission to approach British officials with a similar request.

The February meeting marked a turning point for Foulkes. Three months later, he directed Rear Admiral Harry DeWolf of the Canadian Joint Staff in Washington to approach US officials with a request for increased transparency and cooperation in nuclear affairs.[29] Foulkes wanted Canadian senior staff to observe American nuclear weapons trials and training activities, suggesting one course for navy personnel and four courses each for army and air force personnel. In response, the Pentagon informed Foulkes that information about American activities in atomic defence and tactical training was legally restricted to US military personnel.[30] Progress stalled thereafter, until September, when members of the Canadian Joint Special Weapons Committee met in Ottawa to discuss military participation in American and British atomic trials. At the meeting, chemist Otto Maass reiterated the importance of transparency and cooperation among the North Atlantic partners. Lieutenant-Colonel R.A. Klaehn, who represented the army, confirmed that 1 RDU was ready and enthusiastic to take part.[31]

Searching for ways to participate at Nevada, Foulkes met with US Army General Matthew Ridgway, chair of the Joint Chiefs of Staff (JCS), in early November 1953. Foulkes suggested that American personnel could assist Canadian forces in training radiation soldiers and testing field equipment at an actual atomic weapons trial. Four days later, he provided a detailed list of preferred projects that included 1 RDU training with American soldiers, attendance of Canadian officers and selected military personnel at American instructional schools, observation of the effects of an atomic explosion on Canadian equipment, and observation of soldier trials followed by active participation with platoon and company-size formations.[32] The following May, Ridgway sent a formal offer to Foulkes permitting a small group of Canadian observers to attend an upcoming atomic test.[33] The test was designed to train participating personnel for atomic war, and Ridgway proposed placing the Canadian observers alongside American soldiers in trenches located as close to ground zero as safety permitted. Shortly thereafter Canadian military officials received a formal invitation to observe nuclear trials at the Nevada Test Site, located 105 kilometres northwest of the city of Las Vegas.

The urgency of Canadian participation in American weapons testing and military training increased over the next two years as the Cold War arms race intensified. In March 1954, the United States carried out a series of thermonuclear explosions in the Marshall Islands. The following year, the Soviet Union demonstrated its technological might by successfully detonating a hydrogen bomb and raising the spectre of a full-scale nuclear apocalypse. The threat of mutual assured destruction did not spell the end of radiological military training, though. As Canadians debated the practicality of civil defence in a world of increasingly destructive nuclear weapons, military officials in Ottawa reaffirmed the need for specially trained radiological soldiers. The Canadian Civil Defence Review released a new set of guidelines in February 1955 that called for immediate evacuation during a thermonuclear attack, providing further impetus for military units trained in assessing radioactive hazards over large areas.[34] In hindsight, it is easy to overlook the seemingly slow progression of knowledge about fallout and the residual effects of radiation poisoning, but questions about the actual technological threat and adequacy of Canada's capacity to mitigate the danger of a nuclear attack remained debatable throughout the decade.

In the spring of 1955, the US Atomic Energy Commission (AEC) conducted a series of atomic weapons trials at the Nevada Test Site code-named Operation Teapot.[35] The operation was the single largest series of atomic trials involving human participants to date. American military personnel participated under the designation Desert Rock, named for the US Army's adjacent Camp Desert Rock. The Canadian contingent on Exercise Sapling participated in conjunction with the US Army's Exercise Desert Rock, an atomic experiment conducted as part of the AEC's wider Operation Teapot. Designed to permit soldiers in trenches and armoured vehicles to observe and experience the effects of an atomic explosion at close range, Exercise Desert Rock exposed American soldiers to fourteen nuclear events. Canadian service personnel participated in only one explosion, Shot Apple II, on the morning of May 5, the weapons test lucidly described by RCAF Squadron Leader Greensword at the beginning of this chapter. Soldiers, sailors, and aviators of the armed services witnessed the detonation from trenches and foxholes located at distances ranging from 3,000 to 3,500 yards. "At this range they were close enough to the explosion to appreciate the value of a good trench," commented Lieutenant-Colonel Klaehn of the Royal Canadian Engineers, the director of Exercise Sapling.[36]

Shot Apple II was 1 RDU's first exposure to an actual atomic blast. Military officials considered the test vital for obtaining information about nuclear warfare, the performance of radiological soldiers, and the value of radiation-detection equipment under realistic conditions. "In spite of a great deal of training and a number of exercises carried out by No. 1 RDU, there was still a lack of the final proof – 'baptism by fire,'" Klaehn recalled in the July 1955 issue of *Canadian Army Journal*.[37] Unit personnel put on respirators five minutes before the explosion. "The trench heaved and rocked, chunks of it fell in on top of personnel," recalled the head of the RCN contingent. "Stones, sand and dirt showered into the trench . . . Half an hour after the burst our operational vehicles arrived, the unit embarked and proceeded about ten miles out of the area of the shot."[38] On arrival at the back area, 1 RDU ate breakfast and then deployed to commence the radiological site survey. Equipped with Geiger counters and other radiation-detection devices, the unit proceeded toward ground zero and measured radiation near the epicentre of the explosion.

Exercise Sapling was more than a radiological survey, however. It was an opportunity to test 1 RDU under the conditions produced by live exposure to residual radiation. The US military wanted to determine the maneuverability and operational capabilities of armoured units in a nuclear blast zone. Eight minutes after the detonation of Apple II, an American armoured task force equipped with fifty-five M-48 tanks moved to within 890 metres of ground zero.[39] 1 RDU provided assistance with specially equipped jeeps, helping to predict contamination patterns and conduct the ground radiation survey. While on location, Canadian officers instructed 1 RDU personnel to construct a trench in an irradiated area. Four soldiers wearing protective clothing and respirators worked for ninety minutes, digging the trench in an area of confirmed surface contamination. Unit personnel also conducted an experiment to shield a gamma survey metre with a human body, according to the final exercise report.[40] Both experiments occurred while the unit as a whole completed the on-site survey, working in the highly contaminated blast zone for more than four hours. The soldiers covered their feet and legs with protective plastic designed to prevent contamination from radioactive dust and particles. Under intense weather conditions, the respirators and plastic protective suits worn by the soldiers caused a number of personnel to suffer heat prostration. The unit returned to ground zero in the days that followed, further surveying and monitoring residual radiation during the remainder of Sapling.

Media reports about the Canadian experience in Nevada suggest that the armed services lacked sufficient knowledge about the immediate and lasting health hazards of radiation exposure. One news article distributed across Canada showed a smiling Staff Sergeant Jim Taylor of Ottawa holding a "souvenir" nameplate that he kept to mark his experience participating in a live atomic exercise.[41] Taylor was with 1 RDU for Exercise Sapling at Camp Desert Rock. He covered a wooden plaque with a stencil of his name and placed it about 2,000 yards from ground zero. The raw power and heat of one explosion burned his name into the wood, and he left the test site with his name etched into his own atomic plaque. Each Canadian participant returned home with a similar souvenir, largely unaware of any hazardous radiation absorbed and carried in his body.

Owing to the Canadian experience at the Nevada Test Site, British officials invited the Canadian armed services to participate in nuclear weapons trials at the Maralinga Range in the southern Australian desert. Federal representatives from Ottawa and London first discussed Canadian participation in British nuclear weapons trials during the Ninth Tripartite Conference on Toxicological Warfare, held in London in September 1954.[42] The following April, Canadian officials accepted a formal invitation from the British to participate in Operation Buffalo, a series of trials scheduled for Maralinga in mid to late 1956.[43] Considered a remote area by the British government, Maralinga was the traditional land of the Maralinga Tjarutja peoples. Australian authorities seized the land and handed control over to the federal government for use by the British, who subsequently conducted nuclear weapons tests on-site between 1956 and 1963.[44]

Senior Canadian officials approved the armed services for participation in Operation Buffalo at a meeting of the Chiefs of Staff Committee in late June 1955.[45] The plan included twenty-five personnel of 1 RDU, ten scientific officers from the Defence Research Board, nine service officers to be integrated with the British forces, and an administrative staff composed of one officer and one clerk. British officials also suggested a rotation system to increase the number of Canadian participants, which allowed an additional thirteen participants from the Army, the RCAF, and the DRB. The operation commenced on September 27, 1956, when a Royal Air Force bomber dropped the first of four nuclear weapons, a fifteen-kiloton yield bomb named One Tree. The atomic cloud triggered by the blast reached over 10,000 feet higher than scientists had predicted, and the fallout carried hazardous particles eastward toward populated areas on Australia's east coast. Over the next three weeks, three more detonations followed, with radioactive material registering as far away as Queensland.[46] The British were keen to have Canada involved and utilized 1 RDU as the primary radiation survey team during all four nuclear weapons trials.

Canadian personnel were most active during the final operational blast test. Equipped with protective gear and radiation-detection instruments,

1 RDU personnel rode in jeeps near ground zero and conducted a detailed radiological survey during the day and night. The unit experienced partial communications blackouts and contamination of all vehicles was severe, causing personnel to develop and refine decontamination methods in the field. One report noted that the relatively quick decay of fallout enabled unit personnel to work increasingly closer to the blast zone with normal clothes, gloves, rubber boots, and standard respirators about three to four days after the initial detonation.[47] 1 RDU also carried out a second exercise in an area of confirmed surface contamination, participating with two Australian battalions and reconnaissance troops in a simulated full-scale brigade advance. This exercise enabled unit personnel to test experimental radiation detection and monitoring equipment under design and development for use by soldiers, sailors, and aviators in the Canadian armed services.

Despite the medical advice of scientific authorities in the federal government, Canadian military officials preapproved abnormally high radiation doses for 1 RDU personnel at Operation Buffalo. Provisional radiological safety regulations at the Maralinga Range allowed for a dose of three roentgens with the permission of the British Health Control Officer. In the event that service personnel needed to recover vital records, the Trials Superintendent had the authority to approve individual doses of ten roentgens after consultation with the acting Health Physics Advisor and Medical Officer. The maximum permissible dose was twenty-five roentgens during the entire operation, applicable under the same rules governing the initial increase to ten roentgens, and only in special cases where service personnel had received no prior exposure to radiation.[48]

Because the Canadian armed services had previous experience with exposure to live radiation, British officials requested that 1 RDU be permitted to receive ten roentgens during the operation. Before approving the request, Canadian Army officials consulted scientific authorities from the Defence Research Board. Medical scientists in the DRB recommended the approval of ten roentgens for 1 RDU personnel, but not "without reference to the Trials Superintendent."[49] Officials in the armed services disagreed. "Maralinga Range Safety Regulations are designed primarily for personnel who normally are exposed to radiation, and who must average down to the industrial tolerance over the year," stated a Canadian military brief.

"These personnel will have some 1956 count when they arrive at Maralinga. 1 RDU, with its ability to average down quicker than the AWRE or MOS personnel, would be an invaluable pool of personnel able to take, safely, higher dosages."[50] 1 RDU eventually participated in Operation Buffalo under a maximum permissible dose of fifteen roentgens.[51] Any exposure exceeding six roentgens required the approval of senior service officers, and any dose over ten roentgens required consultation with the Trials Superintendent. To the extent that senior Canadian military officials believed specially trained soldiers could withstand higher levels of radiation, the expectation of risk was considerably greater for 1 RDU personnel. The unit served as a radiological protectorate for the armed services, unknowingly risking personal health and safety in preparation for the nuclear battlefield.

## RADIATION EXPOSURES AND 1 RDU

Although the Canadian Army has no official history of its involvement in American or British nuclear weapons trials, Minister of National Defence Gordon O'Connor commissioned historian John Clearwater to prepare a detailed information report in August 2006. After examining classified documents from government and military sources, Clearwater wrote a report for federal officials involved in decision-making about pensions and benefits for veterans who had participated in atmospheric nuclear weapons tests and decontamination activities during the 1940s and 1950s.[52] He uncovered military records with information about twenty-nine nuclear tests involving 689 Canadian soldiers. He also identified 191 service personnel who had participated in the radiation cleanup activities at Chalk River, as well as information about RCAF intelligence efforts involving the monitoring of fallout clouds and collection of nuclear debris using airborne filters.

Clearwater's report is purposefully descriptive and claims to draw no conclusions about what happened to the Canadian military personnel who participated in the events documented. He describes the invitation, selection, and employment of Canadians during nuclear weapons trials conducted in the United States and Australia, as well as the training methods and safety precautions implemented for the personnel exposed to radiation during the testing and decontamination work. He does not address ethical questions, although he defines human radiation experiments as "tests done on human beings in which the person is subject to radiation exposure for the purpose of some direct medical or operational test." The participation of Canadian service personnel at US and British nuclear weapons trials did not constitute human radiation experiments "in the strict definitional sense," Clearwater contends. "Canadian troops were not 'guinea pigs' of atomic tests, in that the term guinea pig implies the person is a test subject on whom continued medical monitoring will be carried out on pursuit of a scientific outcome."[53]

In contrast, documents released south of the border revealed the frequent and systematic use of American soldiers as guinea pigs for radiation experiments conducted during the earliest decades of the Cold War. A 1986 report of the US House of Representatives titled *American Nuclear Guinea Pigs: Three Decades of Radiation Experiments on U.S. Citizens* described thirty-one experiments involving the exposure of 695 personnel to radiation that provided little or no medical benefit to the research subjects.[54] Several years later, in 1993, the Pulitzer Prize–winning journalism of investigative reporter Eileen Welsome prompted the Clinton administration to establish an Advisory Committee on Human Radiation Experiments.[55] The committee released its final report in October 1995, revealing the full extent of US atomic trials and the unsafe use of American personnel in experimental testing.[56] In one series of human experiments carried out during the Manhattan Project, scientists injected research subjects with plutonium to develop a diagnostic tool for determining the uptake of a radioactive chemical element in the body from the amount excreted in the subject's urine and feces.[57] Researchers wanted to develop this tool to protect workers during the production of atomic bombs by identifying and removing individuals that had received an internal dose that was near or above the recommended safety limit.

Clearwater's report is not a Canadian equivalent of the government investigation that occurred in the United States and it is unfair to draw direct comparisons with regard to semantics or conclusions, but the probability of his assessment of Canadian troops hinges on the wider history of Canada's military participation in Cold War nuclear activities. While members of the Canadian armed services experienced American and

British atomic trials as both observers and participants, the personnel of 1 RDU experienced vastly different circumstances.[58] Unlike the soldiers, sailors, and aviators who participated in nuclear weapons trials or decontamination work, members of 1 RDU received instructional duties designed to expose unit personnel to radiological contamination for training purposes. Canadian military officials believed that 1 RDU personnel could safely receive monthly and yearly maximum permissible doses in a shortened period. At no point was 1 RDU deliberately exposed to unsafe levels of radiation for experiments on the human body, but unit personnel received special treatment as superior radiological soldiers. Despite clear health and safety warnings from medical authorities in the Canadian government, military officials subjected 1 RDU personnel to increased radiation exposures under flawed assumptions about tolerance levels in the human body. Training and expertise distinguished the soldiers of 1 RDU, or so military officials wrongly believed.

Indeed, recently declassified medical records indicate that personnel of 1 RDU received abnormally high radiation doses at Nevada and Maralinga. "Records of the atomic tests at Nevada, in May 55, show that no RDU personnel received more than 2606 mr [2.6 roentgens]," stated a Canadian brief describing the British regulation standards at Maralinga.[59] The recorded dose was an estimate based on film badge and dosimeter readings tabulated at the end of Exercise Sapling. At the recommended international safety standard of 0.3 roentgen per week for whole-body exposure, the soldier or soldiers referenced in this brief received more than two times the level of radiation deemed permissible by the International Commission on Radiological Protection.[60] This suggests that Canadian military leaders overlooked existing scientific and medical advice, believing that specially trained soldiers could withstand greater radiation doses than the average citizen. Recorded exposure levels at Maralinga were even higher, in part because 1 RDU participated in four nuclear trials. Thirteen of the fifty-three unit personnel involved in Operation Buffalo registered individual doses exceeding 2.0 roentgens, five of whom registered over 3.0 roentgens. The highest doses were 3.68 and 3.69 roentgens, which was about three times the international safety standard.[61] Collectively, the unit received an average recorded dose of 1.19 roentgens during the operation.

Despite following American and British safety regulations, Canadian soldiers, scientists, and technical workers participated in atomic trials at Nevada and Maralinga without an official policy for radiation exposure. In fact, the Canadian armed services first adopted a formal policy governing exposure to radiation during training and operational duty in March 1961. The health and safety of Canadian personnel was not the top priority, however. The primary aim of the policy was to ensure the maintenance of maximum force capabilities in peace and war. "The variation in biological responses to radiation does not permit accurate prediction of the effect of any dose," stated the final policy paper. "However, the following radiation exposures are considered to be the *maximum* to which personnel can be exposed without the expectation of some early loss of operational effectiveness . . . a) 100r [roentgens] in under six weeks [and] b) 200r in over six weeks."[62] Approved by the Chiefs of Staff Committee, this policy established maximum radiation exposure levels for non-operational situations, wartime operations, and national survival circumstances.

In line with pre-existing attitudes about the performance and expectation of Canada's radiological soldiers, the newly adopted radiation exposure policy circumvented civilian standards. Under the Atomic Energy Control Regulations (PC 1960-348), personnel of the Canadian armed services were classed as "atomic energy workers" for the purposes and interpretation of the new policy.[63] Although the federal government followed the official recommendations of the International Commission on Radiological Protection that entered into force in September 1958, the radiation exposure policy implemented by the armed services in 1961 followed the ICRP guidelines only in non-emergency situations.[64] The policy established different standards for Canadian military personnel operating in combat zones, national survival operations, and support areas. Whereas the ICRP recommended no single dose greater than 0.3 roentgen per week for whole-body exposure, senior Canadian officials approved soldiers for 100 roentgens over a six-week period and up to 200 roentgens in total. It is unclear why the Chiefs of Staff Committee established such high radiation exposure standards, but the policy seemingly underappreciated the health and safety hazards for service personnel in favour of a policy that prepared the armed services for the

**TABLE 7.1**

Early effects of radiation on individuals and units

| Radiation dose within 24 hours (roentgens) | Probable early effect on individuals | Probable effects on unit efficiency |
| --- | --- | --- |
| 0–100 | No acute effects of military significance. Severity of long-term hazard depends on the dose. | No significant loss in effectiveness of a unit. |
| 100–150 | Acute effects of military significance are improbable. Long-term hazard. | Probably no significant loss in unit effectiveness. A few men may be incapacitated for varying lengths of time. |
| 150–250 | Nausea and vomiting within one day. Minor incapacitation after two days. | The effectiveness of a unit would possibly be reduced by one-third for periods of about 48 hours. |
| 250–350 | Nausea and vomiting in under 4 hours, followed by a symptom-free period, lasting from about the third day to the end of the second week after exposure. Some deaths in four to six weeks and most of remainder incapacitated. | A unit will be greatly reduced in effectiveness during the nausea period, but less reduced if the emergency is great. The effectiveness may return almost to normal in two days and remain so for up to a week but will then fall off to complete ineffectiveness in about two weeks. |
| 350–600 | Nausea and vomiting in under 2 hours. Death is almost certain in four weeks. Incapacitation until death. | A unit *may* be partially effective [for] several hours, but the effectiveness will then be steadily reduced to complete uselessness. |
| 600 | Nausea and vomiting almost immediately. Death in one week. | Any unit will be quickly reduced to complete ineffectiveness. |
| 5,000 | Immediate incapacitation. Death within 24 hours. | Any unit will become ineffective immediately. |

*Source:* Adapted from J.N. Donaldson, Executive Secretary, Joint Special Weapons Committee, "Radiation Exposure Levels for Canadian Forces," RG 24-F-1, acc. 1983-84-167, vol. 7508, file DRBS 1600-3, vol. 1, Library and Archives Canada.

worst-case scenario: a nuclear war. Table 7.1 illustrates the military priorities and medical awareness at the time of the adopted policy. Regardless of intent, for the Canadians who participated in the atomic trials at Nevada and Maralinga, the adoption of an official policy governing radiation exposures for individual soldiers and units occurred several years too late.

The evidentiary record further complicates the health and safety context involving 1 RDU. Unfortunately, the historical record is incomplete because Canadian military officials destroyed a large bulk of records covering the unit's first five years. On January 30, 1959, commanding officer Major R.R. Doddridge convened a board of inquiry at Camp Borden to examine unit records for disposal. Doddridge spent two weeks reviewing files dated three years or older with Captain P.J. Pinsonnault and Lieutenants B.A. Perrin and V.M. Strijack. At the end of the review, the group recommended the destruction of more than 100 files marked unclassified, restricted, confidential, and secret. Brigadier R.L. Purves, commander at Camp Borden, approved the disposal recommendation on May 14, with the exception of sixteen files on unit policies and procedures. Purves forwarded the sixteen files to the Directorate of History for preservation and the remaining lot were destroyed. The discarded records included exercise and live test accounts, procedures for special weapons and radiological materials, and reports about accidents and injuries involving unit personnel. Files titled Radiation Exposures, Health Hazards, Safety Reports, and Casualties Exposure Due to Radiation were among the records destroyed.[65] These files ranged in date from January 1950 to December 1955, leaving significant gaps in the documented record of 1 RDU and the medical history of unit personnel.

Despite an incomplete historical record, the documents that survived suggest that 1 RDU personnel experienced hazardous conditions and high radiation exposures during decontamination work and nuclear weapons trials. Not only were the radiation standards used to determine exposure levels for unit personnel below international safety standards but the actual radiation doses received by the soldiers of 1 RDU were above the maximum permissible dosage standards set by the US Atomic Energy Commission.[66] Furthermore, the scientists who monitored Canadian personnel for radiation did not always monitor the most dangerous exposures. Individual film badges monitored radiation rays produced by the detonation of the atomic bomb, but film badge technology did not detect or measure radiation from internal emitters received into the body through airways or openings in skin. Modern developments in medical science have since confirmed that internal emitters and related sources of radiation not monitored during nuclear trials and decontamination work can and do cause the onset of cancer and other diseases.[67]

## CONCLUSION

Military and defence officials in the Canadian government created No. 1 Radiation Detection Unit in response to Cold War anxieties about nuclear war. The unit conducted decontamination work at Chalk River and participated in atomic weapons trials at Nevada and Maralinga, serving as a valuable asset for the Canadian armed services and representing Ottawa's scientific commitment to Western security and nuclear vigilance. But the history of 1 RDU serves as a potent reminder of military science in the atomic age. Unit personnel experienced direct exposure to dangerous levels of radiation, considered abnormally high by civilian standards. Canadian military officials underappreciated the international safety recommendations for radiation exposure and overlooked the warnings of medical authorities in the armed services, exposing 1 RDU to hazardous conditions despite pre-existing knowledge about the potential dangers of overexposure to radiation. The failure to heed medical advice for the safety of service personnel represents an important and understudied episode in Canadian military history and the history of Cold War science in the atomic age. Canada's top military officials did not conspire against unsuspecting soldiers with the intent to deceive or harm personnel of 1 RDU for military research purposes, but senior decision-makers failed to protect the health and safety of unit personnel and their medical records during and after operational duty.

Interrogating why Canadian military officials made the decisions they did with respect to radiation safety standards and medical expertise is important for understanding the full history of Canada's experience with atomic weapons trials and military preparations for nuclear war. Historians have a responsibility to highlight, consider, and question the complex medical and ethical aspects of this painful and difficult subject. In this regard, John Clearwater's report is indispensable to the history of Canada's involvement in nuclear weapons trials and decontamination work. His efforts supported the compensation payments to Canada's atomic veterans, and he deserves credit for unearthing military records and helping to preserve the documented history for current and future researchers.[68]

Moving forward, historians could consider the role of gender performance and heightened masculinity with respect to the disturbing idea of producing a superior radiological soldier. A gender-based analysis of 1 RDU and the imagined superior being may yield new insights into the history of cybernetics and Canada's experience with the Cold War sciences. At the same time, placing the experiences of Canadian personnel into a wider Cold War context of human radiation exposure will help flesh out and give substance to Canada's role in the broader international history of atomic weapons activities. Personnel of 1 RDU represented Canada on the front lines of military preparations for nuclear war, and their story holds valuable lessons for understanding and investigating the reach and influence of security politics in the Canadian armed services during a significant and volatile period in world affairs.

## NOTES

1 W. Greensword, S/L, SOGD, Report on TD to Canada and U.S. – Atomic Exercise "Sapling," May 31, 1955, RG 24-E-1-c, R112, vol. 42084, file 960-100-Sapling, Library and Archives Canada (LAC).

2 For full details about the AECL, see Robert Bothwell, *Nucleus: The History of Atomic Energy of Canada Limited* (Toronto: University of Toronto Press, 1988).

3 W. Greensword, S/L, SOGD, Report on TD to Canada and U.S. – Atomic Exercise "Sapling."

4 K.C. Maclure, G/C, DArmE, RCAF Member of JSWC re: Exercise Sapling, May 27, 1955, RG 24-E-1-c, R112, vol. 42084, file 960-100-Sapling, LAC. For biographical information about Maclure, see Keith R. Greenaway, "Kenneth C. Maclure, 1914–1988 (Obituary)," *Arctic* 41, 3 (September 1988): 258–59.

5 Record of Participation: Exercise "Sapling," May 20, 1955, RG 24-E-1-c, R112, vol. 42084, file 960-100-Sapling, LAC.

6 Army Headquarters, Exercise SAPLING: AHQ Instructions No 1, Appendix "A," Exercise "Sapling": Preliminary Instructions, February 14, 1955, RG 24-E-1-c, R112, vol. 42084, file 960-100-Sapling, LAC.

7 For the terms of reference describing the official roles and responsibilities of 1 RDU, see Colonel W.S. Murdoch, Director of Staff Duties, Army Headquarters, Appendix "A" – Terms of Reference: No 1 Radiation Detection Unit, Royal Canadian Engineers, January 5, 1953, RG 24 C-1-c, vol. 35801, file 2001-482-1, pt. 1, LAC.

8 For a full record of 1 RDU activities, including decontamination work, radiological field surveying, and observation of nuclear weapons trials, see John Murray Clearwater, *Atomic Veterans: A Report to the Minister of National Defence regarding Canada's Participation in Allied Forces' Nuclear Weapons Trials and Decontamination Work* (Ottawa: Department of National Defence, January 1, 2007), C-4–C-5.

9 Treaty Banning Nuclear Weapon Tests in the Atmosphere, in Outer Space and Under Water, U.S.-U.K.-U.S.S.R., August 5, 1963, 14 UST 1313, https://www.state.gov/t/isn/4797.htm.

10   Clearwater, *Atomic Veterans*, F-3–F-19; Sean M. Maloney, *Learning to Love the Bomb: Canada's Nuclear Weapons during the Cold War* (Dulles, VA: Potomac Books, 2007), 81–97; Andrew Godefroy, *In Peace Prepared: Innovation and Adaptation in Canada's Cold War Army* (Vancouver: UBC Press, 2014), 119–30.

11   See, for instance, Lt.-Col. R.A. Klaehn, "The Story of Exercise Sapling," *Canadian Army Journal* 9, 3 (July 1955): 2–11; Capt. H.E. Cameron, "Some Highlights of Exercise Sapling," *Canadian Army Journal* 9, 3 (July 1955): 11–17.

12   Lieutenant-General Charles Foulkes, Chief of the General Staff, to Brooke Claxton, Minister of National Defence, March 8, 1950, RG 24 C-1-c, vol. 35801, file 2001-482-1, pt. 1, LAC.

13   Clearwater, *Atomic Veterans*, C-4.

14   No. 1 Radiation Detection Unit – RCE: Amendments to Establishment, Lieutenant-Colonel R.A. Klaehn, March 8, 1951, RG 24 C-1-c, vol. 35801, file 2001-482-1, pt. 1, LAC.

15   For the official history of the Defence Research Board, see D.J. Goodspeed, *A History of the Defence Research Board of Canada* (Ottawa: Queen's Printer, 1958). For an updated source, see the recent institutional history written by Jonathan Turner, "The Defence Research Board of Canada, 1947 to 1977" (PhD diss., University of Toronto, 2012).

16   Donald Avery, *Pathogens for War: Biological Weapons, Canadian Life Scientists, and North American Biodefence* (Toronto: University of Toronto Press, 2013), 93. For additional information about the exercise, see Brigadier F.M. Richardson, "Exercise 'Medical Rubicon' D.G.A.M.S. Annual Exercise, 1952," *Journal of the Royal Army Medical Corps* 99, 3 (April 1953): 107–11.

17   Avery, *Pathogens for War*, 93.

18   For a history of the Atomic Energy Project at Chalk River, see Bothwell, *Nucleus*.

19   Ibid., 154–66.

20   Report on Exercise Charity I, Chalk River, Ont., December 15–20, 1952, January 13, 1953, Exercise Charity, Organization and Administration, S-2001-91/C15, 112.3W1 (D 67), Directorate of History and Heritage (DHH), Department of National Defence; Clearwater, *Atomic Veterans*, O-5.

21   Request for Assistance AECL Chalk River, February 26, 1953, Exercise Charity, Organization and Administration, S-2001-91/C15, 112.3W1 (D 67), DHH; Clearwater, *Atomic Veterans*, O-5.

22   H. Smith, "The International Commission on Radiological Protection: Historical Overview," *International Atomic Energy Agency (IAEA) Bulletin* 30, 3 (1988): 42–44; R.H. Clarke and J. Valentin, "The History of ICRP and the Evolution of Its Policies," *Annals of the ICRP* 39, 1 (2009): 75–110.

23   Charles B. Meinhold, "One Hundred Years of X Rays and Radioactivity – Radiation Protection: Then and Now," *IRPA9: 1996 International Congress on Radiation Protection, Proceedings* 1 (April 1996): 29.

24   Brigadier K.A. Hunter, Director General Medical Services, to Area Medical Officer, Headquarters Eastern Ontario Area, re: Medical Boards – No. 1 Radiation Detection Unit, RCE, April 10, 1953, RG 24 C-1-c, vol. 32024, file 2501-482/1, LAC.

25   Colonel S.G.U. Shier, Command Medical Officer, Central Command, to Army Headquarters re: Medical Boards – No. 1 Radiation Detection Unit, RCE, April 21, 1953, RG 24 C-1-c, vol. 35801, file 2001-482-1, pt. 1, LAC.

26  Liaison Report on Exercise Charity III AECL Chalk River, Ont., July 12–15, 1953, July 17, 1953, Exercise Charity, Organization and Administration, S-2001-91/C15, 112.3W1 (D 67), DHH; Clearwater, *Atomic Veterans*, O-10.

27  Klaehn, "The Story of Exercise Sapling," 5.

28  Minutes of the 534th Meeting of the Chiefs of Staff Committee, Item II, February 16, 1953, 2002/17 Joint Staff Fonds, box 78, file 31, DHH; Clearwater, *Atomic Veterans*, C-1.

29  General Charles Foulkes to Chairman, Canadian Joint Staff Washington [Rear-Admiral Harry DeWolf], May 25, 1953, 73/1223 Robert Lewis Raymont Fonds (RLR), file 316, DHH; Clearwater, *Atomic Veterans*, C-1.

30  Canadian Joint Staff Washington to Chairman, Chiefs of Staff [General Charles Foulkes], re: Courses in Atomic Defense Training and Tactical Employment of Atomic Weapons, July 3, 1953, 73/1223 RLR, file 316, DHH; Clearwater, *Atomic Veterans*, C-2.

31  Minutes of the Joint Special Weapons Committee 29th Meeting, September 9, 1953, HQS 200-25-76-2 (JSWC), NSTS 11280-86-2, DHH; Clearwater, *Atomic Veterans*, C-2.

32  General Charles Foulkes to US JCS A/Chairman General Ridgway, November 10, 1953, 73/1223 RLR, file 316, DHH; Clearwater, *Atomic Veterans*, C-2.

33  US JCS A/Chairman General Ridgway to General Charles Foulkes, May 18, 1954, 73/1223 RLR, file 316, DHH; Clearwater, *Atomic Veterans*, C-2.

34  For details about the Canadian Civil Defence Review of 1955, see Avery, *Pathogens for War*, 93–94.

35  For a complete record of nuclear trials conducted at Nevada, see United States Department of Energy, *Battlefield of the Cold War – The Nevada Test Site*, vol. 1, *Atmospheric Nuclear Weapons Testing, 1951–1963* (Washington, DC: Office of History and Heritage Resources, 2006).

36  Klaehn, "The Story of Exercise Sapling," 7.

37  Ibid., 4.

38  Report on RCN Participation in Operation Sapling, HMC ABCD School, Stadacona, Halifax, to Commodore RCN Barracks re: Report on Operation Sapling, June 21, 1955, RG 24-D-10, vol. 11168, file ACS 1660-9, LAC; Clearwater, *Atomic Veterans*, F-15.

39  Maloney, *Learning to Love the Bomb*, 89.

40  Directorate of Weapons and Development, Canadian Army Headquarters, *Report on Canadian Service Participation in United States Atomic Weapons Trials (Operation Teapot) at the Nevada Proving Grounds of the United States Atomic Energy Commission, April and May 55 (Exercise Sapling)* (Ottawa: Defence Scientific Information Service, Defence Research Board, Department of National Defence, c. May/June 1955); Clearwater, *Atomic Veterans*, F-19.

41  Staff Sergeant Jim Taylor pictured in *The Coast News* (Gibsons, BC), June 30, 1955, 1.

42  For information about the Ninth Tripartite Conference, see Ninth Tripartite Conference, September 13–25, 1954, London, Porton, and Langhurst, War Office, Ministry of Supply, Ministry of Defence: Chemical Defence Experimental Establishment, later Chemical and Biological Defence Establishment, Porton: Reports and Technical Papers, WO 189, Reference: WO 189/3151, The National Archives, Kew (TNA).

43  Major JT Redmond, Commanding Officer and Administrative Officer, Op Buffalo Draft Report on Phase I: Notification to Embarkation, 1, RG 24 C-1-c, vol. 6635, file 2001-91/B33, vol. 3, LAC.

44  On the history of British nuclear weapons testing at Maralinga, see, in order of publication date, Roger Cross, *Fallout: Hedley Marston and the British Bomb Tests in Australia* (Adelaide: Wakefield Press, 2001); Judy Nunn, *Maralinga* (North Sydney: Random House Australia, 2009); Frank Walker, *Maralinga: The Chilling Expose of Our Secret Nuclear Shame and Betrayal of Our Troops and Country* (Sydney: Hachette Australia, 2014); and Christobel Mattingley, *Maralinga's Long Shadow: Yvonne's Story* (Crows Nest, Australia: Allen and Unwin, 2016).

45  Major Secretary W.F. Bates, Joint Special Weapons Policy Committee, to Secretary, Chiefs of Staff Committee, re: Operation Buffalo: Participation of 1 Radiation Detection Unit (1 RDU), RCE, March 26, 1956, RG 24 C-1-c, vol. 6635, file 2001-91/B33, vol. 2, LAC.

46  The 1985 McClelland Royal Commission (MRC), an inquiry into the conduct of the British government during the nuclear weapons trials at Maralinga, found that the weapons tested included cobalt pellets, ostensibly to trace yield. This revelation led to accusations from some that the British secretly tested a cobalt bomb, a highly controversial weapon specifically designed to spread an increased amount of radiation and contaminant over a wide area. For information about the MRC, see J.R. McClelland, J. Fitch, and W.J.A. Jonas, *The Report of the Royal Commission into British Nuclear Tests in Australia: Conclusions and Recommendations* (Canberra: Australian Government Publication Service, 1985).

47  For a detailed account of 1 RDU's participation in Operation Buffalo, including the cited exercise report, see Maloney, *Learning to Love the Bomb*, 90–92.

48  For a full description of British regulations and safety standards for the Maralinga Range, see Canadian Administrative Order No. 1 – Op Buffalo, Appendix "A," Maximum Permissible Levels, Ministry of Aviation, OPERATION BUFFALO, Canadian Participation 1953–1957, Reference: AVIA 65/1123, TNA.

49  ISMC [Inter-Service Medical Committee]: Op Buffalo – Permissive Radiation Dosages, April 4, 1956, RG 24 C-1-c, vol. 6635, file 2001-91/B33, vol. 2, LAC.

50  Ibid.

51  E.H. Lee, Surgeon Commodore, Chairman, Inter-Service Medical Committee, to Medical Section, Defence Research Board, re: Permissible Radiation Exposure, August 3, 1955, RG 24 C-1-c, vol. 6635, file 2001-91/B33, vol. 2, LAC; Major J.T. Redmond, Commanding Officer and Administrative Officer, Op Buffalo Draft Report on Phase I: Notification to Embarkation, 6, RG 24 C-1-c, vol. 6635, file 2001-91/B33, vol. 3, LAC.

52  Clearwater, *Atomic Veterans*.

53  Ibid., ix.

54  US House of Representatives, Committee on Energy and Commerce, Subcommittee on Energy Conservation and Power, *American Nuclear Guinea Pigs: Three Decades of Radiation Experiments on U.S. Citizens* (Washington, DC: US Government Printing Office, 1986).

55  Eileen Welsome later published a book about the subject: *The Plutonium Files: America's Secret Medical Experiments in the Cold War* (New York: Dial Press, 1999).

56  Ruth R. Faden et al., *Advisory Committee on Human Radiation Experiments: Final Report, Executive Summary and Guide to Final Report* (Washington, DC: US Government Printing Office, 1995).

57 William Moss and Roger Eckhardt, "The Human Plutonium Injection Experiments," *Los Alamos Science* 23 (1995): 177–223.

58 For information about Canada's atomic veterans, see Charles D. McGregor, *In Peace Prepared (In Pace Paratus): A History of the Queen's Own Rifles of Canada from 1950 to the 21st Century* (Toronto: Regimental Trust, 2009), 109–25; Guylaine Maroist and Eric Ruel, *Time Bombs* (Montreal: Productions de la Ruelle, 2007), DVD.

59 ISMC: Op Buffalo – Permissive Radiation Dosages, April 4, 1956, RG 24 C-1-c, vol. 6635, file 2001-91/B33, vol. 2, LAC.

60 Smith, "The International Commission on Radiological Protection," Clarke and Valentin, "The History of ICRP and the Evolution of Its Policies."

61 Operation Buffalo: Dosage Records – Canadian Personnel, January 9, 1957, RG 24 C-1-c, vol. 6635, file 2001-91/B33, vol. 4, LAC; Clearwater, *Atomic Veterans,* app. 1, 47–48.

62 J.N. Donaldson, Executive Secretary, Joint Special Weapons Committee, Radiation Exposure Levels for Canadian Forces, RG 24-F-1, acc. 1983-84-167, vol. 7508, file DRBS 1600-3, vol. 1, LAC.

63 Ibid.

64 For information about the ICRP, see Smith, "The International Commission on Radiological Protection: Historical Overview"; Clarke and Valentin, "The History of ICRP and the Evolution of Its Policies."

65 Proceedings of a Board of Inquiry assembled at Camp Borden, Ontario, on January 30, 1959, Annex 1 to Board of Inquiry on Obsolete Files, RG 24 C-1-c, vol. 35801, file 2001-482-1, pt. 2, LAC.

66 Clearwater, *Atomic Veterans,* ii.

67 For instance, see John Harrison and Philip Day, "Radiation Doses and Risks from Internal Emitters," *Journal of Radiological Protection* 28, 2 (June 2008): 137–59.

68 In September 2008, the government of Canada created the Atomic Veterans Recognition Program to recognize Canadian military veterans, scientists, and technical workers who participated in allied nuclear weapons testing and/or decontamination efforts during the period 1946–63. The application period closed on December 31, 2009. At that time, the program had received more than 900 applications and the federal government had distributed over 270 *ex gratia* payments to applicants who met the required criteria. See National Defence and the Canadian Armed Forces, "ARCHIVED – Atomic Veterans Recognition Program Application Deadline Approaching," http://www.forces.gc.ca/en/news/article.page?doc=atomic-veterans-recognition-program-application-deadline-approaching/hnps1ui5. Also, note that Clearwater donated copies of his report and supporting documents to the Directorate of History and Heritage, which houses and maintains the archival record of Canada's Department of National Defence.

*Part 4*

# IMPORTING BY ACCIDENT, EXPORTING BY DESIGN

CHAPTER 8

# A NORTHERN NUCLEAR NIGHTMARE?

## Operation Morning Light and the Recovery of Cosmos 954 in the Northwest Territories, 1978

Ryan Dean and P. Whitney Lackenbauer

*The intrusion into Canadian air space of a satellite carrying on board a nuclear reactor and the break-up of the satellite over Canadian territory created a clear and immediate apprehension of damage, including nuclear damage, to persons and property in Canada.*

– CANADA, "STATEMENT OF CLAIM TO
THE USSR FOR DAMAGE CAUSED BY
SOVIET COSMOS 954"[1]

Making an early delivery to Yellowknife airport the morning of January 24, 1978, water truck driver Peter Pagonis observed "three unidentified flying objects streaking across the dark sky," their bluish-red tracings leaving an unmistakable impression that this was no ordinary occurrence. "The object in front was the largest, like a huge pencil, spurting an incandescent jet of such pure brilliance" that Pagonis believed "might be one of those laser beams he had once seen on a television program. The brilliant steaks trailed fiery tails and dove beyond the town in a northeasterly direction."[2]

Unknown to Pagonis and other Yellowknifers at the time, Cosmos 954, a Soviet Radar Ocean Reconnaissance Satellite (RORSAT), had malfunctioned and was burning up in the upper atmosphere. Its power plant, a nuclear reactor fuelled with approximately 45.5 kilograms of enriched uranium-235, had failed to eject from the stricken craft and boost itself into a higher disposal orbit as per its design. During its three-minute burn through the skies of Canada's Northwest Territories, Cosmos scattered radioactive debris from the western edge of Great Slave Lake, east-north-easterly over an 800-kilometre stretch along the Thelon River, through the barrens, to the region just north of Baker Lake.[3]

Authorities, quick to respond to a potential "nuclear nightmare," raced to discern, secure, and define the physical, political, and legal risks that the unexpected arrival of Cosmos 954 posed to Canada. A twenty-two-person Canadian Forces Nuclear Accident Support Team (NAST) began to assess radioactive contamination to recover satellite debris that morning.[4] "The normally easy-going citizens of Yellowknife were startled by the sight of yellow-garbed troops walking the streets, reading radiation meters and taking air samples," Major W.R. Aikman observed.[5] A nuclear threat required a concerted scientific effort, with military personnel supporting Canadian and American scientists who combed the projected debris area for radioactive wreckage.

The recovery effort, Operation Morning Light, unfolded over the next eighty-four days, ultimately spanning 24,000 square kilometres of subarctic and Arctic lands in conditions that dipped below −40°C and recovering 66 kilograms of wreckage (with all but one 17.7-kilogram piece proving to be radioactive).[6] The response to this unconventional Cold War nuclear threat to North America generated intense national and international interest at the time, and modest attention in its immediate aftermath. The cover of Leo Heaps' book *Operation Morning Light*, published in 1978, carries the hyperbolic tag line: "It was a science-fiction nightmare come true!"[7] In contrast with official reports that emphasized the diligence of authorities in successfully assessing, containing, and communicating the short-term risk that Cosmos 954 had posed, Heaps emphasized popular fears and dangers associated with potential, lingering radioactivity (of which no evidence was ever produced). Captain Colin A. Morrison's more technical history, *Voyage into the Unknown*, based upon his official research and unpublished reports produced for the Department of National Defence, treats Morning Light as a prototypical case study – the first mission of its kind to locate and remove radioactive debris from one country that had fallen onto another country's territory from space – wherein searchers overcame environmental and technological challenges to successfully complete recovery operations.[8]

Although Morning Light has not attracted much academic attention (except as a case study in emerging international space law), two recent studies divide along similar lines as Heaps and Morrison. Our introduction to the publication of a recently declassified Canadian Forces Base (CFB) Edmonton report on Morning Light treats it as a successful operation that featured solid bilateral cooperation between Canadian and US experts, a coordinated whole of government approach, and the effective adaptation of operational techniques and equipment to challenging environmental conditions. By contrast, geographers Ellen Power and Arn Keeling assert that Operation Morning Light is best understood as a contest for power and knowledge via scientific authority, wherein "constant technological failures under northern environmental conditions only increased the uncertainty already inherent in determining radioactive risk." They indict the Canadian government for failing to communicate risks to Northerners and denying a sufficient role for Northern traditional knowledge to inform cleanup efforts, suggesting that this produced "uncertainties surrounding radiation detection and mistrust of government communication efforts" that left "many northern residents" worried about lingering contamination.[9] In short, they suggest that the "colonial authority of southern military and scientific experts," predicated on a western-centric "regime of perceptibility" based on a universal science (and heavily reliant on technology), failed to apply appropriate methods and, in turn, fomented "doubt and mistrust" over the long-term health and environmental consequences of Cosmos 954.[10]

Building our analysis around the risks associated with the crash of a nuclear-powered satellite, we contend that Operation Morning Light was much more successful than Power and Keeling allege in their selective and speculative reading of the actual evidence. The simple fact that scientists and military operators had to adapt their techniques and equipment to respond to a nuclear contingency in Northern Canada does not render their scientific methods inappropriate or their actions ineffective. As Morrison insisted in 1983, "those involved in the planning and execution of the search for and recovery of *Cosmos 954* were venturing into a new field of operations – a voyage into the unknown – a process that entailed much trial-and-error." The potential danger to humans, fish, and wildlife in the region gave the operation its driving imperative and demanded a "crisis-management" approach.[11] Crisis was averted, however, through tight binational cooperation, systematic scientific monitoring, and deliberate recovery operations. After-action reports that critically evaluated the methods, equipment, and personnel employed during Morning Light elucidated how a combination of civilian scientific expertise and military capabilities succeeded in effectively locating and recovering the remnants of a downed nuclear-powered satellite scattered across a frigid, subarctic environment. While Keeling and Power build a critical case around *possible* negative environmental and human legacies, they seem to downplay a preponderance of verifiable evidence that points to the opposite outcome: an effective response to a practical nuclear threat that, rather than eroding public confidence, successfully mitigated risks in a timely and cooperative manner.

Nuclear histories, historian Itty Abraham notes, are dominated by a discourse of control that has narrowed the focus to national efforts at non-proliferation and less on the implications of nuclear programs more broadly, including the scientific-technological underpinnings of these programs and the national (and in the case of Morning Light, binational) response systems set up to deal with nuclear disasters and accidents.[12] While accidents at the SL-1 (1961), Three Mile Island (1979), Chernobyl (1986), and Fuku-shima Daiichi (2011) power plants, as well as those associated with nuclear-powered submarines, have been subjected to significant analysis and debate, the application of science and technology to the detection and cleanup of small nuclear incidents has received less attention. We argue that, by adapting responses that had been developed in southern laboratories and offices and devised for global application to an austere Arctic environment, Operation Morning Light demonstrates the transferability and application of Cold War applied science in the Canadian North. While civilian scientists and military operators had to render the Arctic scientifically "legible" to identify and clean up nuclear debris, this knowledge and concomitant use of technology was not used to reshape Arctic environments during the operation and in its aftermath.[13] Instead, an immediate joint Canadian-American effort, involving multiple government agencies, was coordinated to protect the landscape and Northern peoples from radionuclide contamination. In our assessment, Morning Light offers an important case study in practical government action to respond to nuclear risk and prevent toxic legacies – environmental, diplomatic, or between Northern residents and the Canadian government.

## SETTING THE CONTEXT

The United States became aware that Cosmos 954 was in trouble in late October 1977. Fourteen metres long with a mass of 3,500 kilograms, the nuclear-powered RORSAT was built around a powerful X-band radar that could look through thick cloud layers to scan the world's oceans for naval vessels. The small Romashka reactor on the spacecraft, which was powered by 90 percent enriched uranium-235 embedded in carbide and surrounded by a graphite moderator, also allowed the satellite to send its observations back to Moscow or directly to Soviet naval units and possibly even Tu-22 "Backfire" bombers.[14] Given that this mission had obvious implications for American security in a Cold War context, US officials noted its launch on September 18, 1977, with interest. Five weeks later, North American Air Defense Command (NORAD) noted Cosmos 954's slowly decaying orbit and began updating plots of when and where the satellite would re-enter the atmosphere.[15] Most of these calculations were done at the Lawrence Livermore National Laboratory by engineer Milo Bell and mathematician Ira Morrison, supported by engineer Robert Kelley. The trio had access to the highly sophisticated Control Data Corporation 7600 supercomputer, with its C-shaped frame stretching twenty feet and filling an entire room at the laboratory.[16] The problem was clear: "What does one *do* about a live nuclear reactor re-entering the earth's atmosphere aboard a Soviet surveillance satellite?" Gus Weiss, a special assistant to the secretary of defense, explained how "a quick scan of literature showed no textbook answer, nor even a textbook question. It remained for the National Security Council (NSC) Staff to put together a group to cope with the problem."[17]

On December 19, the NSC formed a working group (the Ad Hoc Committee on Space Debris) to prepare contingency plans and prepare to mount a quick search-and-recovery operation of Cosmos 954 if needed, thus birthing Operation Morning Light. Contributing agencies included the Central Intelligence Agency (CIA), the Department of Defense (DoD), the

Department of Energy (DoE), the State Department, the Environmental Protection Agency (EPA), the Federal Preparedness Agency, and the Office of the Attorney General. The NSC placed the DoE's nuclear emergency response capabilities on alert "to assist in the protection of public health and safety should radioactive debris from Cosmos 954 come to earth in the United States." This included organizations such as the Accident Response Group (ARG) and the Nuclear Emergency Search Team (NEST), which had the expertise and equipment necessary to find and recover radioactive materials. Due to the "uncertainty in determining when or where (in the world) Cosmos 954 would reenter," experts anticipated "that there was no preventative or preparatory action that could be taken by the public." Subsequently, both the American public and the United States' allies were kept in the dark until experts could plot a more accurate projection of Cosmo 954's return.[18]

In early January, the satellite's orbit decayed precipitously. Updated calculations estimated a re-entry date of the twenty-fourth of that month, but *where* the satellite would crash remained hazy. American authorities summoned the Soviet ambassador to secure information on the radioactive hazard that Cosmos 954 posed. The USSR's response was rather sparse, noting that the power plant on the satellite was "explosive-proof" and had been designed to burn up when it entered denser layers of the atmosphere. Nevertheless, the depressurization (for unclear reasons) that had caused the satellite to lose control meant that some destroyed parts of the plant could still reach the earth's surface, and "in that case an insignificant local contamination may occur in the places of impact with earth which would require limited usual measures of cleaning up." One US official remarked that he was not sure what "'usual measures of cleaning up' a reactor crashing in from outer space might be, and there was also some ambiguity in the meaning of 'explosive-proof.'"[19]

By this time, computer modelling discerned that the wavelike orbital path of the doomed satellite overflew Australia, Britain, Canada, Japan, and New Zealand, and the United States notified its allies accordingly.[20] Canada first learned that Cosmos 954 could crash in its territory on January 19, and the Department of National Defence alerted all regional commanders and the NAST of the impending threat the following day. Air Command Headquarters alerted CFB Edmonton base commander Colonel

D.F. Garland on January 23 that Cosmos would be entering Edmonton's Search and Rescue Region the following day, and the NAST was informed and placed on two-hour standby. At this time, the Prime Minister's Office notified several civilian departments of the threat that the satellite posed to the country and of their responsibilities in the response effort. This meant that many of the key agencies and actors who became involved had less than twenty-four hours' notice, and some did not receive notification until after the satellite had crashed.[21]

As soon as American experts confirmed Cosmos 954's re-entry over the Northwest Territories on the morning of January 24, President Jimmy Carter contacted Prime Minister Pierre Trudeau and offered American assistance. Trudeau immediately accepted. The principal mission for the US Nuclear Emergency Search Team was to help the Canadian government locate radioactive debris. Accordingly, they enlisted American experts to provide technical assistance in calculating the re-entry of Cosmos 954 and the ballistics properties that various pieces of it would likely exhibit in their fiery plunge back to earth. This involved sophisticated re-entry calculations and computer modelling, establishing the perimeters of the search area, and estimations of where larger pieces of debris would land. NEST also operated aerial measuring equipment and assisted with ground recovery activities. At the request of the Defense Department, the Department of Energy provided two gamma ray spectrometers and operating personnel, who arrived in Edmonton on January 24 to install their equipment on Canadian Hercules aircraft. Canada provided the technical assistance to mount the detection equipment onto the aircraft, as well as on-site logistics support such as providing NEST with military clothing for subarctic operations.[22]

Despite having received little to no warning, Canadian civilian scientists responded immediately and began arriving in Edmonton on mid-morning of January 24 – at roughly the same time as NEST, which had had seven weeks of forewarning and preparation. The first of these scientists was Dr. Bob Grasty of the Geological Survey of Canada (GSC), whose expertise in aerial surveying for naturally occurring uranium was mobilized to detect Cosmo 954's highly enriched uranium-235 core. A GSC gamma ray spectrometer designed for uranium exploration and mapping was quickly shipped, along with Grasty, from Ottawa to Edmonton to enable the search.[23]

NORAD had provided Operation Morning Light with projections of Cosmo 954's probable debris field between Great Slave and Baker Lakes, delineated as an area 800 kilometres long and 50 kilometres wide. The first phase of the operation called for CC-130 Hercules aircraft, specially equipped with gramma ray spectrometers to detect radiation emitted from the surface, to fly a grid pattern 1,000 feet above ground level over the suspected satellite crash area.[24] While the pilots focused on carefully flying their intended search tracks under difficult conditions, "back in the cargo compartment, the [NEST] scientists took turns watching several needles as they slowly swayed up and down across a piece of graph paper, waiting for the telltale swing that would indicate a hit."[25] NEST members operating these devices quickly began registering "hits" along the search area, which were recorded on data tapes and then fed into NEST computer vans at Yellowknife and Baker Lake for analysis. "Each hour of search flight time for each of the C-130s created four hours of computer analysis time, creating a major assessment backlog," the US Department of Energy's official report recounted.[26] "Hits" would then be located on navigation charts and helicopters fitted with detection equipment would be sent to these sites to precisely locate the radioactive source. One helicopter would drop a brightly coloured streamer on the suspect site, and a second helicopter carrying a three-person recovery team would follow to inspect the area on the ground and recover any radioactive materials.[27]

## SOVEREIGNTY AND CANADA-US COOPERATION

Interestingly, the dominant historiographical theme emphasizing Canadian sensitivity over US "threats" to Arctic sovereignty from the Second World War onward is conspicuously absent in the case of Operation Morning Light.[28] While wartime defence projects such as the Alaska Highway, Canol pipeline, and various remote airfields had prompted concerns about US designs on parts of the Canadian North, and Cold War defence projects such as the Distant Early Warning (DEW) Line had fed popular concerns about the erosion of Canadian sovereignty,[29] media coverage and internal government memoranda related to Morning Light are remarkably free of this usual worry. Instead of construing an American presence in the Canadian North as a *risk,* Canadian officials embraced it as an operational necessity and benefit. The American contribution reached its zenith two weeks into the operation, when 120 specialists in various fields were participating. Author Leo Heaps, in his dramatic account, observed:

> When the Americans went into full gear with their immense back-up resources, there was very little in the world that would be able to equal them. The motive of competition, of sensitive pride where the Americans were concerned, was all one-sided. Canadians are traditionally apt to have some acute feelings in these matters. However, this was an emergency and the clear-headed Garland and his team appreciated the assistance. The American scientists and technicians stayed out of sight in spite of the urgings of their public relations man, allowing the Canadian scientists and military to make all the announcements. They would have their turn when they arrived home.[30]

In the face of a tangible Cold War nuclear threat, a joint effort was politically and popularly acceptable to complete the search, recovery, removal, testing, and cleanup of radioactive fragments. Rather than the United States being seen as encroaching on Canadian sovereignty, in this case a Soviet satellite had violated it – and a combined Canada-US effort was well justified to assess the implications.[31]

When the Department of Energy eventually published its official "non-technical" summary of the operation, it highlighted Morning Light as an "example of international cooperation for the protection of the health and safety of the population of North America."[32] An internally directed Canadian report also affirmed that the two countries' intimate cooperation during the operation proved seamless and effective. "The American agencies provided excellent technical support (equipment and equipment employment) plus the all important scientific expertise for re-entry, health physics and radioactive material recovery advice and support," it highlighted. From an organizational perspective, this technical support "melded well into an efficiently functioning team that performed the job safely."[33] Furthermore, as more Canadians arrived on the scene, the Americans drew down their assistance as planned.[34] NEST expertise proved to be tailor-made for the Cosmos 954 search. "The much smaller resource base in Canada did force some adjustments on the American time accomplishment expectations," an official Canadian report noted. "Beyond this . . . without reservations, this was an excellent, productive exercise in international cooperation."[35] In the end, the Canadians were saddened to see their American counterparts go.[36]

"There was no historical precedent for Operation *Morning Light*," Lieutenant General (retired) William Carr noted afterwards. "From my vantage point as Commander, Air Command during the events recorded here, I was privileged to see the spontaneous cooperation which invariably surfaces when Americans and Canadians, under pressure, work toward a common goal."[37] Supporting this assessment, the most systematic Canadian report explained that individual responsibilities assigned to Canadian and American participants were well defined from the onset. "The two national teams of the Task Force worked extremely well together . . . [in] a common purpose easily and productively with amazingly few problems," it extolled. "The blend of skills each side brought to the task was essential to the other side's requirement and success, which is an exceedingly important factor. Without reservation, this was an excellent, productive exercise in international cooperation."[38]

For their part, the Americans participating in Operation Morning Light concluded that "the Canadians were outstanding hosts, both in technical support and personnel consideration. This likely represents the best of international assistance conditions that we could ever expect to encounter; many other situations could be far from ideal."[39] While the Canadians provided the bulk of personnel and logistics, the "previous specialized experience of the U.S. team with nuclear radiation search and measurement over large areas was a key Morning Light resource; the operation could not have been completed as expeditiously without it."[40] Accordingly, this case study seems to reinforce our recent work that recasts the Canada-US Cold War relationship in the Canadian North as one of "premier partners" who effectively collaborated on an operational level rather than as competitors either threatening or defending sovereignty.[41]

## NORTHERN POPULAR PERCEPTIONS AND SCIENTIFIC DISCERNMENT OF RADIOACTIVE RISK

Cosmos 954 focused the eyes of the world on the Canadian North – and on the actions of scientists and military personnel in assessing and addressing nuclear risk. International and national Canadian media attention initially fixated on the satellite's nuclear core. Had it survived re-entry and, if so, what threat did it pose? The *New York Times* posed the fundamental question on February 6, 1978: "Is part of the satellite's reactor still out there in the frozen wilderness, undetectable from the air, buried until the summer thaw, but nevertheless emitting dangerous radiation?"[42] Coverage also emphasized the precedent-setting nature of the response, spanning a search area the size of Switzerland or Austria, with frigid, rugged conditions pitting "man against nature" in a primordial struggle "just a dog-sled away from the North Pole."[43] The Canadian national press also situated recovery efforts in a Cold War context. Although some overzealous stories wrongly ascribed to the satellite an offensive capability to shoot down other satellites with lasers, more sober critiques highlighted the Soviet Union's refusal to disclose substantive information about the satellite's reactor core – despite initial promises to lend "full cooperation" to recovery efforts. By withholding valuable information about the design and nuclear fuel, the Soviets thus protected their intellectual property – even when their space vehicle crashed onto the Canadian tundra. When Russian authorities refused to acknowledge that the radioactive debris came from one of their satellites (thus placing potential legal implications over environmental and human safety), Canadian minister of national defence Barney Danson told the USSR to "grow up" and share technical information – although he conceded that the Soviets were "somewhat uneasy about intelligence information which could be collected as the satellite fragments are analyzed."[44]

The major risk posed by Cosmos 954 was that its reactor or part of the uranium-235 core would survive atmospheric re-entry and make landfall, posing a lethal radiation threat to any nearby Canadians and the surrounding environment. Officials had to confirm Soviet assurances that the reactor would disintegrate in the upper atmosphere as per its design. About 250 members of the Canadian Armed Forces mobilized for Operation Morning Light alongside 120 Americans (mostly NEST specialists) and 30 scientists from the Atomic Energy Control Board (AECB), the Geological Survey of Canada, and the Department of Energy, Mines and Resources. The latter were responsible for managing the airborne search for Cosmos 954 wreckage: after scientists aboard CC-130 Hercules aircraft located radioactive hotspots, helicopters would deliver scientists to confirm and recover the debris on the ground.[45]

The recovery of the largest piece of debris, known colloquially as the "stovepipe" and identified by aerial search on February 1, exemplified this method. The head of the search team recounted to excited reporters that it was evident "something [had] really gone through the ice at high speed." Paul Murda, the leader of a five-man American scientific team that analyzed the object, described it as "sort of like a cylinder that got smashed," with what "looks like structural tubing" sticking out the ends.[46] Fortunately it was not radioactive, which made its detection from the air a stroke of luck. Another example of this search method occurred three days later when another recovery team – wearing their trademark thick yellow coveralls, parkas, and Arctic boots, with radiation detectors hanging from their waists – found some of the most radioactive material: a clutch of beryllium rods and cylinders partially embedded in the snow and ice.[47] When the recovery team, led by AECB members Tom Robertson and Wick J. Courneya, cautiously approached the debris, their "Geiger-counter readings exceeded 100 roentgens per hour."[48] Courneya, a health physicist, put this level of radiation into perspective in a later interview. "If a person held [an object measuring some 200 roentgens] for one hour, he would probably get ill," he explained. "If a person held it for two hours, he probably would die."[49] Accordingly, it was standard operating procedure after every mission to check recovery teams and aircrew for radiation, and "any item of clothing which produced a reaction on the meters was immediately removed."[50]

As it became increasingly apparent that neither Cosmos 954's reactor nor a large quantity of its uranium fuel survived atmospheric re-entry – thus dramatically reducing the overall risk – scientists turned to broadly monitoring radiation levels by collecting ground samples along the debris field. This surveying was conducted in two distinct phases under the responsibility of the AECB.[51] Phase I ran from January 24 to April 20 and focused on "all known [areas of] human habitation including towns, cabins and camps," along with "transportation routes of all kinds."[52] Scientists and soldiers conducting these surveys were equipped with instrumentation capable of detecting radiation fields of about one to three micro-roentgens per hour.[53] The overall purpose of this ground search was to determine the density of the radiation dispersed across the search area and to analyze its spread and environmental impact.

While officials were worried about popular paranoia emanating from the "first live nuclear object (spewing deadly nuclear radiation) tumbling in from the cold depths of outer space,"[54] our analysis of regional newspaper coverage suggests that Northerners did not overreact. Jarvis Jason, the manager of a fried chicken outlet in Yellowknife, told a reporter on January 26 that the nuclear fallout threat "doesn't really bother me at all. We've had these arsenic scares and things like that. After all, we're Yellowknifers."[55] More generally, the *Yellowknifer* newspaper editorialized in February 1978:

> It appears that people in the North, and particularly Yellowknife, have done it again. Acted in a peculiar manner. They did not fall apart and get hysterical and start evacuating the city when this newsworthy satellite entered our area. What did they expect the citizens to do? . . . Do you think that it would pose too much of a problem to those Southerners to realize that just to come up here to live – many in small outlying lonesome settlements – takes a certain kind of person – self-sufficient with somewhat fatalistic outlook and plenty of plain intestinal fortitude. Please, you Southerners, stop expecting us to react in a predictable manner – by now – at least the media – should know we are different.[56]

*Yellowknifer* editor Sig Sigvaldason, already disillusioned with the federal government over its treatment of mine-related arsenic contamination in Yellowknife, was skeptical of official reports.[57] Downplaying the threat to human health, he instead trumpeted the economic boost that the influx of authorities and outside media brought to his community. "The Russians have contributed more to the economy of the Yellowknife area in a few days," he quipped, "than the Federal government does in a year." One of his stories suggested that "the only fallout one could observe so far were the media types who filled every available hotel space."[58]

While the debris area was large, barren, and sparsely populated, authorities were highly aware that it was not an empty "wasteland" but a homeland for humans.[59] "The inhabitants of the Northwest Territories in the path of the Cosmos 954 satellite were concerned about their safety and it was necessary to undertake search and recovery operations so that the inhabitants could be assured that all debris dangerous to their health had been recovered," an official summary noted. Dan Billing, the chief of emergency services for the government of the Northwest Territories, explained:

> There are approximately 10,000 persons who reside in the "hit-zone." The municipal councils of the Towns of Fort Smith, Hay River, Snowdrift, Fort Resolution and Pine Point expressed great concern for their citizens about the danger of the radio-active debris in their respective areas. Citizens['] committees were established in some of these municipalities for the purpose of expressing their concern about their safety. Signs were erected in these municipalities alerting the residents to report any sitings of unusual debris and to warn the citizens that this debris may be dangerous. Persons residing around Great Slave Lake were concerned that the drinking water and fish were unfit for human consumption. Residents were concerned that the caribou might be unsafe for human consumption. Residents restricted their normal use of the territory for fear of contact with radio-active material. An area north of the Town of Snowdrift was restricted from any unauthorized travel for approximately one month.[60]

Operation Morning Light crews completed foot searches for radioactive material in the municipalities and around hunting and fishing lodges, finding radioactive debris in several of these locations. Although distance and subarctic operating conditions complicated logistics, authorities were confident they had found all the Northern civilians in the search area by early January 28 and advised them of the possible hazards.[61]

Officials were particularly anxious about how they would explain the situation to the region's Indigenous inhabitants. "There was a common concern and generally not enough known about this strange element . . . translated from English to Chipewyan [as] 'poisonous,'" reporter Robert Blake explained. "There are no words in Chipewyan to adequately describe radioactivity, gamma ray sweepers and the like."[62] When a NAST team (in their trademark suits) first flew to the Chipewyan (Dene) community of Snowdrift (now Łutsel K'e) without advance notice in late January, local residents scattered. The town council held an emergency meeting, passing along fears to the Northwest Territories Commissioner. Canadian Northern Region Headquarters commander Brigadier-General Ken Thorneycroft flew to the village the next day to convene a public meeting, where he explained what was happening and reassured local residents that no radiation had been detected near their community.[63] Afterwards, a local councillor noted that "fear, 21st Century style, [was] easing its grip on the hunters and trappers in the community."[64] Although local concerns never entirely dissipated, Morning Light's coordinated response offered credible reassurance to Northerners that their safety was of paramount importance, and the search and recovery operations for debris appropriately addressed the most serious threats to human and environmental health.[65]

Authorities also responded to Northerners' observations of things out of place in an environment that they knew intimately. A prime example occurred on March 10, when the RCMP detachment at Cape Dorset relayed a report to Edmonton from a twenty-five-year-old Inuk seal hunter. Twenty-five miles northwest of Cape Dorset, the man had observed an eighteen-foot crater in lake ice that "was at least five feet thick and big chunks of it were flung hundreds of feet away like toy blocks."[66] Although Cape Dorset was located at the extreme end of Cosmos 954's calculated debris field, authorities took the report seriously. Within three days, a CC-130 airlifted a CH-135 Twin Huey to Cape Dorset, and a ground team of scientists specially equipped with underwater probes was dispatched to measure radiation levels in the water beneath the ice. After careful analysis, the scientists discerned that the phenomenon was a natural occurrence unrelated to the Cosmos crash.[67] This incident and others like it showed that authorities acted upon Northerners' local knowledge, even though non-specialists were unlikely to have the expertise or ability to discern radioactive contamination (as they might other forms of persistent pollutants).[68]

By early March, aerial surveys and Phase I ground surveys led scientists to conclude that people living in the affected area had little to fear from ongoing radiation.[69] A Phase II ground survey, conducted from July 14 to October 14, reassessed the affected areas after snow and ice had disappeared. Most of this phase was devoted to recovering some 3,500 tiny particles of 90 percent enriched uranium, the remnants of Cosmos 954's reactor fuel, which if ingested by a person would offer a radiation dose akin to a "medical X-ray examination of the gastric area." Furthermore, the particles were steadily weakening in radioactivity as time passed. By September, scientists found that these particles emitted radiation at levels only one-fifth of what they had been in initial measurements.[70] Nevertheless, authorities continued to respond to Northerners' observations and concerns. For example, a family reported finding dead fish floating at Louis Lake in the Northwest Territories on October 14 and suggested that this may have been caused by radiation from Cosmos 954 debris. Although Louis Lake was 130 miles beyond the established debris zone, authorities kept an open mind and dispatched a plane to collect samples. When brought to Winnipeg for analysis, the fish were found to be completely clean of radioactivity.[71] Northerners' concerns were treated seriously and acted upon, and this fed into a growing sense of confidence that the threat was abating.

In 1979 and 1980, government scientists continued environmental monitoring for radioactivity and restored public confidence that the risk had dissipated. Caribou from across the affected area were harvested and sampled for contamination, as were hundreds of fish from across all species over a period of several months.[72] No radionuclides were detected that related to satellite debris.[73] Radioactive analysis of drinking water confirmed that runoff did not carry residual particles from Cosmos 954 into water supplies. Furthermore, NAST members and AECB scientists ran tests on equipment and facilities that had been used to handle Cosmos 954 debris and found radiation levels to be within acceptable limits.[74]

In the end, Canadian and American scientific crews recovered about sixty-five kilograms of satellite material.[75] The lead effort in recovering, storing, and disposing of the radioactive debris fell to the AECB,[76] which contracted the Whiteshell Nuclear Research Establishment (WNRE) to analyze and store recovered debris.[77] Studies of the radioactive fragments quickly yielded debris of particular interest, including a highly radioactive steel "hotplate" determined to be part of the reactor container, beryllium "slugs" that were thought to be part of Cosmos 954's reactor core, and a series of small cylinders in pristine condition that may have been part of the reactor control device. WNRE staff quickly determined that the reactor core had broken up and pieces of it were distributed across the search area. By analyzing the recovered fuel, staff determined the approximate size and power of the Romashka-type reactor, discerning that the power plant produced an output of 132 kilowatts and would "have left in excess of 13,000 Curies of radioactivity 90 days after re-entry." WNRE concluded that "much of this [radioactivity] may never have reached the ground."[78]

The extensive scientific monitoring of the affected territory gave authorities confidence in concluding that the radioactive risk posed by Cosmos
954 was no longer a threat to Canadians or their environment.[79] While
remaining radioactive particles could pose a hazard to anyone who came
in direct contact with them, this threat was mitigated by Northern demo-
graphics (a small population distributed over a large area), the recovery
efforts in and around populated areas, the natural behaviour of the particles,
and their rapid radioactive decay. Indeed, scientist F.R. Campbell's comments on one draft report suggested that such definitive conclusions might
themselves worry Canadians. "I find the tone of the report . . . [leaves] the
impression that we tried too hard and too often to convince the reader that
we had done a great job and the risks are trivial," Campbell noted. "While
these things are largely true, I'm afraid we 'protest too much' and raise
suspicions. The facts, I believe, speak for themselves; we would be better
not to belabour the point."[80]

## LEGAL RISKS: LIABILITY UNDER INTERNATIONAL LAW

A professional, systematic scientific effort was also essential to secure
compensation from the Soviet Union for scattering radioactive satellite
debris across Canadian territory. Initial Canadian diplomatic overtures
focused on securing information about the design of Cosmos 954, primarily
to confirm that the reactor had disintegrated during atmospheric re-entry.
On January 24 and 27, the Department of External Affairs posed questions
to the Soviet Embassy about the nature and amount of reactor fuel, as well
as the type of reaction, reflector, and shielding, all of which could have
informed the type of detection equipment required to find local debris
before it decayed to a level that made it difficult to distinguish from the
surrounding environment. Furthermore, the chemical or alloy composition
of the fuel would help to determine the probabilities of dispersal and
"general contamination of large tracts of land and the requirement for
extensive monitoring of flora and fauna."[81]

The Soviets proved highly reluctant to pass along any substantive information about the nuclear-powered satellite,[82] dedicating their energy to
protecting intelligence about its design and managing the legal risk that
they faced under the 1972 Convention on International Liability for

Damage Caused by Space Objects.[83] Although Cosmos 954 was the seventh nuclear-powered vehicle to return to earth, it represented the first example of one inadvertently crashing onto another state's territory and would set a precedent as the first operationalization of anticipatory international law.[84] External Affairs decided that "it would seem to be of no advantages to Canada in political, legal or intelligence terms to have their [Soviet] experts or technicians involved in the operation."[85] Accordingly, Canada rebuffed an initial Soviet offer to send technical teams to assist in the recovery of Cosmos 954 debris *after* it had been located. Given the Cold War context, Canadian legal officials were skeptical, concluding from a Soviet aide-mémoire that the USSR "may be laying basis for denying ownership of debris . . . [by] dismiss[ing] photos that have appeared in press as being of things even he could have put together in his backyard. He seemed to hint too that once debris [was] removed from spot there could be some question about its authenticity."[86] For their part, after the initial exchange the Soviets showed no interest in recovering debris or sharing any information on Cosmos 954's design and enriched uranium fuel.[87]

On February 8, 1978, Canada served notice to the Soviet Union of intended legal action to "restore" the environment "to [a] condition which would have existed if the damage [from Cosmos 954] had not occurred."[88] This included reimbursement for the costs of search, recovery, and "clean-up of radioactive satellite debris as to prevent or mitigate future injuries to persons or contamination of the environment."[89] The Canadian claim described as damage to property the "deposit of hazardous radioactive debris from the satellite throughout a large area of Canadian territory, and the presence of that debris in the environment rendering part of Canada's territory unfit for use." Because the territory over which the debris had scattered was largely uninhabited, the degree to which it was "unsafe" was legally ambiguous.[90] In response, the USSR argued that when Canada declined its offer of assistance, it forfeited any right to compensation.[91] Over time, External Affairs was quietly concerned that a steady stream of scientific papers demonstrating Operation Morning Light's *success* in finding, defining, and mitigating the radioactive risk to civilians might jeopardize Canada's upcoming legal claim against the USSR or the amount of reparations that it might secure.[92]

Ultimately, the legal risk was resolved through diplomatic channels. "In the Cosmos 954 claim, Canada had to meet the argument that the Soviet satellite did not cause direct injury to people or damage to property," legal scholars Edward G. Lee and David Sproule explained. "While no persons were directly injured by the debris and, strictly speaking, the land was usable, the public nevertheless would have faced a health risk had the Canadian government not undertaken decontamination measures."[93] Canada presented a bill of $6.1 million to the Soviet Union in 1979, of total estimated costs of nearly $14 million for the recovery and cleanup effort.[94] After three rounds of negotiations, the countries eventually agreed to a lump sum settlement of $3 million in April 1981.[95] "The text of the protocol gave no indication of a basis for agreement," legal scholar Joseph Burke observed in its aftermath. "As a result, the resolution amounts to no more than a tacit admission by the Soviets of their responsibility to the Canadians in the wake of the Cosmos 954 crash."[96]

## CONCLUSIONS

When Cosmos 954 fell to earth on January 24, 1978, the radioactive debris from its nuclear reactor posed a particular risk to Northern Canadians and their homeland. Amid tremendous uncertainty, officials had to decide how to address a potentially acute threat to public safety, acknowledging the location and scale of an unintended but tangible nuclear threat. Nuclear contamination in a remote swath of Arctic and subarctic in Canada's Northwest Territories forced scientists to apply and adapt techniques to identify and manage radionuclide contamination. Canada and the United States were forced to discern steps needed to mitigate the nuclear risk. Fortunately, the absence of long-term radionuclide contamination of air, water, or food supplies has allowed this case study to fade from popular memory. Despite the acute sense of risk perceived at the time, Operation Morning Light has also faded into the broader background of Canada's Cold War history. As a successful operation predicated on effective Canada-US cooperation that dealt with an unintended Cold War incursion into Northern Canada, it lacks the sensationalism of debates over nuclear weapons on Canadian soil or US threats to Canada's Arctic sovereignty. Instead, it serves as a modest reminder of the global reach of nuclear histories and the various scales at which nuclear incidents required emergency responses.

Lying at the intersection of nuclear and technological histories, Indigenous-Crown relations, environmental history, and scientific practice, it is surprising that Operation Morning Light has attracted so little academic attention. Less surprising, however, are differences in interpretation of what the operation meant in terms of risks and responsibilities. In our assessment, the Canadian government demonstrated that its highest priority was protecting the health, safety, and security of Canadians in the face of a nuclear threat. It did so appropriately and proportionately, working in concert with the United States to effectively identify, recover, remove, test, and clean up radioactive debris on Canadian territory. The scenario revealed the permeable boundary between earth and outer space, as well as the Cold War's global nuclear influence, extending into the far reaches of the Canadian North.

## NOTES

1 *International Legal Materials* 18, 4 (July 1979): 905.
2 Leo Heaps, *Operation Morning Light: The True Story of Canada's Nuclear Nightmare* (Toronto: Random House, 1978), 50.
3 US Department of Energy (DoE), *Operation Morning Light: Canadian Northwest Territories, 1978 – A Non-Technical Summary of United States Participation* (Washington, DC: Department of Energy, September 1978), 67, 71; and "The Unscheduled Return of Cosmos 954," *Science News* 113, 5 (April 2, 1978): 69.
4 DoE, *Operation Morning Light*, 8, 11.
5 Major W.R Aikman, "Operation Morning Light," *Sentinel* 14, 2 (1978), reproduced in Adam Lajeunesse and P. Whitney Lackenbauer, eds., *Canadian Armed Forces Arctic Operations, 1945–2015: Historical and Contemporary Lessons Learned* (Fredericton: Gregg Centre for the Study of War and Society, 2017), 247. Aitken noted that "tension dropped when negative results were announced." While Yellowknife was spared from contamination, analysts projected that massive radioactive objects could survive re-entry and reach the earth's surface further down range toward Baker Lake. DoE, *Operation Morning Light*, 12n.
6 "Canada Wants Cash for Cosmos 954 Cleanup," *Science* 203 (February 16, 1979): 632–33; W.K. Gummer, *Summary of Cosmos 954 Search and Recovery Operation* (Ottawa: Atomic Energy Control Board, January 1979), 1; and W.K. Gummer, F.R. Campbell, G.B. Knight, and J.L Ricard, *Cosmos 954: The Occurrence and Nature of Recovered Debris* (Ottawa: Minister of Supply and Services Canada, 1980), iii.
7 Heaps, *Operation Morning Light*.

8　C.A Morrison, *Voyage into the Unknown: The Search and Recovery of Cosmos 954* (Stittsville, ON: Canada's Wings, 1983), 120. For more on satellite failures in general, see Les Johnson, *Sky Alert! When Satellites Fail* (Chichester, UK: Springer-Praxis, 2013).

9　Ellen Power and Arn Keeling, "Cleaning Up Cosmos: Satellite Debris, Radioactive Risk, and the Politics of Knowledge in Operation Morning Light," *Northern Review* 48 (2018): 81.

10　Ibid., 90, 101–2.

11　Morrison, *Voyage into the Unknown*, 4.

12　Itty Abraham, "The Ambivalence of Nuclear Histories," *Osiris* 21, 1 (2006): 49–65.

13　On legibility and Arctic environments during the Cold War, see Trevor J. Barnes and Matthew Farish, "Between Regions: Science, Militarism, and American Geography from World War to Cold War," *Annals of the Association of American Geographers* 96, 4 (2006): 807–26; Matthew Farish, *The Contours of America's Cold War* (Minneapolis: University of Minnesota Press, 2010). On the theme of reshaping, see, for example, Liza Piper, *The Industrial Transformation of Subarctic Canada* (Vancouver: UBC Press, 2010); Dolly Jorgensen and Sverker Sorlin, eds., *Northscapes: History, Technology, and the Making of Northern Environments* (Vancouver: UBC Press, 2013); P. Whitney Lackenbauer and Matthew Farish, "The Cold War on Canadian Soil: Militarizing a Northern Environment," *Environmental History* 12 (2007): 921–50; and Matthew Farish, "The Lab and the Land: Overcoming the Arctic in Cold War Alaska," *Isis* 104, 1 (2013): 1–29.

14　Jeffrey T. Richelson, *Defusing Armageddon* (New York: W.W. Norton, 2009), 48–50; Gus W. Weiss, "The Satellite That Came into the Cold: The Life and Death of Cosmos 954," *CIA Historical Review Program* 22 (1978): 1; Andrew Brearley, "Reflections upon the Notion of Liability: The Instances of Kosmos 954 and Space Debris," *Journal of Space Law* 34 (2008): 294.

15　NORAD was renamed North American Aerospace Defence Command in 1981.

16　"Operation Morning Light: Department of National Defence Final Report," 1, ATIP A-2015-00308, Directorate of History and Heritage (DHH), Department of National Defence; DoE, *Operation Morning Light*, 66; and Richelson, *Defusing Armageddon*, 53.

17　Weiss, "The Satellite That Came into the Cold," 1. See also unclassified cable, Bureau of Oceans and International Environmental and Scientific Affairs, Department of State, to NATO Posts Tokyo, January 24, 1978, https://wikileaks.org/plusd/cables/1978STATE019297_d.html.

18　DoE, *Operation Morning Light*, 2.

19　Weiss, "The Satellite That Came into the Cold," 3–4. Heaps noted that Anatoly Dobrynin, a former aerodynamic engineer, would inform the US National Security Adviser only that "Cosmos 954 was not an atomic bomb": *Operation Morning Light*, 27. On the uncertainty over the depressurization, see "A Tass Correspondent Interviews Academician L.I. Sedov," *Izvestia*, February 5, 1978, 3, quoted in Alexander Cohen, "Cosmos 954 and the International Law of Satellite Accidents," *Yale Journal of International Law* 10 (1984): 80.

20　Weiss, "The Satellite That Came into the Cold," 4. While the countries that received information initiated their own preparations to deal with Cosmos 954, the US

Department of Energy's field units were ready for deployment by January 22, with all personnel on a two-hour alert and NEST equipment loaded onto four Air Force C-141 Starlifter aircraft in Washington, DC, California, and Nevada. DoE, *Operation Morning Light*, 2–3, 5; and Aikman, "Operation Morning Light," 6.

21 Gummer, "Summary of Cosmos 954 Search and Recovery Operation," 2; and Ryan Dean and P. Whitney Lackenbauer, eds., *Operation Morning Light*, Arctic Operational Series No. 3 (Antigonish: Mulroney Institute of Government, 2018), 63.

22 DoE, *Operation Morning Light*, 8–9, 14–17, 62; and Aikman, "Operation Morning Light," 6. Canada's first contribution to this bilateral collaborative effort was meteorological reports to enhance re-entry modelling.

23 Aikman, "Operation Morning Light," 6. On the spectrometer, see Barb Livingstone, "In Search of Radiation in Barren Land," *Edmonton Journal*, February 2, 1978.

24 By January 28, the whole search area had been overflown at least once by CC-130 aircraft. Gummer et al., *Cosmos 954*, 3, 8; Aikman, "Operation Morning Light," 5–6; DoE, *Operation Morning Light*, 25, 39. Ironically, the gamma ray spectrometers aboard the CC-130 Hercules proved much more effective in detecting Cosmos debris than specially equipped US aircraft designed to measure radioactivity in the atmosphere. See DoE, *Operation Morning Light*, 14, 42; Richelson, *Defusing Armageddon*, 55–56.

25 Aikman, "Operation Morning Light," 7.

26 DoE, *Operation Morning Light*, 22. Data were also sent on to Los Alamos and the Lawrence Livermore National Laboratory for further study. Richelson, *Defusing Armageddon*, 64.

27 Gummer et al., *Cosmos 954*, 8; and DoE, *Operation Morning Light*, 53–54.

28 As Canada's statement of claim explained: "The intrusion of the Cosmos 954 satellite into Canada's air space and the deposit on Canadian territory of hazardous radioactive debris from the satellite constitutes a violation of Canada's sovereignty. This violation is established by the mere fact of the trespass of the satellite, the harmful consequences of this intrusion, being the damage caused to Canada by the presence of hazardous radioactive debris and the interference with the sovereign right of Canada to determine the acts that will be performed on its territory. International precedents recognize that a violation of sovereignty gives rise to an obligation to pay compensation." Canada, "Statement of Claim to the USSR for Damage Caused by Soviet Cosmos 954," *International Legal Materials* 18, 4 (July 1979): 907.

29 On these concerns, see, for example, Ken Coates, P. Whitney Lackenbauer, Bill Morrison, and Greg Poelzer, *Arctic Front: Defending Canada in the Far North* (Toronto: Thomas Allen, 2008); Shelagh Grant, *Polar Imperative: A History of Arctic Sovereignty in North America* (Vancouver: Douglas and McIntyre, 2011); and Adam Lajeunesse, *Lock, Stock, and Icebergs: A History of Canada's Arctic Maritime Sovereignty* (Vancouver: UBC Press, 2016).

30 Heaps, *Operation Morning Light*, 76.

31 Annex A: Legal Basis of Canada's Claim: Nature of Damage, to A.E. Gotlieb, Memorandum to Ministers, Cosmos 954 – Claim against the USSR, October 18, 1978, AECB file 15-200-24-12-0 pt.2, ATIP 2016-000082.

32 DoE, *Operation Morning Light*, iv.

33 Dean and Lackenbauer, *Operation Morning Light*, 71.

34 The first NEST left on March 8, and two weeks later the last Americans left for Las Vegas with the remaining US equipment. Mitchell Beer, "Aftermath of Cosmos Crash," *Globe and Mail*, October 25, 1980, 2; DoE, *Operation Morning Light*, 62; Aikman, "Operation Morning Light," 16.
35 Dean and Lackenbauer, *Operation Morning Light*, 92.
36 Aikman, "Operation Morning Light," 6.
37 Lieutenant-General (ret'd) W.K. Carr, "Foreword," in Morrison, *Voyage into the Unknown*, 1.
38 Dean and Lackenbauer, *Operation Morning Light*, 92. Accordingly, Prime Minister Trudeau expressed Canada's appreciation for American assistance in a message to President Carter on March 22. Aikman, "Operation Morning Light," 16; DoE, *Operation Morning Light*, 62.
39 DoE, *Operation Morning Light*, 73.
40 Ibid., 22.
41 See, for example, P. Whitney Lackenbauer and Rob Huebert, "Premier Partners: Canada, the United States and Arctic Security," *Canadian Foreign Policy Journal* 20, 3 (2014): 320–33; P. Whitney Lackenbauer and Peter Kikkert, "The Dog in the Manger – and Letting Sleeping Dogs Lie: The United States, Canada and the Sector Principle, 1924–1955," in *International Law and Politics of the Arctic Ocean: Essays in Honour of Donat Pharand*, ed. Suzanne Lalonde and Ted McDorman (Leiden: Brill, 2015), 216–39; Lackenbauer and Kikkert, "Sovereignty and Security: The Department of External Affairs, the United States, and Arctic Sovereignty, 1945–68," in *In the National Interest: Canadian Foreign Policy and the Department of Foreign Affairs and International Trade, 1909–2009*, ed. Greg Donaghy and Michael Carroll (Calgary: University of Calgary Press, 2011), 101–20; and Daniel Heidt, "Clenched in the JAWS of America? Canadian Sovereignty and the Joint Arctic Weather Stations, 1946–1972," in *Canada and Arctic Sovereignty and Security: Historical Perspectives*, ed. P. Whitney Lackenbauer (Calgary: Centre for Military and Strategic Studies/University of Calgary Press, 2011), 145–70.
42 John Noble Wilford, "Canadians Pick Up 'Hottest' Satellite Fragment Yet," *New York Times*, February 6, 1978, NJ13.
43 Barb Livingstone, "In Search of Radiation in Barren Land," *Edmonton Journal*, February 2, 1978.
44 "Grow Up, Russia Told," *Edmonton Journal*, February 6, 1978.
45 Gummer et al., *Cosmos 954*, 2, 4.
46 Canadian Press, "Searchers Find Satellite Debris," *Fort McMurray Today*, January 30, 1978.
47 Aikman, "Operation Morning Light," 10.
48 Wilford, "Canadians Pick Up 'Hottest' Satellite Fragment Yet."
49 Canadian Press, "Satellite Fragment Is Radioactive," *Fort McMurray Today*, February 2, 1978.
50 Aikman, "Operation Morning Light," 12.
51 Gummer et al., *Cosmos 954*, iii, 2, 4; and DoE, *Operation Morning Light*, 56, 58.
52 Gummer, "Summary of Cosmos 954 Search and Recovery Operation," 4; Dean and Lackenbauer, *Operation Morning Light*, 88.
53 Dean and Lackenbauer, *Operation Morning Light*, 77.

54 Weiss, "The Satellite That Came into the Cold," 6.

55 Hubert Johnson, "The Day Yellowknife Became Famous" *Edmonton Journal*, January 26, 1978, 64.

56 "Yellowknifers Didn't Contract Satellite Hysteria," *Yellowknifer*, February 9, 1978.

57 See, for example, Heather E. Jamieson, "The Legacy of Arsenic Contamination from Mining and Processing Refractory Gold Ore at Giant Mine, Yellowknife, Northwest Territories, Canada," *Reviews in Mineralogy and Geochemistry* 79, 1 (2014): 533–51; and John Sandlos and Arn Keeling, "Toxic Legacies, Slow Violence, and Environmental Injustice at Giant Mine, Northwest Territories," *Northern Review* 42 (2016): 7–21.

58 Cartoons in the Northern media also cast Operation Morning Light in a humorous or cynical light, appropriating the situation to poke fun at the influx of scientists and military personnel into the Northwest Territories and the environmental threats posed by radioactive debris.

59 Power and Keeling, "Cleaning Up Cosmos," 96.

60 Witness Dan Billing, Chief of Emergency Services, Government of the Northwest Territories, AECB 15-200-24-12-2 vol. 2, ATIP A-2016-00082.

61 DoE, *Operation Morning Light*, 25.

62 Robert Blake, "Snowdrift Safer Than Most Places, General Tells Residents," *Yellowknifer*, February 2, 1978.

63 Aikman, "Operation Morning Light," 9. See also the description of the visit (replete with offensive racial stereotypes) in Heaps, *Operation Morning Light*, 117–22. While the reported results were reassuring, mixed official messaging left some observers skeptical. See, for example, Beer, "Aftermath of Cosmos Crash."

64 "Nuclear Fear Eases Its Grip on the North," *Edmonton Journal*, February 1, 1978.

65 A systematic survey of regional newspaper coverage suggested a more reassured response once scientific teams began sharing findings with the public that did not identify an acute threat to humans. See the collection of newspaper stories in *News from the Canadian North*, compiled by Leona Olfert, in 1978 for the Canadian Circumpolar Library collection at the Cameron Library, University of Alberta, Edmonton.

66 Heaps, *Operation Morning Light*, 102.

67 Ibid., 103.

68 Power and Keeling drew a peculiar analogy between concerns about *persistent* organic pollutants (POPs) and radionuclides from satellite debris ("Cleaning Up Cosmos," 102), although the "persistence" of the former makes them materially different in terms of their long-term environmental effects from radioactive contaminants whose potency is measured in half-lives.

69 DoE, *Operation Morning Light*, 56, 58; Gummer et al., *Cosmos 954*, iii; Dean and Lackenbauer, *Operation Morning Light*, 88.

70 Gummer, "Summary of Cosmos 954 Search and Recovery Operation," 4–5. Although some fragments discovered by search teams had proven highly radioactive, emitting enough radiation to kill a person within a few hours of contact, the widespread dispersal of the particles mitigated the risk, making the odds of a person directly encountering one of these fragments very low.

71 "Memorandum: The Louis Lake Fish Story," W.K. Gummer, December 27, 1978, AECB File 15-200-24-0-0, ATIP 2016-00082.

72 "RE: Operation Morning Light," J.H. Jennekens (AECB) to Deputy Minister Grant C. Mitchell (Saskatchewan Environment), January 22, 1979, AECB file 15-200-24-0-0 pt.3, ATIP 2016-000082.

73 G.J. Brunskill and R.H. Hesslein (Fisheries and Oceans) to A.T. Prince (AECB), June 20, 1979, AECB file 15-200-27-7-2, ATIP 2016-0082.

74 See NAST memos from April 7, 1978, to April 7, 1979, on equipment and facilities handling COSMOS debris, AECB file 15-200-27-7-2, ATIP 2016-0082.

75 H.W Taylor, E.A. Hutchison, K.L. McInnes, and J. Svoboda, "Cosmos 954: Search for Airborne Radioactivity on Lichens in the Crash Area, Northwest Territories, Canada," *Science* 205, 4413 (September 28, 1979): 1383–85; and Gummer et al., *Cosmos 954,* 2–5. Small particles measured as low as a few thousandths or millionths of a roentgen per hour, and steadily decayed to below natural background levels. September measurements found radiation levels to be one-fifth of what they were in January. For a more in-depth breakdown of the recovered materials and the nature of their radioactivity, see Gummer et al., *Cosmos 954,* 10–32.

76 Dean and Lackenbauer, *Operation Morning Light,* 64. Much of the material collected by Operation Morning Light, after being flown to CFB Edmonton and then to the Whiteshell Nuclear Research Establishment at Pinawa, Manitoba, for further testing and storage, was later sent for disposal to the Chalk River Laboratories at Deep River, Ontario. Gummer et al., *Cosmos 954,* iii; Dean and Lackenbauer, *Operation Morning Light,* 67; and Morrison, *Voyage into the Unknown.*

77 By the time the project was completed in the summer of 1978, scientists at Whiteshell had examined hundreds of specimens and conducted more than 4,700 analyses. R.B. Stewart, "Russian Satellite Debris: Examination of COSMOS 954 Fragments at the Whiteshell Nuclear Research Establishment," May 1979, 79/528, ATIP A-2015-00298, DHH.

78 Gummer et al., *Cosmos 954,* 9.

79 See, for example, Dean and Lackenbauer, *Operation Morning Light;* and Gummer, "Summary of Cosmos 954 Search and Recovery Operation."

80 "Memorandum: COSMOS 954 FINAL REPORT," F.R. Campbell to W.K. Gummer, October 12, 1979, AECB file 15-200-24-0-0, ATIP 2016-00082.

81 Department of External Affairs Aide-Mémoire of February 8, 1978, *International Legal Materials* 18, 4 (July 1979): 913.

82 Diplomats ultimately secured little additional information on Cosmos 954's design than the Soviets initially shared with National Security Adviser Zbigniew Brzezinski. "Confidential" EXTOTT to Tokyo/Gotlieb, January 24, 1978, AECB file 15-200-24-12-2, ATIP 2016-00082.

83 Diplomatic notes throughout March 1978, AECB file 15-200-24-12-2, ATIP 2016-00082.

84 Morrison, *Voyage into the Unknown,* 3–4. For example, see Edward R. Finch Jr. and Amanda Lee Moore, "The Cosmos 954 Incident and International Space Law," *American Bar Association Journal* 65 (January 1979): 56–59; and R.I.R. Abeyratne, "Environmental Protection and the Use of Nuclear Power Sources in Outer Space," *Environmental Policy and Law* 26, 6 (1996): 255–60.

85 Confidential, BNATO to EXTOTT DFR, February 1, 1978, AECB file 15-200-24-12-2, ATIP 2016-00082.

86  EXTOTT to Pekin/Mindel, February 1, 1978, AECB file 15-200-24-12-2, ATIP 2016-00082.
87  Diplomatic notes during March 1978, AECB file 15-200-24-12-2, ATIP 2016-00082.
88  Confidential EXTOTT to Tokyo/Gotlieb, January 24, 1978, AECB file 15-200-24-12-2, ATIP 2016-00082; and Restricted, EXTOTT to BNATO, February 8, 1978, AECB file 15-200-24-12-2, ATIP 2016-00082.
89  E.B. Wang, Draft "Cosmos Satellite: Proposed Outline Briefing for Soviet Representatives," March 7, 1978, AECB file 15-200-24-12-2, ATIP 2016-00082.
90  Joseph A. Burke, "Convention on International Liability for Damage Caused by Space Objects: Definition and Determination of Damages after the Cosmos 954 Incident," *Fordham International Law Journal* 8, 255 (1984): 277.
91  Edward G. Lee and David Sproule, "Liability for Damage Caused by Space Debris: The Cosmos 954 Claim," *Canadian Yearbook of International Law* 26 (1988): 278.
92  W.K. Gummer (Manager AECB) to Bruce Stewart (AECL, Whiteshell), January 12, 1979, AECB File 15-200-24-0-0, ATIP 2016-00082.
93  Lee and Sproule, "Liability for Damage Caused by Space Debris," 276.
94  See Address by L.H. Legault and A. Farand, "Canada's Claim for Damage Caused by the Soviet Cosmos 954 Satellite," American Bar Association Forum Committee on Air and Space Law, First Annual Forum (February 23–25, 1984); Burke, "Convention on International Liability," 255–85; and Brearley, "Reflections upon the Notion of Liability," 291–318. On costs, see Dean and Lackenbauer, *Operation Morning Light,* 220.
95  Lee and Sproule, "Liability for Damage Caused by Space Debris," 273–80.
96  Burke, "Convention on International Liability," 279–80.

# CHAPTER 9

# STRENGTHENING NUCLEAR SAFEGUARDS

*The Transformation of Canadian Nuclear Policy toward Argentina and South Korea after India's 1974 Nuclear Test*

Se Young Jang

The export of nuclear technologies has been a controversial element in Canada's foreign and economic policy since 1945. Nuclear suppliers including Canada have used their nuclear expertise not only to gain economic benefits in the international nuclear market but also to further their broader political objectives, such as supporting allies or developing countries through the transfer of nuclear technology in the context of the Cold War competition. However, the dual nature of nuclear export policy sometimes creates an ironic situation in which the pursuit of one aim turns out to contradict another. Canada's nuclear export policy after India's Pokhran-I nuclear test in May 1974 is an example of such a situation, in which pursuing economic benefits did not necessarily achieve Canada's political objectives, and vice versa.

Prior to the Pokhran-I test, in which India used plutonium produced in a Canadian-supplied research reactor (CIRUS reactor) to detonate a nuclear device, Canada had been cultivating access to emerging nuclear export markets, including Argentina and South Korea. However, after Canadian nuclear technology was involved in the Indian test, Canada's approach changed. To restore its damaged reputation and dispel domestic and international concerns about any further involvement of Canadian nuclear technology in global nuclear proliferation, Ottawa strengthened its nonproliferation measures, including safeguards on exported nuclear technology and equipment, at the cost of losing potential contracts in the international nuclear market. After the 1974 Indian test, Canada's negotiations with Argentina and South Korea regarding the export of heavy water reactors were regarded as litmus tests of its seriousness about abiding by global non-proliferation norms.

Given the Canadian role in the Indian test, one might expect that Canada's nuclear non-proliferation policy would have been strengthened after 1974, but the reality was far more complex. Canada halted its negotiations with South Korea on the sale of heavy water reactors – the Canada Deuterium Uranium (CANDU) and National Research Experimental (NRX) reactors – and insisted that South Korea adopt much more stringent safeguards on the reactors and ratify the Nuclear Non-Proliferation Treaty (NPT). At the same time, however, Canada moved forward with the sale of a CANDU reactor to Argentina without imposing any conditions related to stronger nuclear safeguards or adherence to the NPT.

Why did Canada adopt and implement these inconsistent approaches toward the two nuclear buyers? While some literature touches upon Canada's nuclear policy toward South Korea and Argentina from historical and policy perspectives, few studies have examined the causes of the contradictions in Canada's non-proliferation policy during the mid-1970s.[1] Using extensive archival sources from Canada, South Korea, and the United States, this chapter identifies the conditions under which Canada chose one policy over the other in its negotiations with Argentina and South Korea. It also shows the key roles economic and political factors played in the Canadian leadership's decision-making process, ultimately constraining Canada's nuclear non-proliferation efforts during this period.

## CANADA'S NUCLEAR EXPORT POLICY BEFORE 1972

The origin of Canada's nuclear program goes back to the Second World War, when Canada joined the Manhattan Project in 1942. With Canada being one of only two uranium suppliers outside of Nazi-controlled continental Europe, its ability to supply and refine uranium in a safe location far from the battlefields of Europe was greatly appreciated.[2] Canada's main task in the Manhattan Project was "to develop natural-uranium-fuelled, heavy-water-moderated reactors for plutonium production, and to provide uranium for the American and British nuclear weapons programmes."[3] Its contribution to the Manhattan Project remained limited, however, because

Washington took almost all control of the project away from Canada and Britain in 1943 in order to develop the atomic bomb on its own.[4]

Canada's junior status in nuclear development continued in the postwar era. Unable to access American-developed technology – uranium enrichment and light water reactors (LWR) – Canada was further constrained by a lack of financial and technical resources to develop new reactor systems. Thus it fell back on its wartime expertise in heavy water reactors (HWR), using natural uranium as fuel and heavy water as the coolant and neutral moderator. While other nuclear suppliers depended on licensed American LWR technology from the beginning or shifted from one reactor model to another, the Canadians adhered to this single heavy water reactor concept and developed some unique design features.[5]

Despite the lack of consensus, some critics argue that those unique features of Canadian heavy water reactors could be exploited by potential proliferators. Canadian reactors use natural uranium as fuel rather than enriched uranium, which makes Canadian HWRs a more attractive option for future buyers who would like to avoid relying on imported enriched uranium and to develop a "safeguard-resistant independent fuel cycle." The online refuelling capability of Canadian reactors is another key feature that has attracted the attention of potential proliferators. Refuelling of the reactors on a continuous basis makes monitoring and verification of fuel more difficult, allowing spent fuel to be clandestinely diversified unless a very stringent safeguard regime is applied. In contrast, American LWRs need to be shut down for several weeks per year to be refuelled, making them easier to safeguard because the fuel assemblies can be inspected underwater. Moreover, LWRs offer another layer of proliferation resistance by complicating a procedure to extract a fuel assembly from the reactor core.[6]

Despite some attractive technical features, Canada had difficulty expanding its market share in the international nuclear trade during its initial stage of nuclear exports. The fact that it was the only supplier specializing in heavy water reactors – both research and power reactors – gave it certain advantages and disadvantages.[7]

First, demand for heavy water reactors was limited. Until the late 1960s, the nuclear reactor market was dominated by gas-cooled reactors (GCR) or LWRs. Out of 182 reactors either in operation or construction or being shut down between 1951 and 1969, only 13 were pressurized heavy water reactors (PHWRs), 1 was a heavy water/light water reactor (HWLWR; Canada's Gentilly-1), and 1 was a steam-generating heavy water reactor (SGHWR). Heavy water reactors represented only 12 percent of all reactors.[8] The American-designed LWRs were the dominant reactor system, and were also produced by other suppliers like France and West Germany.[9]

The 1960s and 1970s were regarded as "the golden age of the nuclear industry," with a boom in the number of reactors ordered.[10] Canada entered this "golden age" later than other nuclear suppliers. It was only in 1968 that it finished its development phase of nuclear technology and was ready for its full-scale power reactors to be commercially deployed abroad.[11] Canada's small domestic market and vast reservoir of uranium led Ottawa to search out international markets.[12] In 1968, James Lorne Gray, the president of Atomic Energy of Canada Limited (AECL), asserted the necessity and importance of an international market for Canada's own nuclear industry.[13]

Against this backdrop, one of the quickest paths to overcoming Canada's handicap – its late entry into the nuclear export competition – was to establish a relationship with emerging customers in the nuclear market. Unless other political or strategic considerations intervene, countries that acquire nuclear reactors are likely to stick to one or a few reactor types, given the considerable financial and technological investment involved in acquiring different types of reactors. Thus, it was relatively easier for Canada to sell its reactors to emerging nuclear customers with limited ties to other suppliers than to court established customers. This also increased the prospect of securing those markets again in future nuclear deals.

Argentina and South Korea were two representative examples of emerging nuclear customers in the late 1960s. They had already signed their first reactor contracts with other suppliers – Argentina (Atucha I) with Siemens from West Germany in 1968 and South Korea (Kori-1) with Westinghouse from the United States in 1969 – but were still in the initial stage of nuclear development when they started negotiations with Ottawa for their next nuclear power plants in the early 1970s. Thus, they were more flexible than other established customers at that time.

Indeed, Canada participated in the bid for Argentina's Atucha I but lost to West Germany. The competition to supply Argentina's first nuclear reactor was intense because major nuclear suppliers – Britain, the United States, and West Germany – all entered the bidding. The Canadian cabinet was aware that it was less likely for the consortium led by Canadian General Electric to be selected, but considered it important to join in the bidding "to maintain the Canadian competitiveness in this field."[14]

This experience taught Ottawa a lesson in how to approach future nuclear customers. It became convinced that it would need a more assertive marketing strategy to attract potential customers, particularly those from developing countries. As domestic doubts concerning Ottawa's ability to conclude foreign sales grew, AECL faced pressure to produce results.[15] A federal Crown corporation, AECL hired an Israeli sales agent, Shaul Eisenberg, in a bid to offset its lack of knowledge and know-how, which private companies would have used to attract foreign nuclear customers.[16] Hiring an agent and paying a fee upon successful conclusion of a business deal was regarded as "a fact of life in the Far East" at that time.[17] Particularly in South Korea, which had no Canadian embassy until 1974, Eisenberg's previous experience in brokering deals between Western companies and South Korea helped Canada get negotiations started.[18] Eisenberg was involved in Canada's negotiations with Argentina and South Korea by directly accessing the two countries' political and nuclear leadership.[19]

By 1972, it was clear that Canada desperately needed an external nuclear market in order to sustain its own nuclear industry. Between 1968 and 1972, AECL bid on sales to Australia, Mexico, Greece, Romania, and Taiwan (Republic of China). Its single success was the sale of one NRX-type research reactor to Taiwan in 1969. Shortly afterwards, however, Canada's diplomatic recognition of the People's Republic of China and the severing of official relations with Taiwan made further nuclear export to the latter almost impossible.[20]

Canada's specialization in heavy water reactors, once an obstacle to finding new customers, began to prove its real merits as Argentina and South Korea became interested in the Canadian reactors, which were known to be less resistant to proliferation than LWRs. Regardless of how the Canadian government felt about this reputation, such interest on the part of the two countries appeared to provide a rare opportunity for Canada to boost its nuclear exports. For instance, according to AECL president Gray's testimony before a parliamentary committee in January 1977:

> We did not like Argentina, but it happened to be the only game in town. It is an advancing country. It would be much better to sell in the United States, or Germany, or France, or Italy. These are the ones we looked at, but Argentina came along and became convinced that a natural uranium reactor was the right thing, so we concentrated on it because we thought it was essential to maintain the Candu system in the future.[21]

This reveals that Canada's nuclear deals with Argentina and other developing countries in the early 1970s were mostly facilitated by Ottawa's focus on promoting nuclear exports, despite some concerns about the unstated intentions of recipient countries.

## CANADA'S ASSERTIVE NUCLEAR EXPORT POLICY TOWARD ARGENTINA AND SOUTH KOREA, 1972–74

Argentina, with the oldest and most sophisticated nuclear energy program in South America, was regarded as a potential nuclear proliferator during the 1970s and 1980s. It was not a party to either the 1967 Treaty for the Prohibition of Nuclear Weapons in Latin America and the Caribbean (Treaty of Tlatelolco), which created a nuclear weapons–free-zone in Latin America, or to the 1968 Nuclear Non-Proliferation Treaty.[22] Worse, Argentina had been developing a policy on attaining complete independence in the nuclear fuel cycle since 1967.[23] To achieve this goal, it initiated an ambitious nuclear energy program – acquiring sensitive nuclear technologies that could be used to produce weapons-grade materials – before international safeguards on such technologies were fully established, fuelling fears about its military intentions.[24]

Argentina's long regional rivalry with Brazil was a main rationale behind Buenos Aires' decades-long interest in acquiring nuclear capabilities in order "to hedge against the possibility of a Brazilian nuclear bomb."[25] By the mid-1970s, most believed that Argentina's nuclear energy program far outpaced that of Brazil. In June 1975, however, Brazil surprised the international community with its multimillion-dollar deal to import two nuclear reactors from West Germany, which enabled "Brasilia to leapfrog Buenos Aires at one go."[26] Amid this nuclear competition, Argentina managed to become the first country in the region to acquire critical nuclear technologies such as spent-fuel reprocessing and uranium enrichment. However, neither Argentina nor Brazil reached a technical level sufficient to produce weapons-grade fissile material.[27]

In early 1972, Canada decided to participate in the bidding for Argentina's second power reactor, the 600 megawatts electric (MWe) Embalse (Cordoba) project, with an Italian company, Italimpianti. AECL assumed the cost and commercial responsibilities for the marketing and supply of the nuclear part of the Embalse plant, while Italimpianti assumed the same for the electrical generating part.[28] Why did AECL make the joint bid for Embalse with an Italian firm? AECL felt that such a partnership with an Italian company would be useful in helping Canada export nuclear reactors to Italy in the future.[29] Learning from its failure in the Atucha I bid, AECL also realized the necessity for a partnership with a company, such as Italimpianti, that was familiar with the South American market. According to Gray, Italimpianti told AECL:

> Look, you fellows are babes in the woods, you will never sell in South America the way you go about selling . . . you better let us take the commercial lead. You have got a good system, we think it is going to go around the world, but if you want to sell in South America you better let us do it for you.[30]

Canada's provision of financial support for the construction of nuclear reactors abroad through the Export Development Corporation (EDC) was a response to the intense competition in the international nuclear market, which saw the United States using its Export-Import Bank to support nuclear exports.[31] For Embalse, cabinet authorized the EDC to provide up to $160 million to support AECL's contract with Argentina – $117 million of this was to cover 90 percent of the contract price, including the initial fuel charge, while the remaining $43 million would cover the local costs, including interest (not less than 7 percent per year) during construction.[32]

Argentina selected the AECL-Italimpianti joint offer for a turnkey CANDU reactor in March 1973, and signed the contract with a total value of $129 million on December 20 that same year. This contract became effective in April 1974 upon ratification by Argentinian president Juan Peron, only two years after the initial decision to submit a bid.[33] AECL also signed a technological transfer agreement with Argentina's Comisión Nacional de Energía Atómica (CNEA; National Commission for Atomic Energy) in January 1974. This agreement aimed to provide information on topics of mutual interest in nuclear technology and equipment and to familiarize Argentinian personnel in various phases of work associated with CANDU power plants.[34] However, no bilateral safeguard agreement between Canada and Argentina was signed prior to May 1974 because Canada had been content with Argentina's bilateral negotiations with the International Atomic Energy Agency (IAEA).[35] Argentina concluded an agreement with the IAEA for safeguarding the Embalse facility only in December 1974, after India's nuclear test.[36]

South Korea also became interested in acquiring its own nuclear weapons during the early 1970s. The difference from the Argentine case was that South Korea's regional competition or adversarial relationship with North Korea was not a main driver of its nuclear endeavours. South Korea began examining a military nuclear option in the midst of US president Richard Nixon's disengagement policy from Asia, which culminated in his 1970 announcement that the US would withdraw a third of its forces stationed in Korea. South Korean president Park Chung-hee's deeply rooted anxiety over possible abandonment by the United States encouraged him to pursue an independent nuclear deterrent.[37] At the beginning of 1972, Park ordered his close aides to acquire the technology necessary to develop nuclear weapons.[38] The South Korean government dispatched delegations to several countries with advanced nuclear technology, negotiating with France for a reprocessing facility and with Belgium for a plutonium fabrication facility.[39]

South Korea expressed interest in the CANDU and NRX reactors as the Park regime pursued its military nuclear options. Eisenberg arranged a visit to Seoul by AECL president Gray in April 1973.[40] Without an embassy in Seoul, Canada's relationship with South Korea was fairly limited at the time, even though the Canadian Embassy in Tokyo was accredited to South

Korea. It is therefore not surprising that the initial breakthrough for the South Korea–Canada nuclear deals were more effectively arranged through personal contacts rather than diplomatic channels.

In a series of meetings with high-level South Korean officials, Gray learned of their interest in acquiring heavy water reactors from Canada in order to diversify the country's nuclear fuel suppliers.[41] For Canada, AECL projects with South Korea were considered to have "a good immediate prospect" because the reactor size was "a repeat of Gentilly 2 and Argentina."[42] Furthermore, there was less competitive pressure in the South Korean market because it was obvious from the beginning that Seoul was willing to import Canadian nuclear reactors. Unlike in the Argentinian case, "the absence of a partner" in Canada's nuclear deals with South Korea also provided greater opportunities for Canadian industries, and "Canadian goods and services were to be supplied on a firm cost-plus-escalation basis with no ceiling." In general, the deal with South Korea was better for Canada than the one with Argentina.[43]

In the early stage of the negotiations in 1973, Canada was eager to sell both CANDU and NRX reactors as a single package.[44] Although Canada inquired whether South Korea planned to ratify the NPT, such ratification was not made a precondition for Canada's nuclear reactor export.[45] Before authorizing the EDC financing, Ottawa wanted to conclude a bilateral nuclear cooperation agreement, including some safeguard measures, with South Korea, similar to Canada's previous agreements with other countries. By early May 1974, negotiations were completed and the agreement needed only to be signed by both countries. However, India's nuclear test on May 18 changed everything, particularly to South Korea's disadvantage, and a series of new negotiations began between Seoul and Ottawa.[46]

## CANADA'S INCONSISTENT APPROACHES TO
## NUCLEAR NON-PROLIFERATION, 1974–76

The realization that India used plutonium diverted from the Canadian-supplied CIRUS reactor in the Pokhran-I test shocked Canada and the rest of the world. In 1955 and 1956, when Canada and India first negotiated over a research reactor, nuclear proliferation was not a serious concern and international agreements for the control of nuclear technology transfer did not exist, since the IAEA was founded in summer 1957. Although Canada attempted to prevent India from fully controlling the spent fuel by having the latter return the irradiated fuel rods to Canada, India adamantly refused the Canadian proposal, asserting its sovereignty in ownership of the fuel. As India began approaching other suppliers, Canada could not help but consider the economic benefits and opportunities that its first reactor export would bring, in addition to other political aspects. As a result, it transferred the research reactor to India with "minimal safeguards." The only safeguard stipulated in the agreement between the two countries was that "the reactor and any products resulting from its use will be employed for peaceful purposes only" – the very loophole India exploited in its 1974 test.[47]

The Indian test made the Canadian government realize that it was "impossible to distinguish a nuclear device for peaceful purposes from one for military uses," even though India tried to justify its nuclear test as a "peaceful nuclear explosion."[48] Accordingly, strengthening safeguards on nuclear exports was a reasonable and easily expected reaction from Ottawa when the Canadians were implicated in India's nuclear weapons program. The Canadian Nuclear Policy Review submitted in late 1974 made exactly this point:

> The dangers of nuclear weapons proliferation make it incumbent upon Canada to take all reasonable precautions to ensure that Canadian exports do not contribute to such proliferation. This requires an assessment of the likelihood of a recipient country moving towards the development of nuclear explosives, as well as assurances from such a country that Canadian exports will not be used for nuclear explosive purposes and international inspection to ensure that this undertaking is honoured.[49]

The nuclear aspirations of South Korea and Argentina came under close scrutiny following the Indian nuclear test. In the Canadian Nuclear Policy Review, Canada fully appreciated that South Korea had been pursuing a military nuclear option, even predicting that infrastructure for developing a nuclear weapon would be in place by the early 1980s if Seoul's ambitious plans were fulfilled. The Canadian government recognized the high possibility that a Canadian heavy water reactor and associated technology would "materially" assist South Korea's nuclear weapons program, providing facilities and fuel.[50]

With respect to Argentina, the Canadian Nuclear Policy Review noted that there was "no indication" that Buenos Aires had reached a decision to go nuclear despite some "evidence of wishing to keep open a nuclear weapons option." Should Brazil go nuclear, however, Argentina would follow its neighbour's path. The Canadians believed that the Atucha I reactor provided by West Germany could "provide Argentina with more than sufficient plutonium for any nuclear explosives programme which that country might decide to undertake." The review also indicated that Argentina had worked on nuclear reprocessing, but not on a commercial scale.[51]

Based on the review's recommendation, cabinet decided to give preference to parties to the NPT when granting concessional financing and direct aid for Canada's nuclear exports. It ordered the Department of External Affairs to "assess the intention of a potential purchasing country to develop nuclear explosives and the geopolitical pressures which might force it to develop them."[52] External Affairs was also instructed to undertake the safeguards negotiations with recipient countries, including specific provisions such as "coverage of all nuclear material (uranium, thorium, plutonium, heavy water) supplied by Canada and future generations of fissile material produced from or with such material," and "coverage of all nuclear materials, of whatever origin, processed or used in the facilities."[53]

Canada concluded nuclear cooperation agreements, including strengthened safeguards, with Argentina and South Korea in January 1976. While both agreements had far more stringent safeguards provisions compared with the ones signed prior to the Indian test, there were some notable differences between the two. Whereas Canada's agreement with South Korea was regarded as "the most stringent of all safeguards agreements to that time," with provisions for full-scope safeguards, its agreement with Argentina was weaker than the one with South Korea.[54]

Most importantly, Argentina was not compelled to sign and ratify the NPT as South Korea was. Canada attempted to justify this difference by stating that South Korea was under a distinctive regional dynamic, but no further explanations followed.[55] Moreover, the "no nuclear explosive devices" clause in the Argentinian agreement was restricted only to items of Canadian origin. Thus, Buenos Aires could exploit other reactors to develop nuclear weapons. Finally, Argentina was "not required to return all Canadian supplied nuclear items" in the case of non-compliance, which meant that Argentina still could retain the reactor even if the country violated its safeguards agreement with Canada. Obviously, Canada's safeguards agreement with Argentina in 1976 was weaker than the one with South Korea, which was concluded at almost the same time.[56] Why did the Canadian government adopt and implement this inconsistent non-proliferation policy toward these two potential nuclear proliferators?

## THREE MAIN FACTORS IN CANADA'S CONTRADICTORY POLICY

### Timing of the Contracts

Canada concluded its reactor negotiations with Buenos Aires and signed the contract for Embalse in December 1973, several months before India's Pokhran-I test. The only safeguard the Argentines were obliged to abide by was "the understanding that Argentina would sign an acceptable agreement with the IAEA."[57] After the Indian test, Canada's urgent task with regard to Argentina was not to decide whether to proceed with the deal with Argentina but to revise the safeguards requirements so that Argentina could meet the newly strengthened Canadian requirements.[58]

At the same time, Canada did not want to risk losing the contract. The Canadian government was concerned that the "cancellation of the CANDU project on safeguards grounds would result in legal action being brought against AECL in an Argentine court, which could award damages of several hundred million dollars." Ottawa was also worried about lawsuits not only by Argentina but also by Canada's Italian partner, Italimpianti.[59] For Argentina's part, the contract had been already signed, and thus there was room to negotiate about safeguards with Canada without raising fundamental questions concerning whether or not to go forward with Canadian heavy water reactors.

In contrast, Canada and South Korea were in the middle of negotiations for the bilateral nuclear cooperation agreement (NCA), including safeguards, when India exploded its nuclear device. The conclusion of the agreement was necessary in order for Canada to grant South Korea loans for nuclear reactors – an estimated amount of Cdn$570 million. No financial commitment had been made to South Korea at that point, and Canada had little to lose even if the deal with Seoul fell through as a result of Canada's position on safeguards.

By early May 1974, negotiations between Seoul and Ottawa were almost complete based on standard safeguards provisions from the pre–Indian test period, and all that was needed was for the agreement to be signed.[60] At this stage, Ottawa was far more eager to complete the NCA negotiations than Seoul, requesting the latter to conclude it as promptly as possible.[61] South Korea's ratification of the NPT was not a precondition for signing the agreement either. When Ross Campbell, the Canadian ambassador to Japan who was also in charge of Korean affairs, visited South Korean officials in 1973, he briefly mentioned Canada's interest in South Korea's ratification of the non-proliferation treaty, but his Korean counterpart made it clear that there were "no immediate plans to ratify this treaty."[62] During subsequent NCA negotiations, the issue of ratification was not raised again by the Canadians until after the Indian test.

India's nuclear test on May 18 took the negotiations in a direction considered unfavourable by South Korea. Canada increasingly demanded that South Korea accept more stringent safeguards requirements in the NCA, while also stepping up pressure on South Korea to ratify the NPT.[63] South Korea wanted to acquire heavy water reactors to reduce its dependence on American light water reactors. It also wanted to keep open the possibility of reprocessing plutonium, which could be produced in those heavy water reactors, even under strengthened safeguards, as its later efforts to purchase a French reprocessing facility showed. Under these circumstances, South Korea had little room to maneuver unless the leadership in Seoul decided to abandon its nuclear ambitions.

As a result, Canada's ultimatum in January 1975 – Ottawa would reconsider the sale of the CANDU if South Korea refused to ratify the NPT – compelled South Korea's decision to ratify the treaty in order to continue its nuclear negotiations with Canada. The Korean government decided to recommend ratification of the NPT to President Park in an interministerial meeting on January 23, Park gave the green light on March 7, and the National Assembly promptly ratified the treaty on March 19.[64] In December 1975, Secretary of State for External Affairs Allan MacEachen stated in the House of Commons that "the Republic of Korea, certainly at our suggestion or at our urging, undertook to ratify the Nuclear Nonproliferation Treaty."[65]

## Hyperinflation in Argentina

Hyperinflation in Argentina played another decisive role by compelling Canada to renegotiate the commercial contract for Embalse. Despite the timing issue explained above – the contract with Argentina had already been signed in 1973 – Canada was still trying to strengthen the safeguards already put on Embalse through renegotiation. In September 1974, both countries exchanged a note providing assurance of Argentina's intention "not to use Canadian-supplied technology, material, or expertise to produce any such device."[66] This first accord appeared to be more like an ad hoc remedy to allay immediate concerns in the wake of the Indian test; an exchange of notes was less binding than formal agreements, and only very limited safeguards requirements were added to the first accord between Canada and Argentina. Revising and strengthening safeguards on Embalse through the second accord, however, became much more complicated than expected mainly because of the simultaneous renegotiation of the commercial contract.

The "escalation ceilings" in the original contract between AECL, Italimpianti, and CNEA were inadequate to offset expected high losses under the hyperinflation. Canada was deeply concerned that "proceeding with the contracts for the provision of CANDU, heavy water and uranium as they now stand, will mean a considerable financial loss to Canada," and renegotiation of the contract was deemed necessary.[67] Some Canadian officials were also anxious about the possibility that their efforts to impose stringent safeguards on Embalse could be interpreted "as an effort to escape the consequence of an unfavorable contract" under hyperinflation.[68] Under the circumstances, imposing stringent safeguards on Embalse was only the secondary objective for Canada. The more urgent objective was to avoid or minimize the expected financial loss in the midst of Argentina's hyperinflation by renegotiating the original contract. To do so, the consent and cooperation of Buenos Aires was indispensable, which accordingly undermined Canada's willingness to push for stringent safeguards on Embalse.

## Role of the United States

Finally, South Korea was to a great extent under the direct influence of the United States (a close ally based on a mutual defence treaty since the end of the Korean War). Any unilateral military provocation from Seoul, including the development of nuclear weapons, could have threatened US forces stationed in South Korea by dragging Washington into an unwanted war. In addition, US non-proliferation policy in Northeast Asia was basically not to allow any further nuclear weapons states since China's first nuclear test in 1964; the United States was seriously concerned about a nuclear domino effect that could reduce its leverage in the region. The stronger interest and power of Washington in South Korea may have contributed, at least partially, to Canada's stringent position toward Seoul after the Indian test.

Despite Washington's general interest in maintaining the nuclear status quo in Northeast Asia, the US government did not begin extensively applying its stronger non-proliferation measures to South Korea immediately after India's nuclear test. The role of the United States in South Korea's ratification of the NPT in early 1975 was more limited than widely thought, and the underestimated role of Canada in such ratification needs to receive more attention. Canada frequently shared information with the United States regarding its nuclear deals with South Korea and was willing to cooperate with Washington.[69] When Washington exerted pressure to prevent a French reprocessing facility from being transferred to South Korea beginning in the summer of 1975, Canada supported the US position and delayed signing the NCA with South Korea until January 1976, when Seoul finally cancelled its contract with France.[70]

As far as Argentina's nuclear program was concerned, the United States appears to have been perceived as more of an arbitrator than a thwarter. South America was also an important region for US foreign policy, but the United States was not directly involved in Argentina's military affairs. With Argentina's nuclear aspirations deeply rooted in its rivalry with Brazil, the role of a third party like the United States would have been more limited than in the South Korean case. According to Canada's 1974 Nuclear Policy Review, Washington only indicated that it would "try to keep open lines of communication between the two countries" so that they would not embark on a nuclear weapons program due to "fears of each other's intentions."[71]

The lack of US pressure on Argentina, combined with the lack of international export control in the mid-1970s, partially enabled Canada to accept less stringent safeguards on Embalse.

## CONCLUSION

India's "peaceful nuclear explosion" in 1974 opened a Pandora's box. Nuclear suppliers could no longer rely on "statements of good intension" from their customers, while the international safeguards system built up by the NPT and the IAEA remained weak.[72] A handful of nuclear suppliers in the 1970s, including Canada, were pressured to strengthen their bilateral safeguards measures and to design a multilateral export control regime that later became the Nuclear Suppliers Group (NSG).

To attract emerging nuclear customers and maximize commercial advantages, Canada, a relative latecomer in the international nuclear market, assertively sought nuclear reactor deals with Argentina and South Korea, both of which were also interested in the military use of nuclear technology. However, the involvement of Canadian technology in India's nuclear test shifted the priority of Canada's nuclear policy toward a greater non-proliferation orientation, as widely publicized by numerous statements of Canadian government officials.

Despite Canada's intention to strengthen nuclear safeguards, the transition did not take place overnight. Canada's contradictory approaches to its nuclear deals with Argentina and South Korea demonstrate the complex reality faced by Canada in the wake of the Pokhran-I test. While Canada pushed for South Korea's ratification of the NPT and acceptance of the stringent safeguards agreement, Argentina was not forced to ratify the treaty and signed a less stringent agreement with Canada. As explained above, three main factors – the timing of the contracts, the necessity of reducing Canada's financial loss amid Argentina's hyperinflation, and the relationship of the United States with these two countries – influenced Canada's inconsistent non-proliferation policy. Ultimately, Canada participated in creating the NSG and has remained a sincere non-proliferation advocate to the present, but an examination of the transitional period from 1974 to 1976, in which Canada made contradictory choices, sheds new light on Canada's nuclear histories.

## NOTES

1 Robert W. Morrison and Edward F. Wonder, *Canada's Nuclear Export Policy* (Ottawa: Norman Paterson School of International Affairs, Carleton University, 1978), 69–78; Robert Bothwell, *Nucleus: The History of Atomic Energy of Canada Limited* (Toronto: University of Toronto Press, 1988), 426–27, 435; Duane Bratt, *The Politics of CANDU Exports* (Toronto: University of Toronto Press, 2006), 112–16, 128–37.

2 Bratt, *Politics of CANDU Exports*, 8.

3 Morrison and Wonder, *Canada's Nuclear Export Policy*, 12.

4 Bratt, *Politics of CANDU Exports*, 9.

5 Morrison and Wonder, *Canada's Nuclear Export Policy*, 12–13.

6 Bratt, *Politics of CANDU Exports*, 46; Jacques Bouchard, "The Future of Nuclear Power: Reducing Risks," in *Routledge Handbook of Nuclear Proliferation and Policy*, ed. Joseph F. Pilat and Nathan E. Busch (New York: Routledge, 2015), 372.

7 Some countries, such as Sweden, Switzerland, France, and West Germany, had worked on heavy water reactors, but only West Germany managed to build commercialized HWRs and exported two reactor units to Argentina. Since HWRs were not Germany's specialty, however, Canadian HWRs were more competitive in price than German ones. Ministry of Energy, Mines and Resources (MEMR), *Nuclear Policy Review Background Papers*, Report No. ER81-2E (Ottawa: MEMR, 1980), 264; Bratt, *Politics of CANDU Exports*, 24.

8 "Reactor Database," World Nuclear Association, http://www.world-nuclear.org/information-library/facts-and-figures/reactor-database.aspx.

9 MEMR, *Nuclear Policy Review Background Papers*, 260; Bratt, *Politics of CANDU Exports*, 24.

10 Bratt, *Politics of CANDU Exports*, 24.

11 Morrison and Wonder, *Canada's Nuclear Export Policy*, 14.

12 MEMR, *Nuclear Policy Review Background Papers*, 260; Bratt, *Politics of CANDU Exports*, 16–17.

13 Bothwell, *Nucleus*, 407.

14 Cabinet Conclusion (29245), July 26, 1967, RG 2, vol. 6323, access code: 90, Library and Archives Canada (LAC).

15 Bratt, *Politics of CANDU Exports*, 112.

16 Professor Robert Bothwell explained the rationale behind AECL's decision to hire an agent for its sales abroad in an interview with the author on September 21, 2018, Toronto.

17 Bothwell, *Nucleus*, 427.

18 Eisenberg had brokered a number of industrial projects with loans between South Korea and Western companies since the 1950s, building a close relationship with South Korean officials. He was involved in a British firm's bid for South Korea's first commercial reactor, but lost to the American Westinghouse. To appease him, South Korean officials promised to purchase the British advanced gas-cooled reactor (AGR) next time. See Jeong-hun Lee, *Hangugui Haekjugwon* [South Korea's Nuclear Sovereignty] (Seoul: Gulmadang, 2009), 161–64. The Koreans did not have to keep this promise because the AGR design was soon found to be flawed. However, they were probably

not free from their close relationship with Eisenberg, who switched to Canada in the bid for Korea's second commercial reactor.

19  The high fees paid to Eisenberg caused scandal later. Part of the fees were possibly handed over to high-level South Korean officials. See more in Morrison and Wonder, *Canada's Nuclear Export Policy*, 70; Bratt, *Politics of CANDU Exports*, 114–15.
20  MEMR, *Nuclear Policy Review Background Papers*, 265.
21  Quoted in Morrison and Wonder, *Canada's Nuclear Export Policy*, 20.
22  Argentina signed the Treaty of Tlatelolco in 1967 but did not ratify it until 1994. Argentina also acceded to the NPT only in 1995.
23  Daniel Poneman, "Argentina," in *Limiting Nuclear Proliferation*, ed. Jed C. Snyder and Samuel F. Wells Jr. (Cambridge, MA: Ballinger, 1985), 100.
24  Mitchell Reiss, *Bridled Ambition: Why Countries Constrain Their Nuclear Capabilities* (Washington, DC: Woodrow Wilson Center Press, 1995), 46.
25  Other factors, such as the traditional Argentinian desire for "exceptionalism" or the securing of public approval for illegitimate military regimes, also affected Argentina's decision to pursue a military nuclear project. Ibid., 45.
26  This "nuclear deal of the century," the largest transfer of nuclear technology to a developing country up to that point, included an option for Brazil to purchase six additional nuclear reactors in addition to the two reactors already purchased, which were expected to produce up to 10,000 megawatts of electricity by 1990. Ibid., 49–50.
27  Ibid., 66.
28  MEMR, *Nuclear Policy Review Background Papers*, 266.
29  Memorandum to Cabinet, "Policy Relating to AECL Nuclear Power Export Programme," May 31, 1973, RG 2, vol. 6428, file 548-73, LAC.
30  Quoted in Morrison and Wonder, *Canada's Nuclear Export Policy*, 20.
31  Memorandum to Cabinet, "Policy Relating to AECL Nuclear Power Export Programme," May 31, 1973, RG 2, vol. 6428, file 548-73, LAC.
32  Cabinet Conclusion (36500), November 23, 1972, RG 2, vol. 6395, access code: 90, LAC.
33  MEMR, *Nuclear Policy Review Background Papers*, 266; Memorandum to Cabinet, "Sale of CANDU to Argentina: Negotiation of Safeguards," October 27, 1975, RG 2, vol. 6472, file 602-75, LAC.
34  Atomic Energy of Canada Limited (AECL), *Annual Report 1973–1974*, CA.1.1062.c.2, LAC.
35  Morrison and Wonder, *Canada's Nuclear Export Policy*, 72.
36  Memorandum to Cabinet, "Sale of CANDU to Argentina: Negotiation of Safeguards," October 27, 1975, RG 2, vol. 6472, file 602-75, LAC. See the full text of the safeguard agreement between the International Atomic Energy Agency (IAEA) and Argentina (INFCIRC/224) at https://www-legacy.iaea.org/Publications/Documents/Infcircs/Others/infcirc224.shtml.
37  Se Young Jang, "The Evolution of US Extended Deterrence and South Korea's Nuclear Ambitions," *Journal of Strategic Studies* 39, 4 (2016): 507–17.
38  Interview with Won-cheol O (in Korean), *Weekly Chosun*, January 12, 2010.
39  Se Young Jang, "The Development of South Korea's Nuclear Industry in a Resource- and Capital-Scarce Environment," in *Economic Development and Environmental History*

*in the Anthropocene: Perspectives on Asia and Africa,* ed. Gareth Austin (London: Bloomsbury Academic, 2017), 254–55.

40  Memorandum from R.C. Lee to File ck-151-1 (c.c. Campbell), May 7, 1973, RG 13629, Ross Campbell Fonds, vol. 8-1, folder "Posting to Korea 1972.07–1974.01," LAC.

41  Ibid. Under the US–South Korea Nuclear Cooperation Agreement, South Korea was not allowed to enrich uranium but could only purchase US-origin low enriched uranium (LEU).

42  Memorandum to Cabinet, "Policy Relating to AECL Nuclear Power Export Programme," May 31, 1973, RG 2, vol. 6428, file 548-73, LAC.

43  Morrison and Wonder, *Canada's Nuclear Export Policy,* 71.

44  Memorandum by Kaufmann, August 15, 1973, RG 13629, vol. 8-1, LAC; Memorandum, Kaufmann to Johnson, August 9, 1973, RG 13629, vol. 8-1, LAC; Se Young Jang, "Bringing Seoul into the Nonproliferation Regime: The Effect of ROK-Canada Reactor Deals on South Korea's Ratification of the NPT," *Nuclear Proliferation International History Project (NPIHP),* Working Paper Series No. 10 (Washington, DC: Woodrow Wilson International Center for Scholars, 2017), 14.

45  Memorandum, Kaufmann to Johnson, August 9, 1973, RG 13629, vol. 8-1, LAC; Jang, "Bringing Seoul into the Nonproliferation Regime," 14–15.

46  Jang, "Bringing Seoul into the Nonproliferation Regime," 15–16.

47  Bratt, *Politics of CANDU Exports,* 90–95.

48  "Background Information on Safeguard," March 11, 1975, RG 2, vol. 6562, file 167-75, LAC.

49  "Nuclear Policy Review," attached to Memorandum to Cabinet, November 13, 1974, RG 2, vol. 6451, box 15, file 646-74, LAC.

50  Ibid.

51  Ibid.

52  Record of Cabinet Decision, "Nuclear Policy," December 5, 1974, RG 2, vol. 6541, box 15, file 646-74, LAC.

53  Ibid.

54  Bratt, *Politics of CANDU Exports,* 130–31.

55  Telegram, ROK [Republic of Korea] Ministry of Foreign Affairs (MOFA) to ROK Embassy Ottawa, January 21, 1975, classification no. 741.61CN, microfilm roll no. J-06-0102, file 5 (hereafter 741.61CN/J-06-0102/5), ROK Diplomatic Archives (ROKDA).

56  Bratt, *Politics of CANDU Exports,* 133.

57  Ibid., 131.

58  "Nuclear Policy Review," attached to Memorandum to Cabinet, November 13, 1974, RG 2, vol. 6541, box 15, file 646-74, LAC.

59  Memorandum to Cabinet, "Sale of CANDU to Argentina: Negotiation of Safeguards," October 27, 1975, RG 2, vol. 6472, file 602-75, LAC.

60  Summary of Meeting, Gyeong-cheol Kim, Director for International Investigation (MOFA), and Geoni Seo, Desk Officer in Division of Economic Investigation (MOFA) with D. Gordon Longmuir, First Secretary, Canadian Embassy Seoul, May 7, 1974, 741.61CN/J-06-0102/4, ROKDA; Jang, "Bringing Seoul into the Nonproliferation Regime," 16.

61  Transcript of Telephone Conversation, Seo with Longmuir, April 23, 1974, 741.61CN/J-06-0102/4, ROKDA; Jang, "Bringing Seoul in the Nonproliferation Regime," 16.

62 Memorandum, Kaufmann to Johnston, August 9, 1973, RG 13629, vol. 8-1, LAC; Jang, "Bringing Seoul into the Nonproliferation Regime," 14.

63 Jang, "Bringing Seoul into the Nonproliferation Regime," 16–21.

64 Summary of Meeting, Foreign Minister Dong Jo Kim with Canadian Ambassador John Alexander Stiles, January 20, 1975, 741.61CN/J-06-0102/5, ROKDA; Report on Interdepartmental Meeting, Bureau of International Economy (MOFA) to Bureau of International Relations (MOFA), February 6, 1975, 741.61CN/J-06-0102/5, ROKDA; Telegram 01529, US Embassy Seoul to State Department, March 8, 1975, Access to Archival Database (AAD), US National Archives and Records Administration (NARA); Jang, "Bringing Seoul into the Nonproliferation Regime," 23–28.

65 *House of Commons Committees*, "Minutes of Proceedings and Evidence of the Standing Committee on External Affairs and National Defence," 30th Parliament, 1st Session, vol. 1 (December 2, 1975), 32:10.

66 Morrison and Wonder, *Canada's Nuclear Export Policy*, 72.

67 Memorandum to Cabinet, "Sale of CANDU to Argentina: Negotiation of Safeguards," October 27, 1975, RG 2, vol. 6472, file 602-75, LAC.

68 Ibid.

69 Jang, "Bringing Seoul into the Nonproliferation Regime," 28–30.

70 Telegram 9224, US Embassy London to State Department, "Nuclear Export Policy: Bilaterals with Canada," June 17, 1975, NARA; Telegram 5016, US Embassy Seoul to State Department and US Embassy Ottawa, July 8, 1975, NARA; Telegram 6495, US Embassy Seoul to State Department, August 23, 1975, NARA; Cabinet Conclusion (41637), "Sale of CANDU to Korea," January 15, 1976, RG 2, vol. 6495, access code: 90, LAC.

71 "Nuclear Policy Review," attached to Memorandum to Cabinet, November 13, 1974, RG 2, vol. 6451, box 15, file 646-74, LAC.

72 Ibid.

# CONCLUSION

## Nuclear Victorians

### Timothy Andrews Sayle

I n 1982, Canadian officials in Ottawa drafted speaking notes for the diplomats at the High Commission in London. The notes were intended to clarify Canada's nuclear status for the British government. "It is well known," read the remarks sent by cable, and with the standard repetition of negatives, that Canada "is not/not now and never has been [a] nuclear power and that we withdrew from [a] nuclear role in Europe in [the] early 70s." Furthermore, the "nuclear role in NORAD will end with introduction of CF18 aircraft" that would be incapable of carrying nuclear weapons. Canada, the notes went on, "participates in nuclear strategies of Alliance," that is, NATO.[1]

The 1982 speaking notes, then, were as clear as mud: Canada was not and had never been a nuclear power – but it had equipped and trained Canadian artillery and air units to employ nuclear weapons in Europe until the early 1970s, and at the time of the cable, Canada maintained air defence aircraft that would protect North America by firing air-to-air nuclear weapons against Soviet bombers. Canada also remained a part of NATO's Nuclear Planning Group, which managed the nuclear strategies of the alliance, and maintained agreements to enable the basing and overflight of the bombers of the US Strategic Air Command.[2] In the meantime, uranium was mined from Canadian territory, nuclear reactors powered parts of Canada's electrical grid, and Canadians sold reactor designs around the world. The government of Canada planned for nuclear war, and Canadians worried about what any such war might bring.[3]

Not now or ever a nuclear power? Just what makes a state a nuclear power?[4]

Several scholars have suggested that the "atom bomb has become the ultimate fetish of our times."[5] Some nuclear states had made a public exposition of their nuclear status: one need only think of the British Foreign Secretary's insistence that Britain must have the bomb with "the bloody Union Jack on top of it."[6] No Canadian minister has ever been eager to stencil a Maple Leaf on any of Canada's nuclear armaments. If anything, Canadian impulses have been the opposite. The government of Canada has been eager to downplay any connection to nuclear weapons. The criteria for success in Canada's participation in Strategic Air Command exercises, for instance, had been that they occurred unnoticed and with an absence of public criticism.[7] If the bomb is a fetish, the Canadians have kept their devotions quiet, becoming the nuclear equivalent of that hypocritical "Victorian culture, which said one thing about sex while doing another."[8]

Even beyond "the bomb," however, Canada's nuclear history stretches far and wide. Canada produces about 15 percent of the total global output of uranium.[9] In the 1980s, Canada possessed the second-largest number of nuclear industrial firms among non-nuclear weapons states – eighty in total, second only to the Federal Republic of Germany.[10] If one counted nuclear weapons states, Canada still ranked fourth in the world (with the superpowers taking first and second place).[11] As of 2016, nineteen nuclear reactors provided 16 percent of Canada's power. In Ontario, 60 percent of electricity needs are met by reactors.[12] Just as Canadians depend on nuclear power, others outside of Canada depend on Canada's nuclear production. Canada has been the site of innovation in radiation cancer treatment, and exports isotopes for treatment and research around the globe. The unexpected shutdown of a Canadian reactor at Chalk River in 2009 led to a global shortage of isotopes used for medical procedures.[13] How did Canada get to this point if not by being a nuclear state?

Canada's identity as a nuclear power or nuclear state has remained obscure for a number of reasons, the most important of which is the Canadian government's preference – and indeed, likely a preference reflecting the majority of the electorate – that Canada should act, and be seen acting, as a champion of disarmament and arms control. This even if Canadian officials privately admitted to themselves during the Cold War that the "chief means" of preserving peace was the "capacity to retaliate instantly against aggression with nuclear weapons," and that Canada must contribute to that capacity.[14] According to the 1967 Nuclear Non-Proliferation Treaty (NPT), for instance, Canada was and is not considered a "nuclear-weapon State," and yet if war had come in the years after the signing of the NPT, Canadian pilots assigned to the First Air Division would have been flying over the Iron Curtain looking for targets of opportunity to destroy with their nuclear bombs.[15] One cannot be half-pregnant, of course, but Ottawa figuratively came about as close as possible.

In some cases, the presentation of Canada's face to the world as a non-nuclear one was deliberate and shameless politicking, designed to burnish reputations or win elections; in other cases, it was the result of the fact that Canada's nuclear policies were complicated and confusing. Gabrielle Hecht, a leading scholar of nuclear history, observes that trying to answer the question of whether or not a state is "nuclear" is a mug's game; there is no final and definitive ruling. Partially, she writes, this is because "the degree to which – and the purpose for which – a nation, a program, a technology, or a material counts as 'nuclear' is not always a matter of consensus."[16] And so it is with Canada. In each of the chapters in this volume, there is room for interpretation or reinterpretation, and opportunity for different perspectives and differing conclusions as to whether Canada was and is, indeed, a "nuclear" state.

Consider the special status Canada sought and seeks for itself in the international organizations concerned with nuclear weapons. In the diplomatic wrangling of the United Nations Atomic Energy Commission (AEC), Canada secured an important place, helping to manage negotiations between one atomic state, the United States, and an atomic hopeful, the Soviet Union. Canada's place on the AEC, as Katie Davis explains in Chapter 1, was due to Canada's contributions to the wartime nuclear project. And yet Canada had no atomic weapon and had already promised not to build one. It was a nuclear state in that it had been close enough to the production of the first atomic weapons that it held a special status, a legitimacy conferred through participation – yet at the same time it was not a nuclear state in that it had no bomb. Decades later, Canada would use its assigned nuclear role in NATO's strike plan to maneuver its way into a seat on

NATO's Nuclear Planning Group (NPG). Even as Canada was in the process of abandoning that nuclear role, the ambiguity of its position allowed it to present itself simultaneously to its allies as a nuclear-capable state worthy of continued representation in the NPG. Canada has maintained its place in high councils related to nuclear weapons: both at the Conference on Disarmament in Geneva and on NATO's Nuclear Planning Group. The tension between Canada's continued interest in arms control and disarmament and its subscription to an allied strategy dependent on nuclear deterrence is contradictory.[17] But this contradiction is not new and lies in decades of history.

Those operating in the political arena often see benefit in blurring contrasts and contradictions. As Michael Stevenson has pointed out in Chapter 3, while Howard Green pressed for disarmament, the Progressive Conservative government in which he served would ultimately fall on nuclear issues – only to be replaced by a series of Liberal governments that would end up, by the 1970s, adopting the disarmament policies he had advocated in the 1950s. Closely connected to the fate of John Diefenbaker and Howard Green's PCs was the election of Lester Pearson's Liberals. As Jack Cunningham explains in Chapter 5, the Pearsonian nuclear legacy – of a Liberal Party that swore off acquiring nuclear weapons in opposition, only to accept a nuclear role for Canada while in government – really is the quintessential example of the elasticity of Canada's nuclear identity. Asa McKercher, in Chapter 4, along with Cunningham and Stevenson, offers Canadian evidence in support of Hecht's point: there was little consensus in Canada in the 1950s and 1960s about the appropriate nuclear role for Canada, and even less consensus as to just what type of role was nuclear and what was not. This lack of consensus allowed for political pirouettes (and belly flops) but also prevented any agreement among Canadians as to whether or not Canada was a nuclear state.

Politics and military planning and procurement often combine in combustible form, and the Canadian Submarine Acquisition Program offers another example of the confusing and confused nature of discourse and debate about Canada's nuclear role. As Susan Colbourn makes clear in Chapter 6, the acquisition of submarines with nuclear propulsion systems was unacceptable to anti-nuclear protesters, many of whom mixed up or elided the significant difference between nuclear propulsion and nuclear weapons. Would nuclear-powered submarines, unarmed with nuclear weapons, be "nuclear"? Was a nuclear-powered fighting vessel a nuclear weapon? Would Canada with such submarines become a nuclear state? Intriguingly, many on the government side argued that Canada's unique attributes – its large Arctic territory and coast – demanded that Canada have submarines propelled by nuclear power so they could operate under the Arctic ice: that Canada, by its very nature, must be nuclear. Matthew Wiseman's history of No. 1 Radiation Detection Unit (1 RDU) in Chapter 7 reveals another split lens for understanding Canada's place in the atomic age. Although at the time of the unit's creation Canada had no responsibility for delivering atomic weapons, it was expected that a Canadian Army at war would be in the thick of nuclear destruction. Even if the bombs were not dropped by Canadians, Canada was living in an atomic age and needed to be prepared to operate in a world that was recovering from atomic blasts.

On occasion, the nuclear age came to Canada unwanted and entirely by accident. In Chapter 8, Ryan Dean and P. Whitney Lackenbauer reveal how Canada was the site of nuclear accidents. However, not only could dangerous debris from nuclear satellites come to Canada unexpectedly but Canada was prepared, with its American allies, to clean up in the wake of disaster. If Canada was an accidental importer of nuclear matter, it was also the purposeful exporter of nuclear power. In Chapter 9, Se Young Jang has explained how Canadians designed and sold nuclear reactors around the world – sometimes with unintended consequences. Canadian efforts to proliferate nuclear technology, via the sale of reactors to India, led to Canadian efforts to tighten its non-proliferation safeguards. Canada helped export nuclear power – leading, ultimately, to the proliferation of nuclear weapons – even though Canada itself swore off the developments of such weapons and urged others against any such step.

In keeping with the spirit of open academic inquiry it would be possible – just possible – to develop a theory in which the above evidence could be construed in such a way as to demonstrate that Canada was not a nuclear power. But such a finding would fly in the face of overwhelming evidence that Canada was both shaped by, and helped to shape, the atomic age – that Canada is and was a nuclear state. This conclusion is not intended to snap the case shut, but to stimulate new arguments and new areas of research. Going forward, scholars of Canadian history will continue to engage with each other about the role of nuclear power in Canada, but must also seek a way to include Canada in the broader international and transnational accounts of nuclear history.

## NOTES

1 EXTOTT DFR3384 to LDN, October 18, 1982, RG 25, file 27-11-1, pt. 4, Library and Archives Canada (LAC).

2 David J. Bercuson, "SAC vs. Sovereignty: The Origins of the Goose Bay Lease, 1946–52," *Canadian Historical Review* 70, 2 (June 1989): 206–22; Timothy Andrews Sayle, "A Pattern of Constraint: Canadian-American Relations in the Early Cold War," *International Journal* 62, 3 (2007): 689–705.

3 Tarah Brookfield, *Cold War Comforts: Canadian Women, Child Safety, and Global Insecurity* (Kitchener, ON: Wilfrid Laurier University Press, 2012); Andrew Burtch, *Give Me Shelter: The Failure of Canada's Cold War Civil Defence* (Vancouver: UBC Press, 2012).

4 Itty Abraham, "The Ambivalence of Nuclear Histories," *Osiris* 21, 1 (January 2006): 49–65, esp. 51; Gabrielle Hecht, "Nuclear Ontologies," *Constellations* 13, 3 (September 2006): 320–31, esp. 321; Gabrielle Hecht, "A Cosmogram of Nuclear Things," *Isis* 98, 1 (March 2007): 100–8.

5 Hecht, "A Cosmogram of Nuclear Things," 100.

6 Jonathan Hogg and Christopher Laucht, "Introduction: British Nuclear Culture," *British Journal for the History of Science* 45, 4 (December 2012): 482.

7 Asa McKercher and Timothy Andrews Sayle, "Skyhawk, Skyshield, and the Soviets: Revisiting Canada's Cold War," *Historical Journal* 51, 2 (2018): 472.

8 Carol Sizowitz Stearns and Peter N. Stearns, "Victorian Sexuality: Can Historians Do It Better?" *Journal of Social History* 18, 4 (Summer 1985): 625–34, quote at 626.

9 "Uranium in Canada," July 24, 2014, Natural Resources Canada, https://www.nrcan.gc.ca/energy/uranium-nuclear/7693.

10 Simon Rosenblum, *Misguided Missiles: Canada, the Cruise and Star Wars* (Toronto: James Lorimer, 1985), 144–46.

11 Robert Penner, "Can Canada Risk Being Nuclear-Free?" *Globe and Mail*, December 26, 1986.

12 "The Canadian Nuclear Industry and Its Economic Contributions," December 19, 2016, Natural Resources Canada, https://www.nrcan.gc.ca/energy/uranium-nuclear/7715.

13 Mohamed Zakzouk, "The 2009–2010 Medical Isotope Shortage: Cause, Effects and Future Considerations," Publication No. 2009-04-E, Library of Parliament, revised November 7, 2010.

14 "The Policy Implications of the Nuclear Deterrent," July 15, 1955, updated draft of "The Strategic Concept of the Nuclear Deterrent," by George Ignatieff, March 26, 1955, both in RG25, vol. 6069, file 50333-40, pt. 2.2, LAC. Regarding disarmament, see Albert Legault and Michel Fortmann, *A Diplomacy of Hope: Canada and Disarmament, 1945–1988* (Montreal and Kingston: McGill-Queen's University Press, 1992); Joseph

Levitt, *Pearson and Canada's Role in Nuclear Disarmament and Arms Control Negotiations, 1945–1957* (Montreal and Kingston: McGill-Queen's University Press, 1993).

15  On the Canadian role in negotiating the treaty, see Legault and Fortmann, *A Diplomacy of Hope,* 229–80.

16  Hecht, "A Cosmogram of Nuclear Things," 101.

17  Paul Meyer, "Folding the Umbrella: Nuclear Allies, the NPT and the Ban Treaty," Policy Brief No. 58, Asia-Pacific Leadership Network for Nuclear Non-Proliferation and Disarmament, February 26, 2018.

# CONTRIBUTORS

**Robert Bothwell** is Professor and May Gluskin Chair in Canadian History at the University of Toronto. He is the author of *Eldorado* (1984), *Nucleus* (1989), *Canada and the United States* (1992), *Canada and Quebec* (1995), *The Big Chill* (1998), *The Penguin History of Canada* (2006), *Alliance and Illusion* (2007), and *My Country, Your Country* (2015). He co-authored *C.D. Howe* (1979), *Canada 1900–1945* (1987), *Canada since 1945* (1989), *Pirouette* (1990), *Our Century* (2000), and *Trudeau's World* (2017). He is working on a book on Canadian foreign relations since 1984.

**Susan Colbourn** is the Henry Chauncey Jr. '57 Postdoctoral Fellow in International Security Studies at Yale University. Her research focuses on the Cold War, transatlantic relations, and the politics of nuclear weapons. She is currently completing a book on NATO and the struggle over the Euromissiles.

**Jack Cunningham** holds a PhD in History from the University of Toronto, where he is now Program Coordinator of the Bill Graham Centre for Contemporary International History. His publications include co-edited collections on the conflict in Afghanistan and the 2003 invasion of Iraq.

**Katie Davis** is a PhD candidate in the Department of History at the University of Toronto. Her research examines the intersection between public opinion, atomic culture, and US diplomacy in the United Nations Atomic Energy Commission during the early Cold War.

**Ryan Dean** is a PhD candidate in the Department of Political Science at the University of Calgary. His doctoral dissertation examines the development of Canadian Arctic security policy since 1985. His recent co-edited volumes include *(Re)Conceptualizing Arctic Security: Selected Articles from the Journal of Military and Security Studies* (2018) and *Canada's Northern Strategy under the Harper Conservatives: Key Speeches and Documents on Sovereignty, Security, and Governance, 2006–15* (2016).

**Se Young Jang** is assistant professor of Korean Studies at Leiden University. Her primary line of research centres on the history of South Korea's military and civil nuclear development. She holds a BA and an MA from Seoul National University and a PhD in International History from the Graduate Institute of International and Development Studies, Geneva. A former South Korean diplomat, she was also Stanton Nuclear Security Fellow at the Massachusetts Institute of Technology; Nonresident Scholar in the Nuclear Policy Program, Carnegie Endowment for International Peace; and Albert Gallatin Fellow at George Washington University.

**P. Whitney Lackenbauer** is Canada Research Chair (Tier 1) in the Study of the Canadian North and a professor in the School for the Study of Canada at Trent University, Peterborough, Ontario. His recent books include *Breaking the Ice Curtain? Russia, Canada, and Arctic Security in a Changing Circumpolar World* (co-edited, 2019); *China's Arctic Ambitions and What They Mean for Canada* (co-authored, 2018); and *Canadian Armed Forces Arctic Operations, 1945–2015: Historical and Contemporary Lessons Learned* (co-edited, 2017). His research focuses on Arctic policy, sovereignty, security, and governance issues; modern Canadian and circumpolar history; military history and contemporary defence policy; and Indigenous-state relations in Canada.

**Asa McKercher** is assistant professor of History at the Royal Military College of Canada. His books include *Canada and the World since 1867* (Bloomsbury, 2019), *Camelot and Canada: Canadian-American Relations in the Kennedy Era* (Oxford University Press, 2016), and *Mike's World: Lester B. Pearson and Canadian External Affairs* (UBC Press, 2017).

**Timothy Andrews Sayle** is assistant professor of History at the University of Toronto. He is the director of the International Relations Program,

Trinity College, and a senior fellow of the Bill Graham Centre for Contemporary International History. He is the author of *Enduring Alliance: A History of NATO and the Postwar Global Order* (Cornell University Press, 2019) and editor, with Jeffrey A. Engel, Hal Brands, and William Inboden, of *The Last Card: Inside George W. Bush's Decision to Surge in Iraq* (Cornell University Press, 2019).

**Michael D. Stevenson** is an associate professor in the Department of History at Lakehead University, specializing in diplomatic and military history. Among his publications are *Canada's Greatest Wartime Muddle: National Selective Service and the Mobilization of Human Resources during World War II* (McGill-Queen's University Press, 2001) and three edited volumes of diplomatic correspondence in the *Documents on Canadian External Relations* series covering the government of John Diefenbaker. His current projects are a biography of Howard Charles Green, Canada's foreign minister from 1959 to 1963 (with Eric Bergbusch), and a study of Canadian-American relations during the Eisenhower administration (with Greg Donaghy and Asa McKercher).

**Matthew S. Wiseman** is an Associated Medical Services Postdoctoral Fellow in the Department of History at Western University. He studies the history of science in the Cold War and recently completed a forthcoming book about military research in northern Canada between 1947 and 1975. His work has appeared in the *Journal of the Canadian Historical Association*, *Canadian Military History*, and *Canadian Historical Review*.

# INDEX

*Note:* NPT stands for Nuclear Non-Proliferation Treaty; NRX, for National Research Experimental (nuclear reactor); UNAEC, for United Nations Atomic Energy Commission

Abraham, Itty, 184

Acheson-Lilienthal Report, US, 22

Advisory Committee on Human Radiation Experiments, US, 167

Advisory Panel on Atomic Energy (Canada), 22

Aikman, W.R., 182

Air Defense Initiative, 144

Alsop, Stewart, 99–100

*American Nuclear Guinea Pigs: Three Decades of Radiation Experiments on U.S. Citizens* (US House of Representatives report), 167

Anderson, John, 137

anti-Americanism, 88, 92, 95–96, 98, 100, 102

Apple II (atomic bomb tested in Nevada), 153–54, 155, 162–63

Argentina, Canada's sale of nuclear reactor to, 210–22; in aftermath of India's nuclear test, 11–12, 207–8, 214, 215–18, 220, 222; and Argentina's non-ratification of NPT, 208, 212, 217–18, 222; and Argentina's proliferation potential, 7, 211–13, 217; as conducted with less stringency than South Korea sale, 11–12, 207–8, 216–22; as following Canada's unsuccessful Atucha I bid, 210–11, 213; hyperinflation as factor in, 220; Italimpianti as Canada's partner in, 213–14, 218, 220; US influence as non-factor in, 221–22; weak safeguards agreement governing, 208, 214, 217–18, 220–22

Argue, Hazen, 93, 100

arms control. *See* disarmament, *and entries following*

Armstrong, Willis, 68, 118

atomic bomb, viii–x; Canadians' work on, ix–x, 3, 4, 5, 7, 18, 19, 21, 35n4, 208–9; as dropped on Nagasaki, 7, 153; first test of, 3; international control of, 8–9, 17–35, 229. *See also* nuclear weapons testing; United Nations Atomic Energy Commission (UNAEC), *and entry following*

Atomic Energy Act, US (McMahon Act), 160

237